Other Ways of Reading

Other Ways of Reading: African Women and the Bible

Musa W. Dube, editor

Society of Biblical Literature
Atlanta

WCC Publications
Geneva

OTHER WAYS OF READING:
AFRICAN WOMEN AND THE BIBLE

Copyright © 2001 by the
Society of Biblical Literature

Copublished by the Society of Biblical Literature,
825 Houston Mill Road, Suite 350, Atlanta, GA 30329, USA,
and
WCC Publications, the publishing division of the World Council of Churches,
150 route de Ferney, 1211 Geneva 2, Switzerland.

SBL ISBN: 1-58983-009-1
WCC ISBN: 2-8254-1340-2

Library of Congress Cataloging-in-Publication Data

Other ways of reading : African women and the Bible / edited by Musa W. Dube.

   p. cm. — (Global perspectives on biblical scholarship ; no. 2)
   Includes bibliographical references.
   ISBN 1-58983-009-1 (pbk. : alk. paper)
   1. Bible—Criticism, interpretation, etc.—Africa, Sub-Saharan. 2. Bible—Feminist criticism—Africa, Sub-Saharan. I. Dube Shomanah, Musa W., 1964– II. Series.

BS521.4 .O84 2001
220.6'082'096—dc21

                                            2001020562

Chapter 3, "Fifty Years of Bleeding: A Storytelling Feminist Reading of Mark 5:24–43," appeared originally in *Ecumenical Review* 51, no. 1 (1999): 11–17. Chapter 6, "Cultural Hermeneutics: An African Contribution," appeared originally in *Women's Visions*, ed. Ofelia Ortega (Geneva: WCC, 1995). Both are used by permission of the World Council of Churches.

Chapter 10, "Divining Ruth for International Relations," appeared originally in *Postmodern Interpretations of the Bible—A Reader*, ed. A. K. M. Adam (St. Louis: Chalice Press, 2001). Used by permission of Chalice Press.

09 08 07 06 05 04 03 02 01   5 4 3 2 1

Printed in the United States of America
on acid-free paper

Contents

Acknowledgments

More than three hundred women who associate themselves with the Circle of Concerned African Women Theologians (henceforth, the Circle) will welcome this volume. Many want to write, but the reality of the African continent stagnates the best intentions. Some of the budding scholars in the Circle live in war-torn zones. Others have no libraries or no typewriters, and computers are something of which they have only heard. A majority are consumed by the daily cares of sustaining life on our struggling continent. Yet when a book about issues close to their hearts is published, it gives each and every member a chance to read herself into these texts. Thanks to all who have contributed to the articles in this volume.

Realizing a volume like this for Africa is a milestone achievement. We are much indebted to all who have made this possible. We realize that communication with the authors is a luxury not readily available in Africa. Therefore much appreciation goes to the editor for the intense and frustrating work of verifying bibliography, facts, and dates, and for putting the final touches that go into such a publication. The production of *Other Ways of Reading*: *African Women and the Bible* has been possible because of the leadership of Dr. Musa W. Dube. On behalf of the Circle and indeed of all contributors to this volume, I acknowledge with much thanks her determination to do what it takes to conquer the barriers that keep the voices of African women out of print. Members of the Circle continue to lament the dearth of published research and theological reflection by African women on subjects of concern to Africa. Contextual African feminist reading of Scriptures is new. It brings new voices to the table and challenges readers of theology to hospitality beyond mere words. This volume continues the expression of African women's will to arise that began in 1989, when the Circle was launched.

But such a task requires solidarity and practical support from various people. Foremost, we thank Professor Sharon H. Ringe for trusting us and investing in us, the African women of the Circle. The limitations of the research and analysis in this volume remain our responsibility, but we celebrate the solidarity and support of Professor Ringe with joy and ululation. Her immense practical support in editing the manuscripts for language, content, and theory was a gift of great price. Her pioneering feminist biblical work has formed many of us, and she remains a mentor and a teacher much admired and respected by members of the Circle of Concerned African Women Theologians.

A manuscript needs contributors, publishers, editors, readers, typists, and mentors. Thanks to all who fit these categories. More specifically, much thanks to Rex Matthews for agreeing to publish this work. Appreciation is also due to respondents, Nyambura J. Njoroge, Phyllis A. Bird, and Tinyiko S. Maluleke for agreeing to begin the dialogue solicited by this volume.

Other Ways of Reading is fundamentally about insight and perception of truth—truth about ourselves, about the world in which we live, and about our understanding of the God we confess. *Other Ways of Reading* is an offering from African women to the global community. The contributors are women of Africa, inspired by the Christian faith and living that faith in their cultural, geographical, racial, political, and socioeconomic contexts. This volume brings new voices into the conversation about theology and biblical interpretation. It brings to the table stories of women told in a different way. It affirms unity in diversity and challenges readers to create space at the table for a new community of Bible readers and Bible users. Thanks in advance to those who will provide this hospitality.

Musimbi R. A. Kanyoro, Circle Coordinator
Geneva
January 29, 2001

Introduction

Musa W. Dube

This volume represents an ongoing effort of the Circle of Concerned African Women Theologians (henceforth, "the Circle") to promote research and publication in biblical and cultural hermeneutics. At the March 1998 consultation on research, the Circle was divided into four study commissions and research leaders identified;[1] African biblical and cultural hermeneutics was selected as one of the four research areas.[2] Combining Bible and culture is a recognition that authoritative texts for African women are more than just the written religious texts. Rather, African cultures remain vibrant and authoritative texts in the lives of women, and they need to be studied, analyzed, and reinterpreted for the creation of a just world and the empowerment of women.

In reviewing the study of African biblical and cultural hermeneutics, the consultation noted that the discipline

- lacked trained women scholars; consequently, training more African women is crucial;
- needs to develop African women's ways of reading the Bible and culture;
- needs to compile subaltern African women's readings and the cultural canon itself;
- should interrogate colonial translations and how they have disadvantaged women;
- would benefit from producing videos on teaching methods.

Related to developing African women's ways of interpreta-

1

tion, two methods were discussed: storytelling and divination. Participants were particularly keen on storytelling method, noting that

- in many African cultures, it is a role for women;[3]
- the method could be useful to ordained, academic, and lay readers;
- reading biblical stories with African cultural folktales can be a form of cultural hermeneutics;
- the stories of Africa should also be explored for particular themes and characters, which women could use to read and interpret the Scripture critically;
- storytelling and retelling of biblical stories would have to be informed by and grounded in critical theories that seek to avoid all forms of oppression.

Divination was also discussed as another African way of reading.[4] It was suggested that readers would have to thoroughly research the assumptions and skills of divination, and how these ancient ways of interpretation can be used to read Scriptures and social reality for the empowerment of women and the creation of a just world.

Musimbi R. A. Kanyoro and I were responsible for stimulating and encouraging members of the Circle to research and publish in this area of African biblical and cultural hermeneutics. Following this consultation, I identified three areas for research in biblical and cultural hermeneutics. I wrote a call for papers in these three areas, which sought to encourage research and writing in

- African women's Bible commentary from a storytelling perspective;
- translating the divine: postcolonial feminist readings of colonial Bibles;
- reading with grassroots or subaltern readers.

The invitation was sent to all potential writers in the Circle, in the continent and beyond. It is important that I elaborate on these focus areas, for they encapsulate the African women's ways of reading texts that inform this collection. The areas also reflect an ongoing research agenda in biblical and cultural hermeneutics. Our hope is that research will be undertaken by African women individually and collaboratively, wherever they are. This volume, therefore, represents the first fruits of these collaborative efforts. It is a pointer to a larger and ongoing program.

Storytelling Methods and Interpretations

In the first area identified for research—African women's Bible commentary from a storytelling perspective—the call for papers noted that stories and storytelling are central to African societies.[5] Stories are told and retold repeatedly to depict life, to transmit values, and to give wisdom for survival in life. The art of telling and retelling stories remains central to African societies. For example, a grandmother can tell the same story differently depending on her audience and the issues she wants to address. Thus characters in a story may change to suit the listeners and their circumstances, as the teller sees fit. A story may also be told to a group of listeners who add their comments and questions. This makes storytelling itself (and the story itself) a moment of community writing or interpretation of life, rather than an activity of the teller or author.[6] The teller or writer thus does not own the story or have the last word, but rather the story is never finished: it is a page of the community's fresh and continuous reflection.

Further, a number of characteristics of African stories make them useful in building biblical and cultural hermeneutics that empower women. First, a substantial body of African stories are gender-neutral. Stories do not always feature men and women or girls and boys. Instead, they might feature animals whose biological sex is not specified. The story thus manages, to some degree, to pass wisdom and values indiscriminately to its listeners. Second, African stories also carry "flat" characters, such as Hare in southern African and Spider in western Africa, which represent values and philosophies of survival. Both ani-

3

mals are tricksters, representing the art of survival as small, powerless individuals among big and powerful animals. African stories (including proverbs and idiomatic sayings) constitute a part of the African cultural canon. With the coming of Christianity, sub-Saharan Africa received an additional body of wisdom, namely, the biblical stories.

The task of commentators, therefore, is to read the Bible with African tales or through methods of African storytelling, which could include the following:

- retelling a story or stories, once or many times, with different or new characters, to address a certain audience, circumstances, or contemporary or historical issues;[7]

- retelling a biblical story by including listeners who, through comments and participation, take a fixed story and make it open for continuous and fresh retelling. The author either can create the characters or invite colleagues or a community of interpreters to a participatory retelling;

- doing a comparative reading of biblical and African oral stories, to assert the cultural validity of our dual or triple canonical heritage;

- using the gender-neutral techniques to retell biblical stories to counteract patriarchal and colonizing ideology;

- reading as tricksters, using the strategies of Hare and Spider in African folktales in order to subvert powerful and exploitative powers.

In this volume, one narrative poem and two essays have begun to use storytelling methods to read the Bible and African cultures together. In her narrative poem "I Am the Woman," Rose Teteki Abbey enters the biblical narratives of women and retells them as an insider, claiming that she is that woman. Abbey retells the stories of these biblical women by seeing them through her own life and through the biographies of women living in patriarchal societies. She reimagines the experiences of biblical women and articulates what the patriarchal authors did not bother to explicate. Thus, her poem tells the

4

story of the Samaritan woman, of her lonely walk to the river, and of her five husbands. Teteki also tells the story of the woman who was caught in adultery, explaining the situation that led her to engage in adultery. She also captures Mary's desire to study. Yet in retelling these stories, Abbey seeks not only to expose their oppression, but also to show that the encounter with Jesus brought a new world—the liberation of women from patriarchal cultures and laws. This she reclaims as our right to empowerment, for we are these women.

In her essay "Esther and Northern Sotho Stories: An African South African Woman's Commentary," Mmadipoane Masenya reads the book of Esther with and through Northern Sotho folktales while integrating the analysis of class, gender, and power in the reading. Masenya's approach closely follows that of a comparative reading, but the stories from each tradition serve as a lens of social analysis. The stories also illuminate each other, giving women techniques of survival and resistance. Masenya's interpretation also includes Northern Sotho proverbs to illuminate the meaning of the stories. Although it may not be evident in this written form, Masenya's methods are performative and communal. Those who attended this presentation at the Society of Biblical Literature meeting in Cape Town in August 2000 will recall that the audience was expected to participate, and what an experience it was!

The second essay that employs storytelling methods of reading the Bible and African cultures is my "Fifty Years of Bleeding: A Storytelling Feminist Reading of Mark 5:24–43." The article combines three stories—Mark 5:24–43, a southern African resurrection folktale, and a contemporary (his)story of Africa—to depict how African women have survived during the pre-colonial, colonial, postindependence, globalization, and the HIV/AIDS eras. My storytelling interpretation retells African history by placing African women at its center.

As in Abbey's approach, I use storytelling as a feminist theory of analysis and as a method of rewriting the patriarchal silences about women's lives in the biblical texts and African history. The article, therefore, tells us about the bleeding woman's encounter with the many doctors who took her money, but

5

who did not deliver health to her body (Mark 5:26). It names the doctors and their exploitative deeds. It also names the woman, who is called "Mama Africa." The essay, however, depicts not only African women's oppression, but also their acts of resistance, as we find the words *Talitha cum*, which are uttered by Jesus in the text, pronounced by Mama Africa. The story is thus a subversive rereading underlining African women's full understanding of their political, economic, and social positions, in both historical and contemporary times, and showing that they are taking hold of their own destinies.

Patriarchal and Colonizing Translations

The second research area, postcolonial feminist readings of colonial Bibles, highlights that, in the nineteenth and twentieth centuries, Bible translations were carried out primarily by foreign missionaries and were heavily informed by colonial ideology. The subversion of African deities was often carried out in these translations by equating them with demons.[8] Further, while most African languages are gender-neutral, with names of deities and other divine figures bearing gender-neutral names, deities in the Bible were given male genders. This area thus encourages research on the following questions:

- how these translations subvert the power and autonomy of African cultures and religions;
- how the new male gender attached to African deities in colonial Bible translations affected women's position in the society and the church;
- how these translations endorse or introduced the marginalization of African women in the spiritual and social arena even where such marginalization had not existed;
- how African women, who largely enjoyed what Amadiume has termed a "flexible gender system" in the spiritual and social arena, have worked to sidestep the imposition on them of a patriarchal worldview;[9]
- how local male revisers of colonial translations have dealt

with the gendering of God, either to maintain the gendering of God or to fight it, as they resisted the colonizing of African deities;

- how to suggest gender-neutral translations that would reflect the native languages and empower both women and men;

- how to discern the strategies of resistance, both oral and written, that have been used in reading these colonizing and patriarchalizing translations;

- how to develop a fair, gender-neutral, and decolonizing reading.

This research area seeks to document and expose colonial and patriarchal translations, reading them against their times and with the colonial, collaborating, and decolonizing ideologies that shaped their formulations. The research area calls on African women, from the continent and beyond, to examine the translations in their own languages and to reread the colonial biblical translations of the divine from postcolonial feminist perspectives.

Two essays in this volume have begun to address the above concerns. Dora R. Mbuwayesango's essay, "How Local Divine Powers Were Suppressed: A Case of Mwari of the Shona." Mbuwayesango begins by asserting that Mwari, the Supreme Being of the Shona, had no specific gender and could speak through both women and men. She produces evidence that when Christianity arrived in Zimbabwe, it came with and implemented colonizing strategies of subverting the native powers and their institutions, as attested by the archival information of colonial missionaries. Turning to the translations, Mbuwayesango shows persuasively that when the colonial missionaries chose to use Mwari as the equivalent of Yahweh—rejecting all other traditions, institutions, and myths that accompanied this Supreme Being—Mwari had been colonized, and the Shona people had been robbed of their traditions. Moreover, Mwari had been transformed to a male God. Mbuwayesango calls for the unshackling of Mwari from colonial and gender bias through another "writing pen."

7

Gomang Seratwa Ntloedibe-Kuswani's essay, "Translating the Divine: The Case of Modimo in the Setswana Bible," researches the Setswana Bible translation. According to Ntloedibe-Kuswani, the word *Modimo* is used by Batswana to name the divine, and it bears no gender. Modimo has no human characteristics, including that of gender. Similarly, *Badimo*, the intermediaries between Modimo and people, bear no gender. Ntloedibe-Kuswani asks what happened when the earliest translators adopted Modimo as the equivalent of Yahweh in the Bible. She asks if Modimo transformed the biblical God, or it was the other way around? Ntloeidbe-Kuswani argues that the now-gendered Modimo in the Setswana Bible translations distances women from power roles in the public and in the church. The translation also undermines Setswana traditional religions. Ntoedibe-Kuswani closes her essay by suggesting a gender-neutral translation.

Reading with and from Non-academic Readers

The third research focus, reading with grassroots and subaltern readers, encourages learning from these groups of non-academic readers. This method of reading is motivated by several factors:

- There are very few academic and literate biblical interpreters on the African continent, given the orality of African societies and its economic status.

- The majority of African women biblical interpreters are oral hearers or readers.

- Most African academic scholars are trained in the Western schools and methods of reading that often fail to speak to African situations, thinking, and students. Hence there is the need to search for native voices of interpretation.

- Illiteracy affects women and girls more than men, thus decreasing the number of women in the academy.

- African patriarchy is often seen to be supported by bibli-

cal patriarchy; thus, the two collude against the empowerment of women in the process of reading, seemingly
ordaining the oppression of women.

The tasks of researchers in this area, therefore, include the
following commitments:

- to read with non-academic women interpreters, and to
  learn and document their methods of reading;

- to make available to African students, and to all other interested readers in the world's academic halls, non-academic African women's ways of reading;

- to counteract the dominance of Western-oriented methods that are elitist and sometimes irrelevant to some
  African students;

- to conscientize African women readers through bringing
  them to be critical of patriarchy as it is found both in
  African cultures and in biblical texts;

- to document feminist methods of resistance that emanate
  from non-academic readers.

The two essays by Musimbi Kanyoro and Gloria Kehilwe
Plaatjie treat these issues. Kanyoro's essay, "Cultural Hermeneutics: An African Contribution," was first published in 1995.[10]
Together with Kanyoro's other articles in this area, the essay
represents one of the earliest efforts by African women to read
with non-academic women. Kanyoro's aim is to develop cultural hermeneutics. She holds that African cultures remain
alive and authoritative to most African women, and that they
are the lens of reading the Bible for most African women.
Kanyoro thus insists on cultural hermeneutics, that is, that
African cultures should be read, understood, and interpreted.
Their negative effects on African women need to be studied,
and ways should be devised to empower women to free themselves from oppressive cultural traditions.

In her essay, "Toward a Post-apartheid Black Feminist Reading of the Bible: A Case of Luke 2:36–38," Gloria Kehilwe
Plaatjie undertakes to read the story of the prophet Anna with

non-academic black women of South Africa. She writes from a historical situation, in which women were marginalized not only because of gender, but also because of color. The academy in South Africa is, therefore, not only male, but also white. Black women are marginalized from the academy and other positions of power due to apartheid and patriarchy. For Plaatjie, to connect with non-academic women readers is, therefore, an imperative strategy for resisting both patriarchy and apartheid oppression. She thus seeks to "read with and from" communities of black non-academic women. Given that both patriarchy and apartheid were authorized through the Bible, Plaatjie calls for a different canon—the new South African constitution. Plaajtie suggests that black South African women should not only read from the African cultures and the Bible, but that they must also read the post-apartheid constitution, which she regards as sacred.

Womanhood, Womanist, and Divination Methods

This volume also includes two womanist interpretations, those of Mmadipoane (Ngwana 'Mphahlele) Masenya and Sarojini Nadar. Masenya's essay, "A *Bosadi* (Womanhood) Reading of Proverbs 31:10–31," represents a long-standing effort by Masenya to develop *bosadi* (womanhood) hermeneutics, which she distinguishes from the African American womanist hermeneutics, due to their different historical contexts.[11] Masenya's perspective investigates what amounts to ideal womanhood for the South African woman Bible reader. The approach critiques oppressive elements in Northern Sotho African cultures while highlighting aspects of those cultures that empower women. It takes into account the interplay of post-apartheid racism, sexism, classism, and African culture as factors that shape African women's reading. Masenya applies *bosadi* hermeneutics to Prov. 31:10–31 and argues for a close resemblance between the "Woman of Worth" and Northern Sotho expectations of *bosadi*. She holds that they are managers of their households, and that they are industrious. Masenya finds these traits to constitute an empowering and liberating *bosadi*, or womanhood.

In her essay "A South African Indian Womanist Reading of the Character of Ruth," Nadar employs a womanist lens and lays emphasis on race and class. With her Indian cultural background, in which widows were expected to undergo *sati,* she finds the character of Ruth the surviving widow liberating. Both Naomi and Ruth are widows who survive in patriarchal structures. Nadar's contribution is particularly welcome, since we have had very few, if any, Indian women readers of the Bible in the African academy and elsewhere.

In chapter 10, "Divining Ruth for International Relations," I try to articulate and apply divination as a tool of social analysis. I describe *divination,* which is common in southern Africa, as a practice that is tantamount to reading an authoritative social book. Readers consult divining sets in order to diagnose various social problems, to work out solutions, and to maintain healthy relationships.[12] My effort to use divination as a method of reading was inspired by African indigenous churches, which use the biblical text as a divination set. In the essay, I set out to diagnose international relationships by focusing on the relationship between Judah and Moab, which are represented in the narrative by Ruth and Naomi.

Other Contributions and Conversations

African biblical scholarship received a boost in 2000 when two massive volumes were published: *African Americans and the Bible: Sacred Texts and Social Texture,* and *The Bible in Africa.*[13] The first, edited by Vincent Wimbush, is a diaspora work of sixty-three articles. It documents the many ways in which African Americans have interpreted the Bible and used it as a text of social analysis and criticism. The contributors investigate the role of the Bible in the lives of African Americans in the church, visual arts, music, poetry, prose, folklore, spirituals, jazz, rap, politics, and dance through various periods. The volume is not only a contribution to their community, and to Africa, but also to the rest of the guild of biblical interpreters. This volume has shown clearly that biblical studies need not be done only within academic walls, or only by those who hold doctoral degrees. It further demonstrates that vibrant biblical interpretation is being carried out in communities. This interpretation is both analytical and socially engaged, and the academy needs to take it seriously.

On the African continent, *The Bible in Africa,* edited by Gerald West and myself, was compiled by calling for papers from the continent and beyond. It has thirty-nine articles and a long bibliography. As coeditor, I knew we had only nine submissions from African women. This happened despite the open call, and despite the fact that I had announced the call for papers at the Pan-African Circle for Concerned African Women Theologians meeting in Nairobi in 1996 and at the Circle Padare at the World Council of Churches Assembly in Harare, Zimbabwe, in 1998. But, given that the whole of Africa boasts only ten, or fewer, women biblical scholars, there was a limit to what could be done. In the end, out of thirty-nine articles, only six were authored by women. It is, therefore, a delight that this volume, *Other Ways of Reading: African Women and the Bible,* has followed soon after. This volume, which brings voices of African women and their interpretations of the Bible and culture, describes their agenda. It will go a long way to complement *The Bible in Africa,* as well as to equip colleges, seminaries, and universities to engage in a better study of the Bible in Africa.

Other Ways of Reading also contributes to African biblical scholarship by providing methodological tools and by demonstrating their applications. The volume challenges the frameworks of biblical interpretation, as highlighted in Kanyoro's and Plaatjie's articles. While inculturation hermeneutics has insisted on reading both the Bible and culture comparatively, it has tended to be uncritical of patriarchy in both texts. Kanyoro insists that African culture must be read critically, thus exposing silence about inculturation as collusion with patriarchy. Plaatjie's article also takes to task the black liberation biblical hermeneutics of South Africa for its exclusion of women's empowerment. Plaatjie overrides the "biblical entrapment" debate in black hermeneutics on what to do with the Bible, which has legitimated the oppression of black people.[14] She provides a new text, the post-apartheid constitution, as a sacred text born from the human struggle for liberation.

Abbey's, Masenya's, and my own use of storytelling restores to African women the power of interpreting social reality through stories. These articles provide a new tool, insofar as storytelling has not been a central technique in the movements either of inculturation or of black biblical hermeneutics in South Africa.[15] Given that storytelling is a role for women in many African societies, women can reclaim their place as interpreters of social reality and as proponents of their own strategies of resistance and survival. Ntloedibe-Kuswani's and Mbuwayesango's interrogation of interpretation, and their thesis that colonial translation imposed male gender in spiritual spaces and distanced women from the places of power, also challenge the African theological discourse of translation. That discourse, especially as propounded by Lamin Sanneh and Kofi Bediako, has spoken highly of biblical translation, holding that it has preserved African culture.[16] These essays challenge the proponents of translation theologies to revisit their discourse by taking gender into account and by decolonizing their discourse. The contribution of this volume is also evident in African women's insistence on reading with non-academic or grassroots women. As Plaatjie says, she seeks to read "from and with" black South African women outside the academy. For Kanyoro, the method recognizes that African cultures often collaborate with the Bible against women; hence, cultural hermeneutics are essential for studying the effect of African culture on women. My proposal to read the text as divination for the healing of relationships provides an analytical tool that has so far been untapped by academic inculturation and by the black biblical hermeneutics of South Africa.

Among Western feminists, this volume goes a long way to provide one of the missing links. That is, while Western feminists have produced a number of anthologies on feminist biblical studies,[17] *Other Ways of Reading* is the first of its kind. It complements many efforts of Western feminist scholarship by providing new tools and engaging old as well as new themes. One of the controversial issues that surrounded early feminist discourse was that of the authority of the Bible. *Other Ways of Reading* subverts the authority of the Bible in a number of ways. First, it recognizes several canons and gives no particular preference to the biblical canon. There is the canon of African oral cultures, which is read together with the biblical text (Masenya and Dube), and which is also interpreted on its own or together with the Bible (Kanyoro). There are aspects of African cultures that serve as theories for analyzing or reading the Bible (Dube and Masenya). And there is a post-apartheid constitution that is given sacred status (Plaatjie). *Other Ways of Reading* also revisits biblical translations, challenging both colonial and patriarchal ideologies in the translations and proposing that gender-neutral African languages should also inform the decolonization of biblical translations. *Other Ways of Reading*'s conversation with other expressions of feminism is also evident in the womanist and womanhood readers from South Africa (Masenya and Nadar). Writing from a context in which they have been discriminated against based on gender and color, they find a great deal of resonance with African American womanist hermeneutics. The volume also takes up the call long sounded by feminists to rewrite and retell biblical stories from a feminist point of view by placing the presence, contribution, and survival of women in history at the center of the interpretive process (Abbey and Dube). New tools of reading such as storytelling, reading from and with non-academic readers, *bosadi* (womanhood) reading, and divination merit conversations with other feminist scholars.

This volume is also a contribution toward a truly global scholarship that takes into account other methods of reading and other texts. This effort is also represented by such volumes as *Voices from the Margin: Interpreting the Bible in the Third World; Reading from This Place: Social Location and Biblical Interpretation in Global Perspective;* and *Semeia* 78 (with the theme of "Reading the Bible as Women from Africa, Asia, and Latin America"),[18] which have argued that readers from the Two-thirds World have "other" methods of reading Bible, and that their reading may not necessarily focus on the Bible alone.[19] The importance of these methods is that they help us all to have much better understanding of the text and of the world; they help us build a world that accommodates diversity and justice. For Two-thirds World scholars, these methods helps us deal with the realities of our world, to ask questions, and to be engaged with the struggles of our people.

In Response

Since this is the first volume by African women offering methods of reading the Bible, and applying the methods, it seemed important to invite respondents. Three respondents were invited: Phyllis A. Bird, Nyambura J. Njoroge, and Tinyiko S. Maluleke. Their task was to locate the collection along the spectrum of scholars such as Western feminists, African women theologians, and African male theologians, respectively. Except for Bird (whose essay responded to papers by Ntloedibe-Kuswani, Masenya, Plaatjie, and Dube that were presented on July 24, 2000, at the Religion 2000 Congress in Cape Town), all papers were sent to the respondents, but respondents were by no means obliged to respond to all papers. Rather, they were free to address those papers and aspects that they found most striking.

For Bird, the papers to which she was invited to respond redeemed the value of the Congress, by bringing African ways of reading into an otherwise white conference. She highlights the common themes that emerge from the essays, such as colonialism and its legacy and language. She raises a number of questions, but applauds the essays' ethical concerns as a contribution to African scholarship, and she celebrates the authors' continued connection with non-academic readers as an aspect lacking in Western scholarship.

Njoroge's response focuses on three papers (by Dube, Masenya, and Plaatjie) and on the method of "reading with." For Njoroge, to "read with" is to reclaim the legacy of African women, who, since the introduction of Christianity, have read the Bible with each other and with children in church, and composed songs from the Scriptures. My divination essay and its interpretation of Ruth evoked an intense engagement.

15

Njoroge applauds the focus on divination for its connection with African Independent Churches' non-academic readers, its orality, and its ethical commitment to building healthy relationships. Njoroge, however, is uneasy with my interpretation. She engages the "oral-spirit" framework that I have articulated elsewhere, and she reads the characters of Ruth and Naomi differently. Njoroge applauds Masenya's storytelling approach, noting that it underlines the importance of a hermeneutics of orality. She finds Masenya's elevation of African stories to canonical status a radical move, one that should be tested among other biblical readers in Africa to measure their response. Yet she affirms Masenya's standpoint as a challenge to the colonial-patriarchal church that dismissed African cultures. Turning to Plaatjie's essay, Njoroge applauds the strategy of reading the Bible with and from black South African women, and reading the Bible with and through the post-apartheid constitution. Njoroge credits Plaatjie for paving the way to an interdisciplinary approach, which Njoroge advocates in her closing remarks. Likewise, she calls upon Plaatjie to test her proposal among other Bible readers.

Tinyiko S. Maluleke responds as a South African male theologian, and he engages the three South African writers (Plaatjie, Masenya, and Nadar) and myself. Maluleke holds that African women's voices represent the cutting edge, the prophetic voice in African theological and biblical scholarship. For him, the strongest contribution of this collection is in its methodological and theoretical proposals. Yet Maluleke challenges the proponents of these theories and models to sharpen their tools further, to ensure that their tools do not subscribe to the prevailing oppressive thinking. He questions Plaatjie's option for the new constitution as insufficient in itself, for the important issue is interpretation, be it of the Bible or of the post-apartheid constitution. Maluleke challenges Masenya's *bosadi* hermeneutic, urging her to be wary of buying into patriarchal prescriptions of ideal womanhood. He problematizes Nadar's tendency to highlight a few successful women as representative of middle-class women, who have been given some power in patriarchal structures. Turning to my proposed method of divination, Maluleke holds that "we need a critique of national and patriarchal economy within which divination procedures are situated," in order to arrest divination's use against women (in accusations of witchcraft, for example). The association of women with witchcraft, however, is neither limited to Africa nor does it need a divination set. Rather, it is a patriarchal control of women's bodies and labor. The saving grace in divination is perhaps captured best by Njoroge, who says, "I appreciate that Dube mentions that 'all diviner-readers are not healer-readers, save those who regard their reading practices as ethical efforts to contribute toward building better interpersonal and international relations.'"

•

In conclusion, *Other Ways of Reading* is in many ways a contribution to the postcolonial feminist discourse. In many of the essays, Bird notes, colonialism (Ntloedibe-Kuswani, Mbuwayesango, Masenya, and Dube), apartheid (Plaatjie), neocolonialism (Njoroge), and globalization (Dube, Njoroge, and Maluleke) emerge as issues that shape African women's lives and their interpretation of texts. This volume engages the patriarchy of African cultures, the Bible, and colonial masters. It confronts the imperialism of historical and contemporary times, exposing its impact on women's lives and its link with patriarchy. The volume, by offering postcolonial feminist strategies of resistance, seeks to create a space in which women are empowered against the shackles of patriarchy and imperial oppression at various levels and in various forms.[20] It suggests new methods of reading and new interpretations, and it proposes other canonical texts that deserve to be read and heard outside the imposition of imperial culture. By so doing, the volume assumes a postcolonial stance, for it challenges the authority of the Bible and Western methods of reading; it points to a thousand other canons and methods of reading. Its oppositional postcolonial stance is, perhaps, best captured by Maluleke's response:

The contributors are clearly seeking to move us beyond the familiar situation in which the data is African and local, but the analytical theories and methods must come from elsewhere. In that scenario, African contexts provide raw materials and sources, but the explanatory strategies are seldom fashioned out of local practices, beliefs, and cultures. Admittedly a good analytical framework is useful regardless of where it comes from. However, there is something wrong when analytical frameworks almost always come from outside. . . . The essays in this volume make significant contributions in the area of method and theory.

Notes

1. See "Report on Circle Study Commissions," Trinity College, Legon, Ghana, March 1998, 20–25.

2. The other areas of study are African women in religion and culture, theological education and ministerial formation, and African women and history.

3. See Carole Boyce Davies and Anne Adams Graves, eds., *Ngambika: Studies of Women in African Literature* (Trenton, N.J.: Africa World Press, 1986), for a discussion of the role of African women in storytelling.

4. See Philip M. Peek, ed., *African Divination Systems: Ways of Knowing* (Indianapolis: Indiana University Press, 1991), for an extensive discussion of African divination systems.

5. See Isidore Okpewho, *African Oral Literature: Backgrounds, Character, and Continuity* (Indianapolis: Indiana University Press, 1992), for a detailed discussion of African stories and storytelling.

6. See Musa W. Dube, "Readings of *Semoya:* Batswana Women's Interpretations of Matt. 15:21–28." *Semeia* 73 (1996): 121–22, where I encountered this participatory storytelling as used in church preaching.

7. For a good example of this method, see Musa W. Dube, "Five Husbands at the Well of Living Waters," in *A Decade in Solidarity with the Bible* (ed. Musimbi Kanyoro and Nyambura Njoroge; Geneva: World Council of Churches, 1998), 6–26.

8. For example, in Setswana Bible translations, the *Badimo* (sacred intermediaries) of Botswana were rendered "demons." See Musa W. Dube, "Consuming a Colonial Cultural Bomb: Translating *Badimo* into Demons in Setswana Bible," *Journal for the Study of the New Testament* 73 (1999): 33–59, for a study of this rendering.

9. See Ifi Amadiume, *Male Daughters, Female Husbands: Gender and Sex in African Society* (London: Zed Books, 1987).

10. See also Musimbi Kanyoro, "Biblical Hermeneutics: Ancient Palestine and Contemporary World," *Review and Expositor* 94 (1997): 363–78, where she reads the book of Ruth with rural Kenyan women.

11. For further readings on *Bosadi* (womanhood), see Mmadipoane

(Ngwana 'Mphahlele) Masenya, "Proverbs 31:10–31 in a South African Context: A *Bosadi* (Womanhood) Perspective" (Ph.D. diss., University of South Africa, 1996). See also her article, "Proverbs 31:10–31 in a South African Context: A Reading for the Liberation of African (Northern Sotho) Women," *Semeia* 78 (1997): 55–68.

12. For my earlier efforts and a more detailed description of divination as a method of reading, see Musa W. Dube, "Divining Texts for International Relations: Matt. 15:21–28," in *Transformative Encounters: Jesus and Women Re-viewed* (ed. Ingrid Rosa Kitzberger; Leiden: E. J. Brill, 2000), 315–28.

13. Vincent L. Wimbush, ed., *African Americans and the Bible: Sacred Text and Social Texture* (New York: Continuum, 2000); and Gerald O. West and Musa W. Dube, eds., *The Bible in Africa* (Leiden: E. J. Brill, 2000).

14. See Tinyiko S. Maluleke, "Black and African Theologies in the New World Order: A Time to Drink from Our Own Wells," *Journal for Southern Africa* 96 (1996): 3–19.

15. For more information about inculturation and black biblical hermeneutics, see Emmanual Martey, *African Theology: Inculturation and Liberation* (Maryknoll, N.Y.: Orbis Books, 1993).

16. For a critical review of "translation theologians" and their claims, see Tinyiko S. Maluleke, "Recent Developments in the Christian Theologies of Africa: Towards the Twenty-first Century," *Journal of Constructive Theology* 2 (1996): 33–60.

17. One can note such anthologies as Letty M. Russell, ed., *Feminist Interpretation of the Bible* (Philadelphia: Westminster Press, 1985); Adela Yarbro Collins, ed., *Feminist Perspectives on Biblical Scholarship* (Atlanta: Scholars Press, 1985); Elisabeth Schüssler Fiorenza, *Searching the Scriptures*, vol. 1: *A Feminist Introduction* (New York: Crossroad, 1993).

18. See R. S. Sugirtharajah, *Voices from the Margin: Interpreting the Bible in the Third World* (rev. ed.; Maryknoll, N.Y.: Orbis Books, 1995); Fernando F. Segovia and Mary Ann Tolbert, eds., *Reading from This Place: Social Location and Biblical Interpretation in Global Perspective* (Minneapolis: Fortress Press, 1995); and Phyllis A. Bird, Katharine Doob Sakenfeld, and Sharon Ringe, eds., *Semeia* 78 (1997).

19. See Musa W. Dube, *Postcolonial Feminist Interpretation of the Bible* (St. Louis: Chalice Press, 2000), 31–34, in which an examination of the work of non-Western feminists indicates that they insist on the preservation of their canons.

20. See Dube, *Postcolonial Feminist Interpretation*, 23–43, for a more detailed discussion.

Storytelling Methods and Interpretations

1

I Am the Woman

Rose Teteki Abbey

I am the Samaritan Woman.
I am the Woman who met Jesus at the Well.
He asked me for water and I refused.

After all, he was a Jew, I was a Samaritan
But there were other reasons for my refusal.
People condemn me and my lifestyle.
Women shun me for reasons best known to them.
And Men?
Ask the five who have stayed with me.
They use me in secret and despise me in public.

I was used to loneliness, it was welcome to me.
It was better than being condemned by people.
How then was I to socialize with this man at the Well?
How could I add him to the long string of my accusers?
But, before I was aware, he had drawn me into conversation.
He was not ashamed to sit with me.

He sat with me at the Well and had a long conversation with me.
My culture said I was nothing without a husband
But Jesus didn't care that none of the five men was my husband.
He gave me the meaning of true religion.
He corrected my notions about faith.
True worshipers, he said, worship in Spirit and in Truth.

Listening to him, I felt liberated.
It didn't matter any longer that I was a woman—
A woman without a husband.
What mattered was that I was hungry, I was thirsty.
He gave me the living water.
I left my jar and ran to the village.

23

"Come!" I said to the people.
"Come and meet the liberator"
I truly was liberated.
I could talk about my fears to Christ. I still do.
He neither rebuked me nor laughed at me. He still doesn't.
I felt full because Christ gave me the Living Water.
I still feel full, because Christ still gives me the Living Water.
I am the Woman Caught in Adultery
I was brought to the marketplace
They were ready to stone me
My sins, they said, were many.

I wept.
Not because I was to die.
I had died several times already.
I died when society pressured me
To stay in an abusive marriage.
I died when my abusive husband finally
Kicked me out of our home.
Kicked me out with nothing but my hungry children.
I died when I gave myself to a man for money to feed my babies

No, I didn't weep for the life I was about to lose.
I wept for the society that didn't bother to look
For that good-for-nothing man who made me what I had become.
I wept for the so-called religious men
Who used religion to abuse me and condemn me to death.
"Caught in the act of adultery," they said. I smiled to myself.
How does one commit adultery alone?

Oh I was ready to die. I have died so many times already.
One more death, albeit the final, will be accepted.
Even welcomed.
Deep in thought as I was, I didn't hear the stranger speak.
And then I heard him.
He who has no sin, Let him cast the first stone
And then they remembered.
They remembered that they had let the man caught with me
go scot-free.
They remembered that they had committed adultery.
Oh yes, they remembered that they had often used me sexually.
They remembered, and they left.

One after the other, they left.
And then he spoke, the stranger spoke to me
Woman, where are they?
Has no one condemned you? Then neither do I condemn you!
I was free, my sisters, I was free.
Christ saw through their false religion.
True Religion liberates.
Religion that enslaves is false.

I am Mary, the sister of Martha
As a little girl all I wanted was to study.
"Little girls become big girls, Big girls marry.
And married women belong in the kitchen,"
I was told.

I didn't want to obey.
I didn't want to be a "good girl."
It was too suffocating.
Too much of a straightjacket.
My sister was all a girl should be.
That didn't help.

Then he came to our home, that man called Jesus.
I wanted to listen to him to learn at this feet.
"Go and cook for him," I was told.
I pretended not to hear.
"Come and help me," my sister cried.

And then that stranger spoke.
That Jesus called the Christ said words I will never forget.
Leave her alone! She has chosen the best, and it will never be taken from her.
Those words affirmed me.
That wonderful message liberated me and set me
on my journey of discovery.
I have never looked back since then.

No, I don't look back.
Not even when scripture is used to tie me down.
Not even when Paul is used against me.
No! I don't look back
Even male-chauvinist church leaders can't make me look back.

I draw strength from my sister Deborah.

25

I look at her and remind myself that all those men need me.
They need the strength that only a woman of faith can have.

I draw strength from Paul who,
In an unguarded moment, spoke the truth.
There is no male nor female in Christ.

I draw strength from that stranger's words.
She has taken the best, and it will never be taken from her.
I stand on Jesus' words.
I am come to *free the prisoners and to release the oppressed.*

Religion that enslaves us is false.
True religion gives us freedom!

2

Esther and Northern Sotho Stories:
An African–South African Woman's Commentary

Mmadipoane (Ngwana 'Mphahlele) Masenya

Storytelling is a significant art, particularly in the oral and diverse cultures of Africa. This art was and is sufficiently portrayed when stories are told by word of mouth and dramatized in person by the performing storyteller. Telling African oral stories in writing carries potential dangers and or weaknesses. The written story, for example, lacks the vigor and vitality of the narrated story. The "free text" is transformed to a "fixed" text (Mazamisa 1995:11). The necessary modifications and additions that the oral performer can make as he/she retells a story are absent in a written, fixed, "lifeless" story. In this regard, Mazamisa (1995:12) argues: "Oral traditions that are verbally rich and sensuous suddenly become sterile and dead when they are translated into writing."

In the present essay, this situation is exacerbated by several additional factors. First, the written story is retold in a language that is foreign to Africa, the English language. The latter, for example, as compared to many African languages, is gendered. As this essay reveals, certain stories, or even details in some stories,

---

I prefer the term *African–South African* to *southern African* or *black South African*. The word "Africa" in "southern Africa," in my view, defines a cultural group rather than a geographical position. The word *black* is problematic, because it might be understood in some circles to include colored and Indian women in South Africa. I am writing about a *specific* South African woman: an indigenous woman of South Africa, who were historically and are now known as Africans—the blacks of the blacks of South Africa. Included in the African–South African category are the different tribes of South Africa: Zulus, Vendas, Sothos, Xhosas, and so forth.

would read smoothly, without excluding persons of either gender, were the reading done in an African language. Further, some words, phrases, and sentences—such as the African wisdom sayings, many of which form an integral part of the storytelling process, or even the stories themselves—are difficult to translate meaningfully into the English language. One other challenge is that although the written word is immortal and has guaranteed longevity, it is used by a special class of people: the "haves"—the clergy, the officials, and the elite of society. The majority of people (particularly in diverse African contexts) only have access to the original oral literature (Mazamisa 1995:11).

With these and other difficulties in mind, I attempt a rereading of the African (Northern Sotho) stories in conjunction with the biblical story of Esther. Northern Sotho is singled out for more specificity about the African–South African context, although there are close similarities among the many Bantu African tribes in southern Africa. My reading of these stories is shaped by my experiences as an African–South African *woman*. As such, I am led to ask how helpful these stories are to women in patriarchal contexts. Do they have the capacity to provide African women with life and well-being in the midst of oppression, suppression, and death? In an attempt to answer such questions, each set of stories (both from Africa and from the Bible) is accompanied by an African woman's liberationist critique.

As we grapple with bringing the two canons together, it is important to address a number of questions. How may biblical stories meaningfully be read with African stories in mind? Is it possible to marry stories from two different cultures (the Northern Sotho culture and the Israelite culture) and still to end up with a successful union? In the case of these two cultures, it might be possible, since—as several earlier studies have noted—there are close resemblances between the Israelite and African cultures, including a common worldview and a common experience of reality (Masenya 1989:183; see also Masenya 1998; Dickson 1977; Burden and Bosman 1982). My earlier work has demonstrated that, due to those close resemblances, proverbs from the Old Testament can be contextualized with ease in an African (Northern Sotho) setting. Both the biblical proverbs and the African culture share a simplistic, optimistic outlook on life. As Burden observes, "What is important is not a common cultural milieu, or corresponding pivotal points, common customs or even a common belief in a Supreme Being, but rather elements in their world view, a relationship of spirit" (1982:74).

In addition to that common worldview, proverbs from the two cultures share elements of language, style, and subject matter. For example, Victor Zinkuratire (1999) has noted the close resemblances between the Hebrew language and African languages.[1] In addition, proverbs in both cultures are sapiential in orientation, and they reveal a similar structure. They also share the theme of parent-child relationships in a family context. The Hebrew word *mašal*, often translated as "proverb," has a broader meaning as well, encompassing parables or the sort of folktales and stories that are the focus of this study. For that reason, the insights of previous work on proverbs provide an important basis for the current study.

Commenting on the common ground between the Old Testament and Africa, Phillips concludes:

> In short, the church in this continent, though only partially acquainted with this part of the Bible, feels a natural affinity with it, and is not likely to neglect it when the whole becomes more accessible. Misuse, misunderstanding or overemphasis are likely to be more common than rejection or neglect; hence the Church in Africa has much to gain from a clearer and firmer grasp of the Old Testament's true place and function in God's self-manifestation to the world. (1942:13).

Before attempting to bring the two canons together, however, it would be helpful to introduce each canon independently.

A Note on the Story of Esther

This essay is an attempt to reread (not to misuse or misunderstand, to recall Phillips's painful words in the above quotation) the biblical story/narrative of Esther with African stories. Indeed, the book of Esther is a story, not history (see Burger

1988:156). Although it is a narrative partially rooted in history, it has many unhistorical elements, revealing that we are dealing with a story about one of the Jewish heroes or heroines. Burger's remarks are instructive:

> Collectively these historical details would seem to constitute a convincing argument in favour of the historicity of the book, but they do not make it a chronicle. The author uses historical details merely as a background to his story. The arguments against the historicity of the book are far more persuasive. The non-historical elements of the book indicate that the author did not intend to produce a chronicle. (1988:156)

Although the narrative of Esther is not historically rooted, it has realistic elements that lead most modern readers, not excluding the African Bible readers, to identify with the story, or rather with the characters in the story.

The question whether the book of Esther deals with Esther the Jewish heroine or Mordecai the Jewish hero depends on a particular reading. Interestingly, the nationality of Mordecai, much more than that of Esther, is foregrounded in the book of Esther (3:3; 5:13; 8:7; 9:29, 31). One would conclude that although the book bears the name of a woman, it is actually a story about the *man* Mordecai (9:4) and the *Jew* Mordecai (3:3; 5:13; 8:7). It is thus a national male story. Mosala (1993) is right when he argues that, in the book of Esther, Esther is used to achieve the national male agenda.

Even a superficial reading of the story of Esther reveals the androcentric nature of the book and, consequently, the patriarchal nature of the world that produced the book. Elsewhere I have argued:

> Though elements such as these may make our reader (African South African female reader) identify with the story, as a whole she finds the story of Esther offering no liberative possibilities for oppressed women. It does not enhance them as persons in their own right. Instead, it perpetuates stereotyped ideas that women cannot act on their own (cf. Mordecai's influence on Esther's life), that they are evil (cf. Esther's request for a second day of murder) and that they are tricksters (cf. Esther's humility before the king on two occasions. (Masenya 1998:9)

Not only is the story of Esther marred by its male-centeredness, a reading (particularly of chap. 1) reveals that we are dealing with a document that portrays a certain class. The class portrayed in this document cannot be helpful to many African women whose socioeconomic conditions render them largely invisible. In this regard, Mosala (1988:134) contends that the text depicts the surplus of the economy squandered on nonreproductive luxury goods and a luxury lifestyle among the ruling class. It is silent on the conditions and struggles of the nonrulers: peasants, serfs, and the underclass.

One other troubling element as one reads the book of Esther, particularly from an African–South African's perspective, given our history of marginalization as a race, is its foregrounding or "chosenness" of the one race or people (the Jews) over and against the other race or people (the Persians). The problem with the Jewish race's special position in the divine plan is that the "other" race, which is not portrayed as chosen, can be plundered even in their own country, in the name of God. Esther is one of the rare books in which the Hebrew name for God is not used. If one reads the book carefully, however, there are veiled elements of the Divine. God's hand is visible throughout the story (Loader 1998:18–24). It is in the name of the Divine that Esther the Jew—Esther whom we may rightly assume became queen through divine intervention (chap. 2)—can display such cruelty against many innocent Persians, as revenge against the evil plan of Haman against her people. More disturbing is that the evil intentions of Haman against the Jews (chap. 3) were never carried out, yet Esther still had the courage to request a second day of murder—the murder of many innocent people (chap. 9). Given my South African history, this story cannot help but remind us of how native inhabitants were plundered also in the name of God. The "chosen" race came in and found the "heathen" indigenous people, took their land, and colonized their minds and cultures in the name of the God of the Bible. The text of Esther is thus problematic for such factors as its class perspectives, its ethnic biases, and its ideology of colonization.

With these class, gender, and ethnic biases in mind, and given that the Bible is a highly esteemed book in the African–South African context, it is therefore important to think about new, empowering readings for such contexts. This is the main objective of the present essay: to read the book of Esther through the lenses of Northern Sotho stories. We may call it a folklorist reading of the book of Esther. The hope is that such a reading may rescue the story of Esther from the negative biases noted above, so that it can be embraced heartily by many of us, like the women of Africa, at the margins of society.

A Note on the Northern Sotho (Folk)tales

Having said this, it must be acknowledged that although the Northern Sotho language, like many African languages, is gender-neutral, and that many folktales (*dinonwane*), particularly fables, are gender-neutral, many of these stories reveal the patriarchal nature of the culture that produced them. Oduyoye (1994:26–76) also identifies this male bias of African lore in her *Daughters of Anowa*. She therefore approaches the lore with a feminist critique. Such painful elements in the Northern Sotho folk narratives will be dealt with in a critical way below.

In Northern Sotho, there are many folktales (*dinonwane*). In the Northern Sotho language, the word *nonwane* lexically stands for folktale, fable, legend, or fairy tale, and its plural, *dinonwane*, for folklore (Ziervogel and Mokgokong 1975:863). Examples of Northern Sotho folktales include *Nonwane ya kakanyatlhaloso* (myth), *nonwane ya pheteletšannete* (legend), and *nonwane ya tsholo* (fable). Folktales are popular fictional narratives about animals and/or human beings. Unlike myths and legends, folktales need not be taken seriously. That, however, should not perpetuate the unfortunate stereotypes that the "folk" in folktales refers to the "uneducated," irrational, and unimaginative dwellers of small communities (Okpewho 1992:163). Folktales have a role to play in the community. They are handed down from one generation to another, basically for amusement. Apart from amusement, Northern Sotho folktales serve a didactic function; they support the discipline of young

children, and they help to maintain cultural and social con-
formity (Makgamatha 1991:7–9). Some of these functions will
come to light as the Northern Sotho folktales interact with the
biblical stories.

The Two Canons Interact

In this essay, parts of the story of Esther are read in the context of Northern Sotho stories, by virtue of the similarities in
themes and worldviews between the two canons. The identity
of the audiences being addressed in each case is less significant
than the didactic purpose behind the narration. What lessons
do the narrators portray in these stories? Can we then lend
these narrators our ears?

Nonwane! Nonwane! (Tale! Tale!) is an introductory formula
for the Northern Sotho folktales. The implied meaning of *nonwane* appears to be "I want to tell a tale." The audience will then
respond *Keleketla!* The latter, like the word *nonwane,* is difficult
to translate. *Keleketla* is a responsive refrain the audience says
through the narration. Its initial use is assumed to mean "Go
ahead!" Probably the word has the same meaning as the Shona
word *Gweregeta*—that is, "Speak up!" This refrain is helpful, in
that the members of the audience also become active participants in the storytelling process (Makgamatha 1991:45).

Folktale 1: "Tšhiwana ye e sa hwego e leta monono" (An Orphan Who Does Not Die, Awaits Treasure) and Esther the Orphan

The tenor of the proverb is that those who are powerless,
the have-nots (such as orphans), if they remain persistent, will
get out of poverty one day.

Nonwane! Nonwane! . . . Keleketla!

> Long, long ago, there was a widow who had only one son. The
> two lived in severe poverty. So poor were they that the people of the
> village were sick and tired of their requests. In their village, there
> was a sick *kgoši* (chief). All means attempted toward his healing were
> not successful. The *kgoši* sent a word out to inform his people that
> there was only one doctor who could come to his rescue. The doctor

lived in an isolated spot at the outskirts of the village. The men in the village chose two men to go and fetch the doctor. When they arrived, they started singing the song "Tematema re nyaka ngaka, tematema kgoši e a lwala tematema" (Tematema, we are looking for a doctor, tematema, the *kgoši* is sick, tematema). The doctor responded, "If I can come to you, if I can come to you, will you not run away, tematema?" The two replied, "How can we run away while we are looking for tematema? The *kgoši* is sick, tematema." The doctor raised its head and half of its body out of the water. When they saw the big snake with a lamp on its forehead, they were so terrified that they did not have the courage to wait until it reached them, and they decided to run away.

So terrified were they that they went back to the village, admitting their failure to bring the doctor along with them. Then another group of men tried, but with no success. Finally, the orphan boy decided to go and try his luck. On arriving, he shouted the following words to the snake: "Tematema ke nyaka ngaka, tematema kgoši e a lwala tematema" (Tematema, I am looking for a doctor, tematema the *kgoši* is sick, tematema). The doctor responded, "If I can come to you, if I can come to you, will you not run away, tematema?" "How can I run away while I am looking for a doctor, tematema, the *kgoši* is sick, tematema?" answered the orphan.

How was the snake transported to the royal kraal? The snake coiled around the orphan, and he took it there. At the village, the snake licked the *kgoši,* and he was healed. The orphan had to take the snake back to its home. The snake rewarded the boy with a big herd of cattle, goats, and sheep. On arrival at the village, a big feast was made for the orphan, and he was given another herd of cattle, sheep, and goats. The family of the boy came out of their poverty. Then the word spoken by *mogologolo* (the ancestor) was fulfilled: *Tšhiwana ye e sa hwego e leta monono* (An orphan who does not die, awaits treasure). (See Masola 1988:26–28)

Is that not the case? . . . *Keleketla!*

There is yet another story I would like to relate to you. *Keleketla!* This story comes from the Bible. *Keleketla!*

Long, long ago, when the stones were still soft, there was an orphan whose name was Esther. Esther, together with her Uncle Mordecai and fellow Jews, were taken captive to a faraway country [Esther 2:7]. As a result, her situation as an orphan was exacerbated by the fact that they were exiles in a foreign land. They were under oppression. Therefore, they were not free, and hence even their identity was hidden at the beginning of the story [2:10]. However, due to her ability to listen to elders like her guardian, Uncle Morde-

34

cai [children were expected to highly exalt their parents, as in the Northern Sotho culture: see Masenya 1989], and her willingness to take risks, her people were ultimately saved from impending destruction. The risks she took entailed a contest to become queen in a foreign land [chap. 2] and her boldness in approaching King Ahasuerus, even though she knew this could mean her death [chap. 4; see also the risky decision of the boy in the Northern Sotho story, who, although he knew about the potential dangers, was willing to fetch the doctor for the *kgoši*]. Esther, like the orphan in the Northern Sotho story, persevered until the end. She ultimately emerged as a winner.[2]

Esther was rewarded, because she became a queen. Her boldness in risking an appearance before King Ahasuerus was rewarded, because she found favor with the king; the destruction that was to come upon her people was avoided. Due to her persistence, irrespective of her fragile position (her gender, her foreignness, and her position as an orphan), her uncle received a high position at the king's court. Hence we may rightly refer to Esther as *tšhiwana ye e sa hwego e leta monono*. This story has a lesson for those who feel helpless in their difficult conditions. If they persevere, they will be rewarded in the end.

The stories from both canons reveal the patriarchal nature of the cultures that produced them. In the Northern Sotho culture, one is not surprised that the one who fends for the family is a boy. Indeed, in this culture, orphan boys learn at an early age to take control over family affairs. It would appear that society expected women, irrespective of their age and position as parents, to rely on their sons to take care of the needs of the family, particularly needs that had to be met outside the home. Women were expected to operate only in the private sphere of the home. Such an exercise is understandable in the light of male headship typical in patriarchal cultures. Although the Northern Sotho folktale empowers the powerless, including societal outcasts like orphans, the story appears to be biased against female folk.

Folktale 2: "Mokgadi le Mokgatšana" and Esther, the Listener

Nonwane! Nonwane! . . . Keleketla!

Long, long ago there were two daughters in one family. Their names were Mokgadi and Mokgatšana. One day Mokgatšana decided to refresh herself by going outside of her home, so that she could be exposed to life out there. On her journey she had several encounters, the first with an old lady. The lady was struggling through her journey, for she could not see very well. She asked Mokgatšana to remove some matter from her eyes. Mokgatšana did not hesitate to offer her help. The old woman was so impressed by Mokgatšana's kindness that she remarked, "You are a kind-hearted child. Listen to my advice. Offer help to whomever you will meet along the way, just as you have helped me."

Mokgatšana proceeded with her journey, singing a song and admiring the beauty of nature. She met another old lady and asked her, "Where are you going, mum?" The old lady responded, "Far away. Could you please carry my luggage?" Mokgatšana helped to carry the old lady's luggage without any complaint. The two of them reached a place where each had to go in her own direction. The old lady thanked Mokgatšana for her assistance and gave her a packet of salt, and she advised her to help whomever she would meet along the way.

As Mokgatšana proceeded with the journey, she met a frog. The latter requested that she fix a soft porridge for it. She quickly remembered the advice of the first lady whom she had met. She fixed the soft porridge for the frog and put in some of the salt she got from the second old lady. After eating the soft porridge, the frog remarked, "You are a very kind-hearted child. I will give you some advice. Take this mabela meal and proceed to the cave. A big snake lives in the cave. You will not find the snake, but you will find a rock with a hole next to the entrance to the cave. Prepare the soft porridge and put it in the hole of the rock. Wait until the snake comes back."

When she arrived at the cave, Mokgatšana did exactly what she had been told. When the snake came back, it asked her, "Who fixed such a delicious soft porridge? Come out! Come out!" At first Mokgatšana was afraid, but she took courage and showed up for the snake to see her. The snake expressed its gratitude to Mokgatšana for the delicious soft porridge she had prepared, and it said, "You have fed me well. Go inside the cave, and you will find clothes, beads, and necklaces. Take as much as you can carry, for you have pleased me."

On her arrival at home, her elder sister Mokgadi became interested in her gifts. She decided to undertake the same journey. Before she set out on the journey, Mokgatšana advised, "Wait a bit. There is some advice I would like to give you." Mokgadi responded skeptically, "What are you talking about? Young as you are, do you think that I never undertook a journey?" Mokgatšana replied, "You have not undertaken a journey like this one. On this journey there are things that you are supposed to do and those that are not supposed to be done." Mokgadi was fed up with her younger sister. She said, "You are a fool, and you are young." She slapped Mokgatšana in the face and set out on her journey.

Her first encounter was with the same old lady whom Mokgatšana met. She asked her the direction to the cave of a generous snake. The old lady replied, "Wipe away the matter that is in my eyes," pointing at her eyes. Mokgadi answered, "Who are you that I must wipe stuff out of your eyes?" She answered arrogantly and continued with her journey. The old lady shouted at her and said, "Continue to behave to others as you did to me." Later on, Mokgadi met a woman who was carrying a piece of luggage on her head. She refused to listen to the advice of the old lady. She could not understand why a well-dressed girl like her could be expected to carry a dirty piece of luggage belonging to an old lady. She proceeded with the journey, thinking that she was going to receive good gifts. The listeners will recall, however, that before she started her journey, she was not willing to get advice on how she should conduct herself from Mokgatšana, who, though younger, had experienced the journey. To use the Northern Sotho idiom, Mokgadi did not give her ear to *leho le le tšwago pitšeng* (the wooden spoon that comes from the pot), meaning "someone who comes directly from a particular situation or experience unchanged." She thus went out empty-handed.

As she continued with the journey, she met a frog. The latter requested that she fix a soft porridge for her. She replied with ridicule, wondering why a frog would think that a person of her caliber would fix food for frogs. The frog remarked, "Then I will not show you the direction to the cave." Mokgadi became confused. There were different paths, and she did not know which one to follow. She then decided to go and fix soft porridge for the frog. The soft porridge was not as delicious as that fixed by her younger sister, because there was no salt to make it tasty. As a result, the frog did not enjoy it. In spite of that, the frog gave Mokgadi a packet of mealy meal (though it was not as tasty as that which was given to Mokgatšana). The frog directed her to the cave and gave instructions on what to do on reaching the cave.

When she arrived, Mokgadi did not find the snake. She prepared a soft porridge, but there was no salt to make it tasty. Where would the salt have come from, since she neglected the old lady who could have given her some? Even the quality of the mealy meal was not the same as that prepared by Mokgatšana. When the snake came back, it smelled the aroma of the soft porridge and started to help it-self. As it licked the food, the snake found the food tasteless. The snake became angry with the cook and called her. She headed to the snake, being excited and thinking that she was going to receive some gifts. But that was not the case. The snake told Mokgadi that she came, basically, to receive gifts. It condemned her for not being kind and for having cooked a tasteless soft porridge. It promised Mokgadi that it would swallow her up. When Mokgadi realized how angry the snake was, she ran away very fast, continuing until she reached her home. On her arrival, her younger sister asked her about the gifts. So ashamed was she that she could not respond to Mok-gatšana's question. Since that day, she changed her lifestyle. She learned to be kind and compassionate. Hers was a hard lesson, be-cause she did not succeed in obtaining gifts from the snake. (Masola 1988:16–20)

What lesson do we get from this story? To listen is reward-ing. Moreover, learning to cooperate with people—even if it does not seem to make sense at times, or even if the people with whom we are involved are considered "lowly" by soci-ety—can be a rewarding exercise.

The same applies to Esther in her story. She is a listening type, and she therefore proves to be a wise daughter. When her uncle advises her to join the beautiful women who were com-peting for selection as the Persian queen, she does not question it. Instead, she relies on the wisdom of her guardian Mordecai and acts accordingly. It is worthy to note that one of the duties of Jewish or Israelite children was to respect and honor their parents (Prov. 1:8–9; 6:20; Exod. 20:12). The meaning of *parent* extended beyond the blood boundary. Anyone who was the contemporary of blood parents was supposed to be respected as well—an understanding shared also in the Northern Sotho culture (Masenya 1989). When under the custody of Hegai in preparation for the contest, Esther is cooperative (Esther 2:8ff.). When her uncle charges her not to reveal her identity to the people, she obeys (2:10). When Mordecai advises her to appear before the king for the sake of her people, she listens (4:15ff.). Her capacity to listen is rewarded because, in the end, her na-tion is saved.

The moral is the same as that in the Northern Sotho folk-tale: it is not a good idea to despise advice, even if it comes from those who might not meet one's standards, even if it comes from the "powerless" (like the younger sister in the Northern Sotho story), and even if it sounds unwise. But particularly if advice comes from an older party, it is worth listening to; in most cases, the listener will not regret it.

The question worth asking is whether boys or girls in African cultures are still expected to be obedient to their seniors. Although one could argue that, in African–South African cultures, all children regardless of gender are expected to honor their parents (Masenya 1989), it would not be an exaggeration to argue that more was and is expected from the female gender. What was noted in the preceding folktale ("Tšhiwana ye e sa hwego e leta monono")—namely that, in the absence of their fathers, boys could take leadership responsibilities at an early age—points in that direction. In a patriarchal culture, with its emphasis on male leadership and female submission, it makes sense that female folk, regardless of their age, are expected to be more obedient to seniors than their male counterparts. Perhaps it is no coincidence that, in both stories, females are portrayed as models of children who listen.

Folktale 3: "Kgomo ye tšhwana" (The White Cow) and the Story of Haman and Mordecai

Nonwane! Nonwane! . . . Keleketla!

> Long, long ago, when one could still get greens [a relish of some sort] from the stones, there were brothers whose names were Mashilo (the elder one) and Mashilwane (the younger one). One day the two brothers decided to go out of their village to be exposed to life outside the village. As they continued happily with their journey, they came to a point where the road branched into two directions. After an argument, they had to part ways. Mashilo headed in the eastern direction, while his younger brother Mashilwane went in the direction of the West.
>
> As he continued on his journey, Mashilwane saw a big fire in front of him. There were many pots around the fire. He thought to himself, "Perhaps there is some wealth inside these pots." He started picking them up one by one, until he was left with one extraordinarily heavy pot. After a short rest, he started struggling with the pot again. A big sound was heard, and the last pot rolled down, and—surprisingly—a big giant appeared at the place where the pot was.

39

The giant had big eyes and scary teeth. "What are you doing?" asked the giant. "Why do you destroy my home?" The giant continued angrily, "Where do you think I must live?"

Mashilwane, frightened by the scene, replied, "I was not aware that I was destroying your home. Please let me mold your pot again." The giant refused Mashilwane's offer. He instructed Mashilwane to carry him on his shoulders. Mashilwane, realizing that one of the giant's legs was too big, said, "I do not mind carrying you. However, seeing that your leg is beautiful, we will need to wrap it with a beautiful skin." He then took his dogs, and off they went. Where did they go to? To get wild meat and animal skins for the giant. On returning, Mashilwane gave lots of meat to the giant and prepared a beautiful skin coat for him. In the process, the giant, who was full from all the meat, fell asleep. Little did the giant know about the disaster that was to befall him. While he was asleep, Mashilwane's hungry dogs devoured him. Only the big leg was left. Mashilwane then chopped the leg, and a herd of cattle came out of the giant's leg. Among them was a very fat, healthy, well-built white cow, *kgomo ye tšhwana*.

Later when the two brothers met each other, Mashilo, the elder brother, only had a flock of dogs. Mashilwane sympathized with his elder brother. He said, "If I found cattle, you too have found wealth. You may have the whole wealth, only let me have the white cow." Mashilo became jealous. He was not interested in the other cattle. His heart was also on the white cow. Hatred and anger filled his heart. As they continued with the journey, Mashilo told his brother about his thirst. They both planned to go by a fountain of water to help themselves, because Mashilwane also was thirsty. At the fountain, Mashilo, knowing the evil he had plotted against his brother, pretended to be caring by offering Mashilwane an opportunity to be the first one to drink. As Mashilwane bowed down to drink, Mashilo pushed him into the deep fountain.

After arriving home, Mashilo did not survive, for a bird [which in most of the Northern Sotho folktales is a symbol of conscience] kept on singing the following song:

> *Mashilo! Mashilo o na le mona* (Mashilo! Mashilo! You have jealousy)
> *O bolaile ngwaneno Mashilwane* (You murdered your younger brother Mashilwane)
> *Ka baka la mona ka dikgomo tša gagwe* (Because of your jealousy for his cattle)
> *Wa mo kgoromeletša ka bodibeng* (You pushed him into deep waters)

O phaphametše o lewa ke matlapakgerepe (He is on the waters
      eaten by crabs)

In a nutshell, the song revealed that it was Mashilo who
killed his brother. Ultimately, the villagers took Mashilo and
threw him into the same fountain into which he had thrown
his younger brother (Masola 1988:3–7).

The lesson is that people must learn to be satisfied with
what they have. They must remember that what goes around,
comes around: the evil that one plans against someone will ultimately come back to them.

Nonwane! Nonwane! . . . Keleketla!

> Long, long ago, when the stones still could speak, there were
> two men whose names were Haman and Mordecai. The strife and
> enmity between Mordecai and Haman began when Mordecai re-
> fused to bow before Haman. Consequent to Haman's promotion by
> King Ahasuerus to a position above all his officials, the king com-
> manded that all his servants who were at the king's gate should bow
> to this new appointee (Esther 3:2). Because of his Jewish religious
> convictions, Mordecai was not willing to bow to a fellow human
> being. Mordecai's defiance displeased Haman so much that he
> planned not only to murder Mordecai, but also to annihilate all of his
> people.
>
> If Haman's plans would succeed, much innocent blood would
> be shed because of the greed of one man. So greedy for power was
> Haman that the refusal of just one man—Mordecai—was enough to
> make Haman furious. So power-hungry was he that he would do
> anything to keep his status. His greed to have everybody bow to him
> reminds us of the greed for material possessions, and perhaps also
> for power, that is reflected in the above Northern Sotho tale.
> Haman's anger against Mordecai is captured in the following verse:
> "Yet all this does me no good so long as I see the Jew Mordecai sit-
> ting at the king's gate" (5:13). As a response to his anger and frustra-
> tions caused by the uncooperative Mordecai, Haman's wife and
> friends gave the following destructive, or foolish, advice: " 'Let a gal-
> lows fifty cubits high be made, and in the morning tell the king to
> have Mordecai hanged on it; then go with the king to the banquet in
> good spirits.' This advice pleased Haman and he had the gallows
> made" (5:14).

In both tales, the perpetrators of evil do not wait to carry
out their evil plans; they do not waste a minute in deciding to

take the lives of their opponents. Indeed, the gallows were pre-pared for hanging Mordecai. What happens ultimately? *Keleketla!* The tables are turned against Haman, and he is the one hanged on the same gallows. Such an occurrence reminds us of the Northern Sotho proverb that says, *Moepalebitla, o a ike-pela* (The one who digs a grave, digs for her/himself). Haman's greed for power results not only in his own death, but in the deaths of his ten sons and of many innocent Persians. That which goes around, comes around. The same lesson as that de-rived from the Northern Sotho proverb can be derived from the Haman-Mordecai story: The evil that one plans against others will ultimately return against the plotter. Then the word of the ancestor becomes fulfilled: *Le ge o ka buela leopeng, mago-kobu a a go bona* (Even if you can skin it [your victim] in the veld, the wild birds are looking at you).

Both stories shed light on masculine violence—men abus-ing fellow men for material gain and fame. Although both sto-ries remind us that perpetrators of violence, irrespective of their gender, will reap accordingly, the Haman-Mordecai story is problematic because it appears that violence is punished only if exercised by a non-Jew. Violence done by the Jews seems to be tolerated. One may ask why Esther and Mordecai are not punished for shedding innocent blood. When the Jews under the leadership of Mordecai, who is depicted in 9:4 as "powerful in the king's house," used that power and "struck down all their enemies with the sword, slaughtering, and de-stroying them, and did as they pleased to those who hated them" (9:5), it does not seem to cause the narrator concern. Is that because the enemies are not the Jews' neighbors?

We are, however, empowered by the Northern Sotho folk-tale with regard to justice. The story of Mashilo and Mashil-wane teaches readers, including those who identify with Mordecai's and Esther's violence in the biblical story, that greed and power, irrespective of the power wielded by the per-petrator, cannot be tolerated.

Folktale 4: Tricksters at Work (Esther and the Hare)

The hare (*mmutla*) is the most clever character in Northern Sotho fables. It lives on its wits and succeeds in foiling even the lion, who is the leader of the animal world. In most Northern Sotho folktales, the hare plays the role of a trickster. One such tale will suffice.

Nonwane! Nonwane! . . . Keleketla!

One year there was a serious famine for all the animals. A certain hare determined to give a lion a plan to address the problem, because it was scared by the greatness of the lion. The hare advised that a house be built and a hole be dug inside the house. The lion was to get into the hole and let only its teeth show outside. When the exercise was completed, the hare called all the animals to come and witness a miracle: teeth had grown from the ground! The animals came, and they were attacked by the lion's teeth. When the lion came out of the hole in the ground, the hare advised that they prepare a roof for the lion, because the latter, unlike the hare, could not survive rain.

Meanwhile, the meat from the animals killed by the lion was cooking. The lion was on the roof with the hare. While they were up on the roof, the hare decided to nail the lion's tail to one of the roof poles. When the lion felt the pinch, the hare responded: "The louse that was on the tail, Granny, is the biggest of them all." When the hare was satisfied that the lion's tail was firmly nailed, it went down to the pot of meat. The hare started picking different pieces of meat out of the pot and asked the lion, "May I eat this piece?" If the pieces were big, the lion disapproved, but if they were small, the hare was allowed to eat them. The hare then picked one big piece and, disregarding the lion's disapproval, ate it. Then the lion decided to come down from the roof, but in vain. It was held firmly there—hanging—while the hare ate whatever piece of meat it liked.

The lion died there on the roof. Then the hare skinned the lion and put on its skin. The clever animal then went to the place where the baboons lived. They thought it was a lion. The hare found the baboons cooking beer and instructed them to put the beer on their hands and lick it. They did that reluctantly. The following morning the baboons left their house to go to the field. The "lion" was to be left alone in their house. While on the way, they discovered that they had forgotten a sleeping mat for the child. One of them was instructed to go and fetch the mat. The messenger found the hare basking in the sun with the lion's skin off its body, for the skin was making it hot. Was the ancestor not right when s/he said, "Dinaka tša go rwešwa ga di gomarele hlogo" (Artificial horns do not stick on the head)? It is no wonder that at some stage the hare had to take the lion's skin off of its body. The baboon rushed to go and inform the others that it was the hare and not the lion. They came back and began to chase the hare. Along the route, the hare found Mr/s. Protruding Eyes in a cavity in a tree trunk. When the animal was threatened, it left the hole, and the hare got inside. When the baboons came to the tree, they asked Mr/s. Protruding Eyes: "Have you not seen the hare pass here?" S/he responded: "The little dust is the hare's!" They passed and left the hare there. (Makgamatha 1991:137–42)

The lesson of this folktale, of course, is that the hare survived through its tricks.

Nonwane! Nonwane! . . . Keleketla!

Long, long ago, when the rocks were still soft, there was a Jewish girl by the name of Hadassah. Others called her Esther.

Keleketla! Her wits remind us of the wits of a hare. Esther also plays the role of a trickster, the same role played by the hare in the above tale. Small as she is, particularly by virtue of her position as a woman in a patriarchal world—coupled with her "powerless" position as a daughter vis-à-vis her Uncle Mordecai, and her diasporic condition—she manages to manipulate even the king of the empire and emerges a winner. Two examples will suffice to illustrate Esther's role as trickster. In chapter 2, when the beautiful virgins of Persia gather before the king for a contest, Esther, knowing that disclosing her identity would have harmed her chances of winning, hides her identity (2:10). In chapter 4, Esther appears to be "humble" before Ahasuerus the Persian king, not for the sake of the Persians, but for the sake of her own people. Esther does all she can to save her own people (4:16).

In this essay, characters in the Esther story take on the names of the animals. For example, Esther is a hare and King Ahasuerus is a lion, but *tau ya go hloka meno*—literally, a lion without teeth, a harmless lion. We may therefore call Ahasuerus an old lion. Although Ahasuerus has a powerful position as a king (like the lion, which is a leader of the animal world), Ahasuerus is inefficient and thus can be easily manipulated by his subjects. Haman can be referred to as the snake:

Haman *ke noga* (is a snake). If a person is metaphorically referred to as *noga* in the Northern Sotho language, it means that s/he is the embodiment of evil. Mordecai is the kind of person who likes to be in the background, but Mordecai has the capacity to exercise silent influence behind the scenes. Mordecai thus assumes the role of the elephant.

Nonwane! Nonwane!. . . Keleketla!

> Once upon a time, there was a Hare in one of the villages in the South of Judah. It happened that its animal family [race] was carried over to another country as captives. The Hare had neither mother nor father. However, as always is the case in the Hare's culture [and also in the African culture], the Hare had a guardian to look after it. The name of the guardian was the Big Elephant. Off they went to exile together with other animals. While they were in the foreign place, a word went out that the king, the Old Lion, wanted the different animals to come to a contest to become queen. What happened to the former queen? In her attempt to be *serokolo se sennyane sa go ikoketša ka go nkga* (a small herb that increases itself by smelling badly), by her refusal to appear before the Old Lion, she was dismissed from her position as queen.
>
> The Big Elephant called the child that was in its charge and advised it to join those who were to try their luck before the Old Lion. Wisely, the Hare did not disclose its nationality: such is the wisdom that it acquired from the Big Elephant. We are informed that a certain animal by the name of Hegai was in charge of the contestants. Hegai was pleased by the Hare, who thus won Hegai's favor. Who could not show favor to a clever, cooperative creature like this one? When they appeared before the Old Lion, the Hare won the contest. The Hare became a queen in a foreign land, with no one, including the Old Lion, aware of the Hare's foreign identity!
>
> While at the palace, the Hare was made to understand that the Big Elephant was in deep distress, to the point of refusing to eat. How could the Elephant eat while the other animals were about to be destroyed by the Snake's plot? The latter was angered by the Elephant's refusal to bow before him. The understanding of the Elephant was that the only One to whom they could bow was *Modimo*, the One who created all the animals. The Elephant asked the Hare to intervene on behalf of the fellow animals. The whole family of animals was to be destroyed because of the Elephant's refusal to bow before the Snake. The Hare was to appear before the Old Lion to ask for favor in view of the Snake's evil plan against the Hare's animal family. Although the Hare was hesitant at first, it decided to go because of its commitment to fellow animals. The following words re-

veal the Hare's determination: "After that I will go to the [Old Lion], though it is against the law; if I perish, I perish" (4:16). The Hare's initial reluctance to appear before the Old Lion is understandable; in that context, no one would dare appear before the Lion unsummoned. That act by itself could result in their assassination. By its wits, the Hare commanded that a fast be held on its behalf, even as it was about to take the risky step of appearing before the Old Lion.

What happened? A small, powerless, yet clever animal approached a big one—the Lion, the leader of all the wild animals. The Hare found favor in the eyes of the Old Lion. If we know the Hare's wits, we are not surprised by this positive outcome. We are not surprised that, not only did the Old Lion give the Hare an opportunity to speak, but it promised to give the Hare anything, including half of its animal kingdom! A wise and clever being does not jump quickly into serious matters. Instead, it first gives some room in order to prepare the ones from whom it is begging. Or perhaps to give the powerful ones a long rope to hang themselves?

Instead of quickly disclosing the mission, the Hare proposed to organize a banquet for the Old Lion and the Snake. Little did the Snake know that the banquet would lead to disaster. That is how the Hare works: small and harmless though it is, it uses its wits to subvert the powerful and the cruel. The Snake was so happy that it boasted to its friends that it was the only one invited by the Hare to the banquet with the Hare's partner, the Old Lion. On arriving at the banquet, the Hare disclosed the Snake's evil plans against Hare's animal family. The tables turned against the Snake. The deep, big pit into which the Snake had prepared to throw the Elephant was to serve as the Snake's pit! Ultimately, because of the Hare's wits, its family was saved, while the Snake's family was destroyed. By its wits, the Hare triumphed in a situation in which the big, powerful animals had more influence. At the same time, the Big Elephant was also saved from destruction and elevated to the high position that was formerly the Snake's.

The moral is that one should not despise those who appear small or powerless, for through their survival tactics they may take control. Furthermore, the powerful and oppressive people will be overcome, in one way or another, by the powerless and oppressed. The oppressed will always triumph over their oppressors.

A concerned woman may ask why, in Esther, a woman in a world ruled by men is portrayed as a trickster. And a trickster she is. Esther, a foreigner, appears before Ahasuerus as a candidate for queen, and she never discloses her foreign identity (2:10). Supposedly a Persian queen, she appears before a Persian king "unsummoned," in order to pursue her own Jewish agenda against the Persians. She ultimately succeeds in reversing the evil that was supposed to befall her own people by "tricking" the king to join her side. This is one of the survival strategies of the powerless—in this instance, of women in the world of men, and of exiles in the world of their captors.

A folklorist reading of the book of Esther such as the reading above—in which human characters take the names of animals—may, to a certain extent, help to get rid of negative biases like that against "woman as trickster." Thus, the more inclusive narration of the story of Esther may have empowering possibilities for those at the margins of patriarchal societies. The story is even more empowering when narrated in a gender-neutral language like Northern Sotho.

Conclusion

The storytelling approach is helpful in several ways. First, it makes the stories in the Bible—which is an important spiritual resource in African Christian settings—come alive, particularly in oral cultures. As a result, even those who cannot read the biblical story will feel themselves included, because of the similarities between their folktales and biblical narratives. Second, a comparative approach helps confirm close resemblances between the African and Israelite worldviews. That recognition may help many Africans embrace the Old Testament—and not only the New Testament—as a resource. Third, a storytelling approach reminds readers that the Bible is not only history, but that it consists of many stories with lessons behind them. Finally, a narrative approach may help to get rid of some of the Bible's biases against the powerless, such as non-Jews, women, and the poor.

Mpho! Sa mosela wa seripa! (*Mpho!* is an ideophone signifying the spitting of saliva, and *Sa mosela wa seripa!* means "That which has a short tale!") This is the closing formula for the Northern Sotho folktales. By these words, the storyteller is moving from fantasy to reality. With these words the present storyteller would advise those who have been listening not to be preoccupied only with fantasy, but to ponder the lessons behind it. It would be a good idea not only to ponder these lessons, but to make the wisdom portrayed in them an integral part of one's everyday life.

Notes

1. Correspondences and similarities between these languages could be helpful in various ways: (1) for those contemplating writing a Hebrew grammar for Bantu-speaking students; (2) for African Bible translators who will find it easier to translate from Hebrew directly into the Bantu language, without going through a European language; and (3) for African Old Testament scholars who can be encouraged to consider using mainly African Bible translations (in place of European translations), together with the Hebrew Bible.

2. Her endeavors on behalf of her people remind us of the Ghanaian story of how Eku, the matriarch, saved lives by being the first to drink the waters of which the people were afraid. The two women have in common that they are willing to take risks on behalf of their people. The Ghanaian story is more empowering for women, because there is no male figure behind Eku; rather, she acts on her own.

References

Amoah, E., and M. A. Oduyoye. 1989. "The Christ for African Women." Pp. 34–46 in *With Passion and Compassion: Third World Women Doing Theology,* edited by V. Fabella and M. Oduyoye. Maryknoll, N.Y.: Orbis Books.

Burden, J. J., and H. L. Bosman. 1982. *Only Guide for OTB 302–3.* Pretoria: Unisa.

Burger, J. A. 1988. *Biblical Studies: Only Guide for BSB301–6.* Pretoria: Unisa.

Dickson, K. A. 1977. "Continuity and Discontinuity between the Old Testament and African Life and Thought." Pp. 95–108 in *African Theology en Route,* edited by K. Appiah-Kubi and S. Torres. Maryknoll, N.Y.: Orbis Books.

Loader, J. A. 1998. Biblical Studies 111 (BSB 301–6): Tutorial Letter 103.

Makgamatha, P. M. 1991. *Characteristics of the Northern Sotho Folktales: Their Form and Structure.* Johannesburg: Peshkor.

Masenya, M. J. 1989. "In the School of Wisdom: An Interpretation of

Some Old Testament Proverbs in a Northern Sotho Context." Master's thesis, University of South Africa, Pretoria.

———. 1998. "Reading the Book of Esther through the Lenses of an African–South African Woman." Paper presented at the NICTE Conference, Johannesburg.

Masola, I. S. 1988. *Bohwa bja rena*. Pretoria: Palm.

Mazamisa, W. 1995. "Re-reading the Bible in the Black Church: Towards a Hermeneutic of Orality and Literacy." *Journal of Black Theology in South Africa* 9:1–26.

Mosala, I. J. 1993. "Implications of the Text of Esther for African Women's Struggle for Liberation in South Africa." *Semeia* 59:129–37.

Oduyoye, M. A. 1994. *Daughters of Anowa: African Women and Patriarchy.* Maryknoll, N.Y.: Orbis Books.

Okpewho, I. 1992. *African Oral Literature: Background, Character, and Continuity.* Indianapolis: Indiana University Press.

Phillips, G. E. 1942. *The Old Testament in the World Church.* London: Lutterworth.

Ziervogel, D., and P. C. Mokgokong. 1975. *Comprehensive Northern Sotho Dictionary.* Pretoria: Van Schaik.

Zinkuratire, V. 1999. "Morphological and Syntactical Correspondences between Hebrew and Bantu Languages." Paper presented at the International Symposium on Africa and the Old Testament, Nairobi.

3

Fifty Years of Bleeding:
A Storytelling Feminist Reading of Mark 5:24–43

Musa W. Dube

This essay is based on three texts: (1) an oral African tale of a young girl buried by her friends but who sings from her grave, telling her story; (2) a biblical tale of a bleeding woman (Mark 5:35–43) who had visited many physicians, spending all her money while getting worse; and (3) the story of Africa in the past fifty years (and before), covering the pre-colonial and colonial periods, the struggle for independence, and the influence of neocolonialism, globalization, and HIV/AIDS. The essay views this history through a gender lens and places a woman in the middle of Africa's story. The woman exists both as one who defies death by continuing to sing from her many graves and as a bleeding woman who fully participates in the search for healing[1] and survival on the African continent.[2] Evidently, it is still *a luta continua!*—the struggle continues.

Mama Africa as a character thus personifies the story of Africa. Her role exposes gender oppressions and other forms of oppression encountered by African women (and the people of Africa in general), yet highlights their will to arise. This will is dramatized by the repeated song and by Mama Africa's surprising assumption of power, when she calls *talitha cum!* ("Little girl, arise!") to those buried by various forms of oppression. While the essay does not expressly describe its method and theoretical basis, it draws on the theories of social location, reader-response, gender-feminist, and contextual biblical reading. These theories hold that all readers interpret the text according to their social experiences and contexts.[3]

A large crowd followed him and pressed in on him. Now there was a woman who had been suffering from hemorrhages for twelve [fifty] years. She had endured much under many physicians, and had spent all that she had; and she was no better, but rather grew worse. She had heard about Jesus, and came up behind him in the crowd and touched his cloak, for she said, "If I but touch his clothes, I will be made well." (Mark 5:24b–28)

Scene 1: Dr. Colonial Master, before 1949

Ngubani o gamla lapha, nqo ("Knock, knock, who is there?")
Yimi e ngamla lapha, nqo ("It's me cutting firewood around")
Ufike utshele uMama lo Baba ("Please, take a message to my parents")
Uthi uAfrica/nthenthlezandleni ku sekho ("Tell them that I am no
   more")
Ngoba banqebhela e mhlathini we bundla ("For they buried me here")
ka ku sa iyewa ("And abandoned me here")

Once upon a time, there was a beautiful princess called Africa. She built her summer palace on the Great Zimbabwe by the art of patience and endurance, cutting, carrying, and laying one little rock after another. She built her winter parlor in the golden sands of Egypt by the community spirit of all her children, who cut and pulled heavy rocks in the sand for years. She grazed her cattle on the Great Lakes of the East and plowed her fields on the sand banks of the Nile. There she struggled, living with and in the land, fighting and surviving many natural disasters of floods and droughts. She showered in the waterfalls of Mosi oa thunya (Victoria Falls), and she painted her art on the rocks of the Tsodilo caves of the South. She took walks on the seashores of the West. Africa, a tall and bouncy girl, walked freely from one end of her land to another, visiting the shrines, offering sacrifices to the Divine, fighting and surviving disasters, but always bringing enough food for her household.

During the day, Africa's children played under the bright and blue sky that was graced by the unfailing sun. During the night, her children slept under the luxurious roof of a million stars. In their dreams, Africa's children laughed with the moon.

When morning came, Africa's children woke up singing with a million birds of the valley. In the midmorning, Africa's children went down to the river to play with the frogs. When the sun went down, Africa's children danced to welcome each star in the sky. And when all the stars were planted in the sky, the moon emerged to tell them tales around the fire. Her brothers, uncles, husbands, and fathers spent their days tending their animals and plants, mining and carving, hunting and watching the children as they played. And always bringing sufficient food to the household. Africa blossomed in self-sufficiency, survival, health, and peace.

But in the year 1939, Africa woke up severely ill. She felt walls had entered into all of her body. She felt fenced, bound. Africa cried out, saying, "Take this thorn of suffering away from my flesh! Take it away!" And as she spoke, she began to bleed nonstop. Just then Dr. Colonial Master appeared, saying, "I am the healer of all diseases. But in order to heal this kind of disease, I have to take you into my hospital. I have to watch you very closely, teach you what you need to learn and what you need to know. Basically, what you need most is the medicine of civilization."

Africa entered Dr. Colonial Master's hospital, and she was put to sleep with heavy medication. She slept for ten years. Lying limp, she heard the distant sound of her children's joy disappear into the air. She heard no more the voices of her brothers, uncles, fathers, and husbands, for they had disappeared into the mines, the plantations, and the farms to work for Dr. Colonial Master. But in the year 1949, Dr. Colonial Master seemed preoccupied by his homeland. He no longer had enough time to treat Africa in the mornings. Picking up her clothes and still bleeding, Africa escaped into the bush. This is how she came to meet her new physician, Comrade Dr. Struggle-for-Independence.

Scene 2: Dr. Struggle-for-Independence, 1949–69

When Africa escaped from her captor, she yearned for a revitalizing shower in the waterfalls of Mosi oa thunya. As she got closer, she heard the soothing sound of the falls. But when she arrived there, she found Mosi oa thunya fenced in, with a sign posted: "Victoria Falls."

"Victoria? Who is Victoria?" Africa muttered audibly. And off she went to her palace in the Great Zimbabwe. But when she arrived there she found that it too was fenced in. A porter standing by the gate said to her, "This is the home of Dr. Colonial Master. Are you one of his domestic servants or are you seeking to be one?"

Shaking her head, and still bleeding, Africa headed to her grazing lands in the Great Lakes of the East. She wanted to find her people, her cattle, and her farms. As she came closer, she saw the beautiful valley that stretched peacefully in front of her. She saw her cattle grazing in the green pastures. The memory of happy times gripped her. She ran down, but a young herdsman—who looked just like one of her many children—came hurriedly to meet her. "Mum," he said, "this land and these cattle belong to Dr. Colonial Master. Are you one of his domestic servants or do you seek to be one?"

"Are you telling me that this very land and cattle belong to Dr. Colonial Master?"

"Yes, Mum. It is so."

"Then tell me how I can get to my farms along the fertile banks of the Nile and to my winter home in the golden sands of Egypt."

"Your farms? Along the Nile? There is the missionary road to the North."

Africa turned to the North. As she came close to the Nile, the sweet smell of its fertile sandbanks tingled her nose, and the memory of happy times gripped her. She began to run with excitement. But as she was running, she was brought to a sudden stop by a fence with a large sign announcing in bold letters: "No trespassing. This territory belongs to Dr. Colonial Master." Africa turned back toward the rocks of Tsodilo in the South, where she decided to express her fears in a painting. But there, too, a porter met her by the gate, declaring, "Mum, black people are not allowed in this resort area. Are you one of Dr. Colonial Master's domestic servants or do you seek to be one?"

Shocked, shaking, and still bleeding, Africa turned toward the West. The sun was setting when she began to cut firewood in the rocky and barren land where she found herself. The pain of the capture of her children, people, land, and property was excruciating. Africa cried out from her anguish, saying, "Take this thorn away from my body! Take it away!" Just then a voice broke her despair, singing and saying:

Ngubani o gamla lapha, nqo
Yimi e ngi gamla lapha, nqo
Ufike utshele umama lo baba
Uthi uTentelezandleni ka sekho
Ngoba bamqebela emhlathini
we bundla ka kusaiwa

She heard her own beloved child singing, calling out, saying, "Who is there? Who is there? Who is cutting here? Please, go and inform our parents that we have been buried right here in our own land and left to die."

Seized by anger, Africa called out, "Talitha cum," which means "Little girl, arise!" And behold, the bellies of the earth opened. UTentelezandleni jumped out. She was followed by all the beloved old women and men. Miriam Makeba emerged with her new song: Mozambique (*A luta continua*), Botswana (*A luta continua*), Zimbabwe (*A luta continua*), Namibia (*A luta continua*), South Africa (*A luta continua*).

As she sang, the ground shook and broke open again. And there came from the ground the many handsome sons and daughters of Africa: Kwame Nkrumah, Nehanda, Julius Nyerere, Hastings Banda, Chinua Achebe, Kenneth Kaunda, Ngugi wa Thiongo, Milton Obote, Seretse Khama, Joshua Nkomo, Buchi Emecheta, P. G. Matante, Samora Machel, Robert Mugabe, Winnie Madikizela, Nelson Mandela, and others. There was much joy and weeping as they saw each other again after such a long time. They told each other the stories of how Dr. Colonial Master had captured and confined them. Yet many more daughters and sons were missing or dead. Africa wept. She wept for the lost children of her womb.

Seeing her tears, all the able-bodied young adults said, "We cannot live like this. We have to fight for our liberation." Many of her children who lived in North America were also heard saying, "Back to Africa! Harambee! Africa shall be free!" Just then the booming voice of Mzwake Mbule, yet to be born, was heard shouting from the future: "Do something to facilitate change in Africa. Let it be done before dawn."[4] And the children of Africa rose and said, "We must go out and fight Dr. Colonial Master. We must recapture all that belongs to us. It is the only solution."

"Do you want to leave me again?" Africa asked.

Kwame, her firstborn son, turned to her and said, "Mama Africa, stay right here in this infertile land with the young children and the old people. Take care of them while we fight for independence. It is the struggle for independence that will give you healing. It is the only solution to your suffering."

And her last-born son, tall and regal, Nelson Mandela, said, "Mama Africa, the struggle is my life, for my freedom and that of my people cannot be separated."[5] From that day on, Africa became Mama Africa: the strong black woman who carries us all on her back.

Shaking and still bleeding, Mama Africa was left in the barren, crowded lands to plow and fend for her young children, old people, and all those who were struggling in the guerrilla warfare for independence. For many years she took care of everyone to ensure that independence would come to heal the land and all the peoples. Guns would sound, bombs would explode, and the heart would shudder in fear during the night. Slogans would be chanted: *Kwacha-ngwee! A luta continua! Bambiri ne chimurenga! Amandla nga wethu! Mayibuye iAfrica!*

And many more of her boys and girls would disappear and join the shouts of the comrades, of the struggle for independence. While many others were forced to work in the farms, plantations, and mines of Dr. Colonial Master, Mama Africa herself labored both in the farms of Dr. Colonial Master and in her own fields. She produced food for those at home and for those at war—for the oppressed and for the oppressor.

The years of the struggle dragged on. Blood flowed from her body until all the rivers of Africa were red and the land began to stink with the stench of death. That is when Mama

Africa stood up and shouted, "Take this thorn away from my body! Take it away!" Just then a horn sounded, and liberty was announced throughout the land. Viva! Victory was certain! And that is how Mama Africa came to meet her new physician, Dr. Independence.

Scene 3: Dr. Independence, 1969–79

Weak and still bleeding, the heart of Mama Africa rejoiced in hope. Independence was here! *Amandla nga wethu!* Power to the people! Healing was certain. She rejoiced at the prospect of getting all her children back again, getting back her power, her honor, and her share in the struggle for independence. Mama Africa was ready for the healing of her own body.

Indeed, her sons and daughters did arrive in the crowded villages, singing songs of victory. Drums were sounded. There was dancing. There was singing. There was joy. Mama Africa ululated, *Alelelelele!* She sang along and danced along. Thanksgivings were offered to the Divine.

When the day ended, her sons pulled away, back to the towns and cities, back to sleep in the fortresses built by Dr. Colonial Master. Mama Africa and her daughters were left in the rocky, crowded, and barren lands to produce food for those in towns and in the villages. Her grazing land, her fields, her palaces, her caves did not return to her. "Plantations produce the crops that we need to export. Mosi oa thunya, the Great Zimbabwe, the Egyptian pyramids, and Tsodilo are essential to attract tourists," she was told. "Stay where you are and produce food for the nation, Mama Africa." Most of her daughters who were in the struggle for independence were also left at home, alongside their mother.

Weak and still bleeding, Mama Africa struggled and toiled in the hospital of Dr. Independence. Again there were wars. Now the sons of Mama Africa were fighting among themselves. Guns and bombs exploded. Young boys and girls disappeared. Her children dodged death or died in the very air they breathed. Young children took arms, went to war, and were killed. The genocide of Tutsis in Rwanda claimed multitudes.

Mama Africa's Somalian children starved until they were bones, while warlords made war, not love. Land mines were planted, and boys and girls lost their limbs and legs until they learned how not to play. Mama Africa could not plant more crops for the fields had already been planted—with mines. She could not walk freely again, for her body was full of explosives. She was confined, afraid to set one foot outside her yard lest she step on a mine. Once more, she was buried in a hole. But one day she heard in the distance the sound of someone chopping, and she cried out, saying:

Ngubane o gamla lapha, nqo
Yimi engamla lapha, nqo
Ufike utshele umama lo baba
Uthi Africa ka sekho
Goba ba nqibhela e mhlathini
We bundla ka kusayiwu

And, indeed, help came. International organizations arrived. Church organizations arrived to facilitate reconciliation. International financial bodies arrived to lend money. International donors were ready to give aid to resuscitate the devastated economies. Mama Africa was ready for a much-needed rest. That is how she met a new physician: Dr. Neo-colonialism, who also goes by the name Dr. Global Village.

Scene 4:
Dr. Neo-colonialism/Dr. Global Village, 1979–89

Still sick and bleeding, Mama Africa heard about the miracle of external aid, which would bring an end to the poverty that had befallen her land and children. The qualified players and planners were numerous, among them the International Monetary Fund and the World Bank. Soon Mama Africa was receiving millions of dollars. She was even wearing the imported garments of Democracy.

Mama Africa heard of the millions of dollars that were flowing in to build roads and bridges. She heard about the Structural Adjustment Programmes. She heard how money would also be coming her way for development and how plans were being made for the kind of projects she should undertake: projects that were familiar neither to her nor to her ancestors. Not even to her land. And that is how she used the aid that came—as a medicine prescribed by Dr. Neo-colonialism, the physician.

Still bleeding, Mama Africa partook of the prescribed medicine of developmental projects. But aid turned to debt. Africa had received millions of dollars and now owed billions of dollars. Her economies had been bad, but now they were ruined. Africa and all her people now were laboring to pay enormous debts, working simply to pay off this new physician, for he is the new colonial master. Dr. Neo-colonialism continues to give Africa and her children some medicine to keep them alive and working: to keep them paying the debt.

Shaking and still bleeding, Mama Africa was visited by a new physician. Dr. Global Village offered a different medicine. "I can heal you, Mama Africa, just like I can heal the world of all its pains. My prescriptions are simple: I will do away with national boundaries. I will strengthen regional trade. I will prescribe unlimited trade across the globe. I will require competition, and my multinational corporations will create jobs for you."

Mama Africa made her last bet—taking the prescriptions of Dr. Global Village. Mama Africa also saw with her eyes the arrival of chain stores and foreign companies. Suddenly, there was Coca-Cola and Pepsi, Kentucky Fried Chicken and McDonald's and Wimpy, BP, Hyundai, CNN. The colors were the same everywhere. They brought the touch of foreign sophistication. When the multinational companies came, bringing jobs for Africa, the local companies were bought out. Mama Africa and all her people began to work for the big multinational companies. But soon after, high-tech machines rolled in, replacing her children. They were retrenched, asked to go home to their cramped lands.

That is when Mama Africa realized that Dr. Global Village was a twin brother of Dr. Neo-colonialism and a grandson of Dr. Colonial Master. Africa's currencies suffered major devaluations. And while Asian economies were catching the flu from the impact of globalization, Africa caught a more deadly disease: HIV/AIDS. And Mama Africa had no more money to buy prescriptions from the doctor.

HIV/AIDS: Mama Africa Is Coming Up Behind Jesus! 1989–98

Still bleeding and searching for healing, Mama Africa has been struck by a new disease: HIV/AIDS. She is now a nurse. She runs home-based care centers for her dying children and people. She washes them, feeds them, holds them in her arms, and rocks them, singing a little song, while she awaits their death. And when they finally die, she rises to close their eyes, to wrap them and bury them. Mama bears in her own flesh the wounds of their suffering. And they die in her loving arms.

Mama Africa was burying this morning, and this afternoon she will bury again. And tomorrow morning she will bury yet another of her gems. In the afternoon she will bury again. At this moment, Mama Africa is nursing a sister, an uncle, a brother with one hand; with her other hand she is holding a dying child and feeding many, many orphans. She has closed many homes and villages, and she will close many more. Mama Africa is once more confined, caring for the sick and dying. Just a few minutes ago, she was sitting in her home, feeling like a motherless child, when she heard a crowd in the distance streaming into Zimbabwe, into Harare. Africa, in dire straits, stood and began to sing:

Ngobani o gamla lapha, nqo
Yemi e gamla lapha, nqo.
Ufike utshele uMama lo Baba
Uthi uTentelezandlene ka sekho,
Ngoba ba nqebhela emhlathini we bundla ka kusaiwa

When she called out, "Who is there? Who is there?" she was told, "Jesus Christ, the healer of all diseases, is passing by." She heard that Jesus was on his way to heal a little child already dead, the daughter of Jairus.

Mama Africa is standing up. She is not talking. She is not asking. She is not offering any more money—for none is left.

59

Mama Africa is coming behind Jesus. She is pushing through a strong human barricade. *Weak and still bleeding but determined, she is stretching out her hand. If only she can touch the garments of Jesus Christ.*

Notes

1. *Healing* in this essay denotes a person's entire well-being: economic, political, social, spiritual, the physical body, and so on.

2. This essay cannot pretend to speak for the whole continent of Africa, and it cannot pretend that African women are identical. Africa and African women are extremely diversified by class, race, education, ethnicity, culture, nationality, religion, region, and so on. The "Africa," "African woman" or "Mama Africa" in this essay should be seen as a gender-feminist view or construction of one African woman of Botswana. Many will empathize and identify with some parts of this perspective and story; many more will feel estranged from it, for it does not and cannot speak for all African women and people. I am grateful to Peter Mikwisa, Seratwa Ntloedibe, and Dumisani Mmualefe, who read this essay and have enhanced it with their useful comments.

3. While twelve years in the biblical story (Mark 5:25) is recognized to represent Israel, the fifty years in the title of this essay represents Africa and interweaves Africa's story with the fifty years of World Council of Churches, for whose fiftieth-anniversary assembly this essay was written.

4. From Mzwake Mbule, *Mzwake: Now Is the Time*, BMG Records Africa, 1994, a compact disc of poetic music.

5. See Nelson Mandela, *Long Walk to Freedom: The Autobiography of Nelson Mandela* (London: Little & Brown, 1994), 455–56.

Patriarchal and Colonizing Translations

4

How Local Divine Powers Were Suppressed: A Case of Mwari of the Shona

Dora R. Mbuwayesango

Before the colonization of Zimbabwe by the British in 1890, the country comprised many different political entities that were united religiously by the belief in a Supreme Being. This Supreme Being was commonly known by the personal name "Mwari." The different political entities paid allegiance to Mwari in different ways. Zimbabwe can be divided into two major superficial regions, that is, Mashonaland and Matabeleland. In Mashonaland, the language is mainly Shona, although with different dialects. The language in Matabeleland is predominantly Ndebele. The Ndebele, to a limited extent, respected the Mwari cult that was centered in Matopo Hills in Matebeleland.[1] The Shona understand Mwari to be a genderless spirit, neither male nor female. The attributes of Mwari all have to do with Mwari's transcendence and creative activities.[2] Thus, these attributes include *Nyadenga* (of the sky), *Mutangakugara* (the first to exist), *Muumbi* (the one who forms), and *Musikavanhu* (the creator of humanity). Also, Mwari does not discriminate and can speak through women and even through objects, as well as through men.

Colonialism and Christianity came to Zimbabwe simultaneously. In fact, the two aided each other in "christianizing" and dominating the indigenous peoples. The partnership of colonialism and Christianity is well expressed in one of David Livingstone's letters, discussed by John Kirk:

> That you may have a clear idea of my objects, I may state that they have more in them than meets the eye. They are not merely exploratory, for I go with the intention of benefiting both the African

and my own countrymen. I take a practical mining geologist to tell of the mineral resources of the country, an economic botanist to give full report of the vegetable productions, an artist to give the scenery, a naval officer to tell of the capacity of river communications, a moral agent to lay a Christian foundation for anything that may follow. All this machinery has for its ostensible object the development of African trade and promotion of civilisation; but what I can tell none but such as you, in whom I have confidence, is this. *I hope it may result in an English colony in the healthy high lands of Central Africa.*[3]

Robert Moffat, one of the great missionary pioneers, also expresses the connection between missionary and colonial ventures in Africa:

> It is where the political organization is most perfect, and the social system still in its aboriginal vigour, that the missionary has the least success in making an impression. Where things have undergone a change and the feudal usages have lost their power, where there is a measure of disorganization, the new ideas which the gospel brings with it do not come into collision with any powerful political prejudice. The habits and modes of thinking have been broken up, and there is a preparation for the seed of the word.[4]

The European settler group that succeeded was the British South Africa Company (BSA Company) under Cecil Rhodes, after whom the country was later named Rhodesia. There were several European missionary organizations involved in Zimbabwe, although the initial missionary ventures had little success. The first missionary to operate in the country was Gançalo da Silveira, a Portuguese Jesuit, who was killed. The second phase of missionary activities in the country took place in the seventeenth century, when the Dominicans set up missions in the eastern part; by the end of that century, they had abandoned the missions. The next to attempt the evangelization of the Shona peoples were the Congregationalists, who worked among the eastern Shona in the 1870s. The Dutch Reformed Church, the Berlin missionary society, and Anglicans also made tentative efforts in Mashonaland in the 1880s, but these missionary ventures were unsuccessful. It was only after Cecil John Rhodes had occupied Mashonaland that the missionaries started to experience success. Rhodes personally encouraged missionary work by allocating generous tracts of land to thirteen different societies during the 1890s. Later the Methodists and other missionary groups entered the country.

The missionaries found no need to explain the concept of God to the Shona people. In fact, they discovered that the Shona were a very spiritual and monotheistic people who believed in the Supreme Being by the name of Mwari, whose cult flourished in the Matopo Hills near Bulawayo. This cult seems to have been one of the strongest elements that united the different groups comprising the Shona.

> So many different clans are presented among the staff at each shrine as to make it likely that the location of the cult in the Matopos is to be regarded as an ancient structural feature. We find that priests, dancers, consecrated women and messengers are drawn from such diverse groups as the Karanga, Kalanga, Mbire, the Hera, Rozvi, and the Venda.[5]

The widespread belief in Mwari in the Matopo Hills is demonstrated by Daneel, who records finding a system of messengers and tribute in operation among Matonjeni and the districts of Chilimanzi, Gutu, Victoria, Melsetter, Bikita, Ndanga, Chibi, Chipinga, Belingwe, Gwanda, Plumtree, Nyamadlovu, and centers in Vendaland both north and south of the Limpopo.[6]

The Quest for a Shona Word for the Biblical Deity

One of the challenging tasks for the missionaries was to make the biblical deity relevant and acceptable to the Shona. While the missionaries eventually adopted the name Mwari to designate the biblical god (*Elohim* or *Yhwh* in the Old Testament, and God the Father in the New Testament), the history leading to that conclusion is reflected in the translations of the Bible, liturgical texts, and the catechisms of the different missionary organizations operating in Mashonaland.

Before the standardization of Shona language, the missionary groups had different preferences for Shona terms for the biblical deity. The first was *Modzimo* or *Mudzimu*, which was used in writings between 1899 and 1912 by the Lutheran and Dutch Reformed churches operating among the Karangas.[7] The second Shona term to refer to the biblical deity was *We-*

denga, "of the sky." This was found in writings of the Dutch Reformed Church and the Church of Sweden in 1909 and 1927, respectively.[8] The term *Wedenga* was also combined with *Mudzimu* as *Mudzimu Wedenga,* "the Ancestral Spirit of the Sky."[9]

In Shona, the term *Mudzimu* refers only to the ancestral spirit. Its early use among the Karanga seemed to have been influenced by the corresponding Sotho term *Molimo,* due to the missionary misunderstanding of that term. As Smith points out, the Tswana (the people of Botswana) were responding to a specific question posed by the missionaries: What is "the cause of all appearances in nature and the origin of all good and evil that happens to them without any act of their own?"[10] Attempts to correct this misunderstanding, as demonstrated by Louw's qualification with *Wedenga,* did not catch on.[11]

Other missionary organizations used the term *Mwari* exclusively from the beginning, especially the Anglicans, Methodists, and, later, groups such as the Salvation Army, who operated among the Eastern Shona and the Zezuru.[12]

The Roman Catholic Church was characterized by initial diversity in the terms used for the biblical deity before the general acceptance of *Mwari.* Some Catholics—in particular the Dominicans and the Catholic translations at Waddilove—used *Mwari* from the outset.[13] Jesuit Catholic publications, however, used *Yave* from 1898.[14] The first edition of the Catholic Shona-English dictionary gives the following entries as translations of the English word *God: Yave* (a foreign word); *Mwea mukuru* (the great spirit); *Mwari* (the great spirit, according to native understanding); *Murenga* (the god of war, a word introduced from the Matabeleland in the last rebellion: the cry was, *Murenga wamuka* [the God of war has risen]).[15]

Although *Mwari* finally became the accepted Shona term for the biblical deity, the discussion that ensued between 1921 and 1924 in Catholic circles reveals the underlying distinctions between the Shona deity and the biblical deity. For example, Father Richartz argued that, although the Shona gods might be honored as gods or have godlike traits, their names were sullied by unworthy associations, and, if used, they would confuse the simple. The term *Mwari,* he said, would be unsuitable because it did not connote the notion of judge—an essential in-gredient of the Christian belief—nor the notion of creation in the strict sense. He also considered the views of those who went to the Mwari shrines as concerned only for material mat-ters. Thus the use of the term would be bound to bring in many false notions.[16] Also, Father Luobiere objected to the term *Mwari* for the Christian God on the grounds that it lacked moral connotations, in that both the good and the wicked are equally Mwari's offspring, and after death all would be treated alike.[17] Even non-Catholics such as Bullock weighed in on the debate, to express their reservation about the equation of Mwari and the Christian God: "I should be the last to advocate the translation of our word God by the Chishona word *Mwari*."[18] By the early 1960s, however, the Jesuits had joined the other Christian societies in using *Mwari* to refer to the Christian God. For example, one of the most influential persons in the standardization of the Shona language, Father Michael Hannan, used *Mwari* in his New Testament translation of 1966 and listed *Mwari* as one of the Shona terms for God, the Supreme Being, in his Shona dictionary.[19]

The missionary translation of the Bible was aimed at re-placing the Shona Mwari with the biblical God in everything else but the name. If the missionaries had come to introduce a new God to the Shonas, they might have met much resistance, as happened in the earlier mission ventures. The adoption of the Shona name Mwari for the biblical God was in reality the religious usurpation of the Shona. The missionaries took the Shona captive by colonizing the Shona Supreme Being. The re-sults of this religious colonization can be demonstrated by an-alyzing texts that were now taken to speak of Mwari, the Shona God.

The Effects of the Adoption of the Shona Term *Mwari*

Due to the similarities between the Shona culture and the culture depicted in the Old Testament, the effects of the mis-sionary adoption of the term *Mwari* will be considered mainly from the Old Testament context. There are several ways to refer to the deity in the Old Testament. One of the ways is by personal names, such as Elohim as in Gen. 1:1, or Yhwh in Exod. 3:4, or a combination of the two, Yhwh Elohim, in Gen. 2:4. Another way is by a construct chain made up of Elohim with a proper name, such as Elohe-Abraham, Elohe-Isaac, and Elohe-Jacob (Exod. 3:6). In other passages the name El may be juxtaposed to a place name, as in El Shadday or El Bethel.

The direct equation was made between Elohim and Mwari in Shona Bibles. Thus, for example, the first verse in Genesis reads *Pakutanga Mwari vakasika denga nenyika . . .* (In the beginning Mwari created the heavens and the earth . . .). The earlier Bible translation had *Tenzi* in place of *Yhwh,* based on the English use of LORD to signify that divine name.[20] *Tenzi* means a variety of things depending on the context. It can mean "master," or "owner," or even "employer." The earliest and most recent translations use *Jehova,* based on a German transliteration and misunderstanding of the concept behind the vowel pointing.[21]

As a written record the Bible became the authentic voice on Mwari and Mwari's ways. The Shona believe that Mwari is the creator and the ultimate controller of the universe, the Supreme Being. However, the authentic way to describe Mwari's creative activity has come to be understood as that found in the Bible. The equation thus overruled the way the Shona spoke about and dealt with their deity. The missionaries designated the Shona as primitive and uncivilized in their understanding of God. While the Shona believed that Mwari had created everything, the missionaries granted no validity to the myths that describe the details of these creative activities. The equation of Mwari and Elohim resulted in the suppression of the Shona stories about Mwari's activities as creator. The Shona were basically an oral people, with no written documents. The Shona myths and folktales were not given the same status as the written material that the missionaries introduced to the Shona.

The biblical story of creation appears to be in line with the belief of the Shona that Mwari is the creator of the universe and of humanity. The details in the story, however, distort the details in Shona belief. The most evident distortion is found in

Gen. 1:26–28, which depicts the creation of humanity. While to feminists this account provides positive testimony for the equality of male and female before the biblical deity,[22] the depiction of the deity distorts the basic belief about the form of the Shona deity. In the Shona Bible translation, Mwari is given a human form. In the Shona religious traditions, however, Mwari was truly holy, set apart from creation.[23] Mwari had no form or image. Mwari was truly a spirit without sexuality or gender,[24] but, in the Bible, Mwari is given human form (Gen. 1:26–27). Although the story seems to portray Mwari as having both male and female attributes, by the time of the ancestral stories later in Genesis, Mwari has acquired male gender. In Genesis 18, when the deity by the name of Yhwh appears to Abraham, there are three men with whom Abraham carries on a conversation and has a meal. Two of the men, identified as "messengers," leave Abraham and continue to Sodom. The implication is that the third "man" is actually the deity (Gen. 18:22).

In the Old Testament, the deity is presented as male in subtle ways. In languages that have grammatical gender, masculine forms are generally used. In the Prophets in general, and particularly in Hosea and Ezekiel, the metaphor that represents the relationship between the deity and Israel is that of husband and wife. In this metaphor, the deity is the husband and the wife is Israel. The clearest reference to the deity as male in the Old Testament is in Isa. 63:16, in which the term *father* is used to address the deity.

The biblical stories of creation are products of Jews in the exilic period whose basic aim was to preserve their beliefs in the face of the religious and cultural threat represented by the Babylonian environment. It is significant that these "priestly" writers did not replace Elohim with Babylonian gods such as Marduk. *Elohim* is not a generic term for the deity but a specific name, just as *Mwari* is for the Shona. To take over the name Mwari is to rob the Shona of their traditions and to colonize Mwari. The Shona were a people whose traditions were passed orally from generation to generation. With no written records to concretize those traditions, the missionaries replaced the unwritten records of the Shona with the Bible. As a result, the Bible now talks about Mwari, but *whose* Mwari?

In the stories of the Old Testament, Mwari becomes the god of the Hebrews who had dealings with the Hebrews and not with the Shona peoples, and in the New Testament the only way to Mwari is through *his* son Jesus Christ. This pattern is made clear when *Mwari* functions as the term for God in the story of the rise of Israel as a nation. The call of Moses in Exodus 3 needs special attention, because it demonstrates clearly how the biblical god is tied to the nationhood of Israel. That crucial account, however, must be set in its narrative context.

The book of Genesis begins by considering the world in broad spectrum and gradually narrows to focus on a specific family, the family of Abraham, who is promised a land and nationhood (Genesis 12). The story moves through the descendants of Abraham—Isaac and Jacob. The book of Genesis, however, closes with Abraham's descendants in Egypt, where they end up because of famine in the promised land (Genesis 50).

The book of Exodus opens with the *bene yisrael* (children of Israel), at the death of Joseph, as a population of only seventy (1:1–5). When Joseph and his brothers died, the *bene yisrael* experienced a population surge—"they multiplied and grew exceedingly strong, so that the land was filled with them" (1:7). The Pharaoh, who did not know Joseph, saw the *bene yisrael* as a threat and devised measures to keep their population growth and strength in check (1:8–22). The story of the birth and survival of Moses, the founder of Israelite religion, relates to Pharaoh's attempts to suppress the growth of the Israelites. Moses is rescued by Pharaoh's daughter and subsequently grows up in the Egyptian environment (2:1–10). But Moses identified with the Hebrews. One day he saw an Egyptian mistreating a Hebrew man, and he killed the Egyptian and hid his body in the sand. When Pharaoh learned what Moses had done, he sought to kill him, and so Moses fled to Midian (2:11–22).

After a while, the Pharaoh who sought to kill Moses died, but the Hebrews continued to suffer in Egypt and groaned and cried; their cry for deliverance rose to Elohim. "Elohim heard their groaning, and Elohim remembered his covenant with Abraham, Isaac, and Jacob. Elohim looked upon the Israelites, and Elohim took notice of them" (2:24–25). The name Elohim is repeated five times in 2:23–25. More significant, however, is the connection between Elohim and the ancestors of the Israelites. When, in Shona Bibles, Elohim is replaced by the name Mwari, it becomes Mwari who remembers the covenant that Mwari made with the ancestors of Israel, not with the ancestors of the Shona. Thus, the Shona deity becomes the special God of the Hebrews. For the Shona to relate to their deity, they have to adopt the traditions in the Bible. These traditions have no room for the ways in which various groups of the Shona deal with Mwari, such as through the epics or myths about how Mwari, through the leadership of a *mhondoro* (a spirit of the founding ancestors), led each group to its current location.

Exodus 2 concludes by noting what was taking place in Egypt. Chapter 3, however, goes back to the scene in Midian, in which Moses is in exile. While in Midian, herding his father-in-law's flock, Moses has an encounter with the deity. The encounter takes place at a location identified as Horeb, the mountain of Elohim. The story is characterized by interchangeable use of biblical deity's two names, Elohim (*Mwari*) and Yhwh (*Tenzi* or *Jehova*).[25] A messenger of Yhwh appears to Moses in a flame, in a bush that is ablaze but not consumed. Moses investigates this unusual phenomenon, and when Yhwh sees that Moses has turned aside to look, Elohim (Mwari) calls and Moses responds. The voice that calls identifies itself with the construct form of Elohim (*elohe*), juxtaposed with the names of Moses' ancestors, Abraham, Isaac, and Jacob (3:6). Once again the deity is identified in relationship to the ancestors of Israel— Abraham, Isaac, and Jacob. In Shona Bibles, the text reads, "Mwari vaAbraham, Mwari vaIsaka, naMwari vaJakobo." Thus Mwari is identified exclusively with the Israelites, and the connection between Mwari and the Shona is disregarded. The Shona traditions about how different mediators, such as Chaminuka, Nehanda, and Kaguvi, serve as spokespersons of Mwari are discredited and superseded by the biblical traditions. For example, the Mazezuru, a branch of the Shona, have a tradition about how Chaminuka became the link between Mwari and the people. Prior to Chaminuka's time, at a place called Maringari, was a special tree, *muti usinazita* (a tree without a name). According to Shona tradition, the tree fell and became a log from which shoots continued to sprout. The people would hear a voice, giving instructions and providing them with food. The voice was first identified as Mwari's voice and later replaced by Chaminuka, such that Mwari now speaks through Chaminuka and the people speak to Mwari through Chaminuka.[26]

The biblical account of the encounter between Moses and the Israelite God continues with the deity's identification with a people: "I have observed the misery of my people who are in Egypt" (Exod. 3:7). The Hebrew people belong to a specific deity, Elohim, who has come to deliver them from their sufferings at the hands of their oppressors. The connection between the people and this deity is made even clearer. This deity has come down to bring them "out of the land of Egypt to a good and broad land, a land flowing with milk and honey, to a country of the Canaanites, the Hittites, . . . and the Jebusites" (3:8). This deity has a grand scheme for the Israelites—a scheme that involves replacing other peoples in the land. For Africans, this picture of the divine purpose is ironic in the face of the Shona peoples' displacement by the European settlers.

Moses' response to this grand scheme relates to his specific role. He is to go to Pharaoh and demand that Pharaoh give the Israelites freedom. Moses initially wants to know what qualifies him for this role: "Who am I that I should go to Pharaoh, and bring the Israelites out of Egypt?" (3:11). The deity's response is that Moses' qualifications are inconsequential to the grand scheme of deliverance. What is significant is that the deity will be with him.

Moses then wonders how to communicate the identity of the deity. The deity had identified itself as the God of the Israelite ancestors. Moses now says, "If I come to the Israelites and say to them, 'The God of your ancestors has sent me to you,' and they ask me, 'What is his name?' what will I say to them?" (3:13). There are three parts to the deity's response. The first part seems to be the deity's refusal to respond and give its name: *Ehyeh asher ehyeh* ("I am who I am").[27] But this is the not the final response. The second part tells Moses how to respond to the Israelites' question: "Thus you shall say to the Israelites, '*Ehyeh* . . . has sent me to you'" (3:14b). The deity gives its name as *ehyeh*, which means "I am" in English and translates as *ndiri* in Shona. But that is not the final answer either. Moses is again told what to say to the Israelites: "Yhwh, the God of your ancestors, the God of Abraham, the God of Isaac, and the God of Jacob, has sent me to you" (3:15a). The God that Moses brings to the Israelites is none other than the God of their ancestors, who thus will fulfill the promise made to the ancestors. Thus, in Shona Bibles, Mwari becomes the name that stands for the new name revealed to Moses, and Mwari becomes the God of Abraham, of Isaac, and of Jacob, the God of the Hebrews.

This is a direct usurpation of the Shona deity by the biblical deity. Sanneh argues that the translation of Scriptures into vernacular languages assisted the Africans in preserving their names for the deity.[28] In fact, the translation of the Scriptures, at least as far as the Shona are concerned, resulted in the colonization of the Shona God. Mwari ceased to be the God of the Shona peoples and became the God of the Hebrews. Shona ways of relating to their deity are replaced by the new ways of relating to Mwari as Yhwh. The missionaries, and the Bible as the missionaries interpreted it, thus had the final word on what is acceptable and not acceptable for Mwari's new identity; the ways of the Shona were deemed obsolete. The Mwari shrines became an abomination, the connection between the Mwari and the ancestors invalid. The list of activities abhorrent to Mwari, according to Deut. 18:9–13, include most of the ways the Shona people communicated with their God. The equation of *vadzimu* (the ancestors) with the "ghosts and spirits," with whom connection is prohibited in Deut. 18:11, demonizes the Shona ancestors.

Unshackling Mwari from Colonial Chains

The Bible played a large role in the colonization of Zimbabwe. The religious colonization of the Shona began with the colonization of the Shona deity Mwari. This colonization, as detailed above, occurred by equating the name of the Shona deity with the biblical god and by the consequent transformation of the Shona deity. For the Shona to relate to this god, they had to abandon their Shona identity and become Western. Their own religious traditions suddenly were deemed incompatible with Mwari.

There is no doubt that Christianity is now one of the major religions of Africa. Mainstream Christianity, however, is plagued by having remained a foreign religion. It continues to make Shona Christians feel inadequate for being Shona, because Shona understandings of Mwari are suppressed. There are several ways to deal with this problem. The Bible entered Zimbabwe as a propaganda tool. The writing of African languages was developed in order to translate the Scriptures, since the missionaries wanted Shona words to make their message less foreign and thus acceptable to the Shona; that is the basis on which the Shona name of deity was appropriated and transferred to the biblical god. The Bible was also used as a text in schools, so that the adaptation of the deity was imprinted on those learning how to read and write. The power of the written word is demonstrated clearly by how the Bible suppressed oral traditions and led the biblical word to be seen as more authentic than the oral traditions it superseded. Shona values and beliefs had been transferred from generation to generation through folktales, but this process gradually ended and was replaced with the written word. Shona folktales were not accorded the same validity as the Bible, because they were said to be "myths," or unreal stories.

While the past cannot be undone, it is crucial now that the translation of the Shona Bibles be done independent of the evangelization of the Shona. In such a project, as Bird points out,

> The aim of the Bible translator . . . should be to enable a modern audience to *overhear* an ancient conversation, rather than to hear itself addressed directly. . . . It is not the translator's duty to make her audience *accept* the author's message, or even [to] identify themselves with the ancient audience.[29]

This also calls for a move from translating the Bible through European languages such as English, and instead to working directly from the Hebrew and Greek texts. There should be a Hebrew-Shona dictionary and Greek-Shona dictionary to allow the Shona to meet the Bible, not on English terms, but on the terms of Shona and of the original languages.

The inadequacy of the Bible to the Shona people's experience is expressed well by Canaan Banana, a Zimbabwean theologian, who argues not only for a translation from the original languages, but even for a rewriting of the Bible.

> This would include revision and editing to what is already there, but would also involve adding that which is not included. . . . I see that a re-written Bible, one that is more universal, embracing the rich plurality of the human experience in response to God, would be a more authentic and relevant document in today's world.[30]

The assumption behind Banana's proposal is that the Christian deity and the Shona deity are one and the same. This assumption still falls into the trap of making Mwari compatible with Christian concepts. In my judgment, the two should be kept separate and distinct. There should be separate documents containing the Shona stories and traditions about their deity. The Shona traditions should have authenticity apart from the Bible.

In the project I propose, the Hebrew names of God would be maintained in order to maintain the differences between Mwari and Yhwh Elohim. The pen should rescue the Shona deity. Writing merged Mwari with the biblical god, and it is through writing that the identification of Mwari with the genderless Shona deity will be reclaimed.

Notes

1. The limited allegiance of the Ndebele to Mwari can be demonstrated by the function of the Mwari cult during the first Ndebele-Shona uprising against the British settlers in 1896.

2. The claim that Mwari was divided into three—Father, Mother, and Son—is an attempt to make African religions compatible with the Christian concept of trinity.

3. John Kirk, *Zambezi Journals and Letters* (ed. Reginald Foskett; vol. 1; Edinburgh: Oliver & Boyd, 1965), 309. Italics are mine.

4. Cited in J. P. Wallis, ed., *The Matabele Mission* (London: Chatto and Windus, 1945), 70–71.

5. G. Fortune, "Who Was *Mwari?*" *Rhodesian History: Journal of the Central African Historical Association* 4 (1973): 5. Also, J. M. Schoffeleers and R. Mwanza, "An Organizational Model of the Mwari Shrines," in *Guardians of the Land: Essays on Central African Territorial Cults* (ed. J. M. Schoffelers; Gwelo, Rhodesia: Mambo Press, 1978), 308.

6. M. L. Daneel, *The God of the Matopo Hills* (London and The Hague: Mouton, 1970), 56–57.

7. *Buke eo ko Ravisa Tshekaranga* (The book for learning Karanga language) (Middleburg, South Africa: 1899); Rev. Wedepohl, *Mashoko e Buke eo Modzimo* (Compiled Bible stories) (Berlin: Evangelical Missiongesellschaft, 1902); J. T. Helm and A. A. Louw, *Evangeli ea Mattheus* (Translation of Matthew's Gospel) (London: British Foreign Bible Society, 1904); *Nziyo dzechiKaranga dze "De Ned. Ger. Kereke pa Mashonaland"* (Karanga hymns for the Mashonaland Church) (Cape Town: Citadel Press, 1910); *Vunzo dzeshoko ro Mudzimu* (Questions on the Word of God) (Fort Victoria, Rhodesia: Morgenster Mission, 1912).

8. *Vunzo dzeshoko roWedenga* (Questions about the Word of God) (Fort Victoria, Rhodesia: Morgenster Mission, 1909); *Mashoko e Bibele* (The Bible stories) (Belingwe, Rhodesia: Southern Rhodesia Church of Sweden Mission, 1927).

9. C. S. Louw, *Manual of the Chikaranga Language* (Bulawayo, Rhodesia: Philpott & Collins, 1915), 203.

10. E. W. Smith, *African Ideas of God* (London: Edinburgh House, 1950), 116–17.

11. Louw, *Manual of the Chikaranga Language,* 203.

12. For example, for Anglicans: *Minamato neZwiyimbo Yamana we-Sangano* (London: SPCK, 1900); Methodists: H. E. Springer, *A Handbook of Chikaranga* (Cincinnati: Jennings & Graham, 1905); Salvation Army: *Chizezuru and Ckinyanja Songs* (Cape Town: Salvation Army, 1920).

13. *Testamente Itswa ya She Wedu Jesu Kristu no Rurimi rwe Chishona* (The New Testament of our Lord Jesus Christ in Shona) (London: British & Foreign Bible Society, 1907); F. Mayr, *Katekisima re Makristo e Sangano re Katolike* (Pinetown, South Africa: Miriannhill, 1910).

14. A. M. Hartmann, *Rugwaro rgwo Kunamata* (Chishawasha, Rhodesia: Jesuit Mission, 1898); E. Biehler, *Zwinamato Zwineitikwa* (Roermond, Holland: J. J. Romen, 1906).

15. *English-Chiswina Dictionary with an Outline Chiswina Grammar* (Chishawasha: Jesuit Mission, 1906).

16. Fortune, "Who Was *Mwari?*" 8.

17. Ibid., 9.

18. Charles Bullock, *The Mashona* (Cape Town: Juta, 1928), 124; idem, *The Mashona and the Matabele* (Cape Town: Juta, 1950), 147.

19. M. Hannan, *Chitendero Chitsva* (Gwelo, Rhodesia: Mambo Press, 1966); *Standard Shona Dictionary* (Salisbury, Rhodesia: Rhodesia Literature Bureau, 1959 [1st ed.], 1974 [2d ed.]).

20. *Bhaibheri rine Apokirifa* (Harare: Bible Society of Zimbabwe, 1979).

21. *Bhaibheri Magwaro Matsvene Amwari Testamente Yekare Testamente Itsva* (London: British and Foreign Bible Society, 1949); *Bhaibheri Magwaro Matsvene Amwari Namanyorero Anhasi* (Harare: Bible Society of Zimbabwe, 1995).

22. For example, Phyllis Trible, *God and the Rhetoric of Sexuality* (Philadelphia: Fortress Press, 1978), 18.

23. This is contrary to Mbiti's assertion that the Ndebele and Shona have a pantheon of God the Father, God the Mother, and God the Son. This conclusion is actually a distortion that comes from the influence of Christianity. The Shona have never conceived of God in such human terms, which to their traditions would appear to limit the deity.

24. Shona languages lack the complication of grammatical gender.

25. This is sometimes taken as evidence that the story results from the J and E sources, or traditions.

26. Michael Gelfand, *Shona Ritual with Special Reference to the Chaminuka Cult* (Cape Town, Wynberg, and Johannesburg: Juta, 1959), 13–14.

27. Or "I am what I am" or "I will be what I will be."

28. Lamin Sanneh, *Translating the Message: The Missionary Impact on Culture* (Maryknoll, N.Y.: Orbis Books, 1989), 181.

29. Phyllis A. Bird, *Missing Persons and Mistaken Identities: Women and Gender in Ancient Israel* (Minneapolis: Fortress Press, 1997), 243.

30. Canaan S. Banana, "The Case for a New Bible," in *Voices from the Margin: Interpreting the Bible in the Third World* (ed. R. S. Surgirtharajah; rev. ed.; Maryknoll, N.Y.: Orbis Books, 1995), 81.

5

Translating the Divine:
The Case of Modimo in the Setswana Bible

Gomang Seratwa Ntloedibe-Kuswani

How do you translate the God of the Bible in terms of the "god" or "gods" of another culture? How do you change the categories and concepts of biblical religion to terms understood by those of native traditional religions? In general . . . the local gods, religious terminology, and categories are usually hijacked and christianised, or infused with new biblical meaning.

—Aloo Osotsi Mojola

In many African cultures, for example, the name and concept of the deity are often female. It is also women who are responsible for the intervention between people and the deity. This concept was foreign to early missionary Bible translators, and most translations changed the word for God to adapt it to the Western, male God name. These kinds of translations, now accepted by churches, have helped to reverse the status of women in religious spheres, both in the church and in local cultures.

—Musimbi R. A. Kanyoro

Long before the introduction of the Christian tradition in Africa, Africans had their own religious traditions, many of which have concept of the Divine, such as Modimo of Batswana, Unkulunkulu of the Zulu, Mwari of the Shona in southern Africa, Olorun of the Yoruba in West Africa, Ngai of the Kikuyu, Nyasaye of the Luo in East Africa, and many other names in central Africa. The colonial, mission Christianity had

---

The word *Setswana* in the title refers to the language and culture of Botswana. *Motswana* refers to a person who comes from Botswana. The plural of *Motswana* is *Batswana*. Epigraphs are drawn from Mojola 2000:31 and Kanyoro 1996.

first thought that Africans had no consciousness of the Divine or "Something Other Than the Ordinary," but this was a colonial rhetoric of subjugation. The same missionaries later found names of the Divine among African languages, which they used in biblical translations. African scholars' challenge to colonial Christianity also changed many attitudes toward Africa. This is reflected in some later writings of the missionaries and theologians, but the change is minimal in the Book of God, the translated Setswana Bible.

This essay focuses on the Batswana concept of the divine, Modimo. Its usage in Christian theology is different from its usage in African Batswana theology. The difference is articulated by John Hick's thesis (1989) that modern awareness of religious plurality and conceptual relativity has brought about a new situation that sees religious thought and experience as a global continuum containing an immense variety of forms. Consequently, discussions of religion have problems in defining concepts, precisely because each religious tradition has its own patterns. It is always a complex move, as this chapter demonstrates, to define what we mean by Allah of Islam, Brahman of Hinduism, Modimo of Batswana, Ngai of the Kikuyu, Nyasayi of the Luo, Mwari of the Shona, God of Christianity, and YHWH of Judaism. As the above quote from Aloo Osotsi Mojola indicates, this is precisely because we tend to try to understand various cultures' portraits of the Divine through the dominant form of the Divine—in this case, the biblical God. The attempt to study religions as a "global continuum," in other words, consists of suppressing differences by attempting to present a general and a global theory of religion that can be suitable for all religious traditions. As practiced in biblical translations, Mojola terms this suppression the hijacking and christianizing of other cultures. It is, therefore, important for all religious traditions to acknowledge their differences before they celebrate their universality and think that they are coexisting in the so-called global village. Even where there are apparent similarities among concepts, one has to bear in mind that their meaning may be different in different religious contexts. In the light of the global-continuum approach, it is important to grasp the uniqueness of each religion and its beliefs. In this essay, *the Divine* refers to the concepts of "God" listed above, as an attempt to underline the uniqueness of each concept and to avoid its suppression.

As the above quotes of Musimbi Kanyoro and Mojola underline, part of the hijacking, christianizing, westernization, and gendering of African concepts of the Divine and of spiritual spaces was informed by the colonial ideology that believed in the superiority of the Christian religion over the local religions. The Christian God was held to be the only saving God in the world, while African religions, or any other religion for that matter, were seen as the *preparatio evangelica*. That is, they were regarded as lacking completeness and salvation on their own and seen as raw materials that prepared the ground for planting Christianity. One cannot claim, however, that these colonial subjugations ended with colonial times. They continue today, wrapped and girded in translation theory that holds that translation is a communication process that moves the message or meaning "from the source language to the receptor language" (Kanyoro 1996). According to this theory, the source text is the given and cannot be changed. In other words, the Bible is the source text that cannot be changed, while the languages and cultures into which the Bible is translated are "receptor languages" that must and can be changed to make room for the Bible.

In making the so-called receptor language carry and communicate the biblical message, African and other nonbiblical cultures are hijacked. Their identity and authority is sacrificed to make room for the source text. The relationship between source and receptor is not equal. In fact, it smacks of both gender and colonial relationships, in which the man and colonizer are regarded as the sources of knowledge, power, and leadership, while the woman and colonized are the subjugated, the silenced, the ruled, and those guided to receive the colonizer's knowledge. Regardless of how these concepts are defined, whether the terms used are *source text* and *receptor languages* or *source text* and *targeted text*, their relationship is grounded on inequality, on subjugation and domination of the targeted languages and cultures. Thus, within translation theory itself—still used in our day—there is an inherently colonizing and gendered ideology that renders the so-called receptor languages into servants of the "source text," namely, the Bible. As Mojola correctly points out, "Translation is never neutral. It is an instrument of ideological and theological *formation—within the limits of fidelity and faithfulness to the source text*" (2000:31; emphasis mine). The source text is the power, the determinant. While Robert P. Carroll argues persuasively that translation also does violence to the source text itself, the translator starts from the premise that they must be faithful to the Bible, the source text, which is held to be normative or authoritative.[1]

But what of us and African cultures, which are equally normative to us? Who has the right to name us as "receptor languages," or "targeted texts," and to decide that our cultures must lose their authority and identity to the source text, the Bible? Why have translators not regarded both the source text and the receptor languages and cultures as equally authoritative and worthy of preservation? Given that proponents of translation theory cannot be separated easily, if at all, from the colonizer, these questions cannot be deferred any longer if the integrity and human rights of all are to be recognized. It is no longer enough to say that the translator's duty is to be faithful primarily to the source text, nor is it enough to begin with the premise that the source text cannot be changed—unless one espouses the same commitment to the so-called receptor languages. The violence of biblical translations must be revisited and exposed, and alternative theories that respect both the receptor and source languages should be proposed and applied.[2]

This essay pursues some of these concerns by focusing on the translation of Modimo, the divine figure of Batswana, and the ways in which Modimo was colonized and gendered in Setswana biblical translations. At issue is how these translations undermine the positions of women in the spiritual and social spaces. The exploration begins by tracing the earliest "written understanding" of Modimo, in an effort to illuminate the distinction between this concept and the biblical images and concepts of the divine. I then illustrate the gender neutrality of

81

Modimo by examining the contents of the Setswana divining set, *ditaola*, to show that, as a spiritual space, it espouses gender neutrality and resists giving Modimo human traits. This section is followed by an attempt, by briefly following the role of Modimo in Setswana biblical translations, to show how Modimo has been taken from its own people and tradition. In conclusion, I underline the need for biblical translation that takes the gender neutrality of Modimo into consideration, and that respects the differences between Modimo and the biblical concept of YHWH or the Christian God. The essay underlines the differences between YHWH/God and Modimo, even where they appear to be similar. This is a decolonizing strategy, necessary because the colonizing translations subjugate the so-called receptor languages or cultures by ignoring their differences, their uniqueness, and, indeed, by bending them to fit or to receive the so-called source text. It is therefore crucial to begin by acknowledging that the two views of God are different, despite some discerned similarities. Above all, the differences must be respected.

Understanding Modimo of Batswana

J. Tom Brown, a London Missionary Society missionary who wrote the *Secwana-English Dictionary* (1923), was puzzled by the Setswana verb *dima*. He consulted a Motswana old man versed in the traditions of his people. The old man demonstrated *go dima* to him by pouring a drop of ink on blotting paper. The ink penetrated, permeated, percolated, and spread, and the old man explained: "You see, that is *go dima;* and that is what Modimo does" (Smith 1981:51). Tom Brown made this entry in his dictionary:

> *dima*, v.pft *dimile:* the true original meaning of the word is very obscure. Some say it is the verb from which *Modimo* comes or a verb formed from *Modimo*. It carries the force of a searching, penetrating insight into men and things (a kind of X-ray!). It may also mean to excel: *Moea o o dimang;* an excellent and searching spirit in understanding—to create. (Setiloane 1976:25)

Modimo is not only the deity, but also all that pertains to the spirit world; hence, Modimo can neither be personified nor gendered. But other missionary writers of Setswana languages made the concept Modimo to mean man, ancestor, sky, and many other things. In spite of all attempts made to translate and define Modimo, "The fact is that there is much more to *Modimo* than the Christian missionaries dreamed of, rather than the much less which they came to think" (Setiloane 1976:78).

There is an expression in Setswana, *Modimo ke Selo se se Boitshegang*, meaning that Modimo is "Something Mysterious or Awesome." First, the expression tells us that Modimo is not a being or a person but that it is "Something." Second, it tells us that this "Something" is "mysterious" and probably too big to be held captive in any one place, book, or tradition, or to be comprehended by human beings (Smith 1981; Panikkar 1979). By *Selo*—"Something"—the expression does not mean something tangible, but something without form and that cannot be captivated through human gender. Modimo thus, in the Setswana understanding, forever remains in the neuter.

This expression helps to explain the Batswana understanding of and totality of the "Something Mysterious." That is, the characteristics of Modimo do not bear gender. The expression *Modimo ke Selo se se Boitshegang* is further illustrated by an incident that occurred among the Bakgatla people of Botswana. Isaac Schapera has recorded the incident, which reflects the Bakgatla's understanding of the Divine and their early response toward Christian religion, especially their protests against what they understood as the Christian understanding of God. What follows is part of a *kgotla* (public meeting) that took place at Mochudi during the early days of the colonial missionary era:

> It was "wrong" for God (Modimo) to have a house in the town; and they wanted him (the king) to pull it (the Church building) down and expel the Christians. . . . At the meeting several speakers repeated the complaint that Christianity, and especially the Church building, was the cause of drought. . . . There is no God (Modimo) for whom a house has to be built. (Schapera 1971:19)

This quotation is significant, for it highlights that Batswana, and most southern black Africans, never represented the Divine in physical forms, or even put up a physical abode for Modimo. Indeed, when colonial missionaries first thought that the Batswana had no concept of God, they had partly misinterpreted the Batswana's refusal to represent the Divine in physical structures. Colonial missionaries mistook Batswana's respect for the Divine for lack of knowledge of the Divine. The expression *Modimo ke Selo se se Boitshegang*, supported by the Bakgatla's protest, indicates that Modimo is an awesome "Something" that is everywhere and that is larger than life. The word *Something* underlines that Modimo is not human or gendered; Modimo is beyond such representation. Modimo cannot be given human or other specific characteristics (including gender) without distorting the name's original meaning. It follows that Modimo cannot be contained or be fully captured by biblical traditions or by the language of the Divine without a serious hijacking or Christianizing of the word.

Modimo, as "Something Mysterious," has hierophanies. Modimo can be manifest in ways that are gender-inclusive, at different places and times. The "Something" is emphasized to underline that Modimo, above all, resists taking human form, let alone a particular gender, and that Modimo inhabits all space, in whatever form. This is why, for Batswana, the whole environment and other forms of life ("nature") are considered sacred, because Modimo inhabits them and is manifest through them. This further explains that Modimo is for all and in all of us, both in humanity and the rest of the natural order. Modimo is not for the chosen few or a favored gender. It is this understanding of Modimo that translators and theologians of colonial Christianity failed to grasp when they translated the gendered Hebrew and Christian God as Modimo in the Setswana Bible. Gabriel Setiloane has already argued in his book *The Image of God among the Sotho-Tswana* (1976) that the Batswana image of Modimo hardly fits with the biblical pattern of God; he proposed that we will better represent Modimo with the pronoun "It" than "He." In a response to an earlier version of this essay presented at the International SBL Meeting in Cape Town in 2000, Eric Hermanson supports my argument from a linguistic point of view:

Grammatically the word *Modimo* is interesting. From its form, one would expect that it would belong to the Class 1 group of singular nouns, all of which are personal, and which have their plural in Class 2. However, *Badimo,* which is a personal plural in Class 2 and on surface looks as if it is the plural of *modimo,* in fact is used only in plural. *Modimo,* like *moya,* is actually a Class 3, as can be seen from the pronoun used in the above-mentioned verses, viz. *ona,* instead of the Class 1 pronoun *yena.* So, *Modimo* is not placed on the same level as human.[3]

No doubt, many of the above-outlined characteristics of Modimo will sound familiar to a biblical reader or scholar, who may find many similar understandings of the Divine in both Testaments. For example, one may point to the commandment prohibiting "graven images" (Exod. 20:4). The God of the Hebrew Bible is also represented as omnipresent, and in such gender-neutral images as a "small, still voice." In counteracting male images of God, Western feminists' strategy is to argue that this language should be taken metaphorically rather than literally. They have argued that to equate God with the gendered male language would be idolatry—equating God with the image of a man, although this is strongly forbidden in the second commandment. Western feminists have also noted that God is sometimes referred to in feminine images such as midwife (Ps. 22:9); mother (Jer. 31:15–22; Isa. 66:7–14); coin seeker (Luke 15:1–10); and baker woman (Matt. 13:33) (Anderson and Moore 1992:108–9). Some have resurrected the Goddess as a spiritual figure that empowers women (Eller 1996). Others have imagined God as friend, lover, or wisdom.[4] Western feminists insist on searching "for a viable term for divine mystery, redemptive for women as well as men" (Johnson 1996a:129). Their struggle with the naming of God comes with the realization that the dominant male gender associated with God has been and still is read literally, and it is used to marginalize women from themselves and from positions of power in social and spiritual spaces.

While many of the divine traits highlighted by Western feminist readers indicate similarities with Modimo, it is important to respect the differences. It is important to resist collapsing Modimo into YHWH/God. To emphasize only the similarities easily legitimates the practice in translation of treating Setswana as a receptor language that has no right to exist on its own in front of the biblical source text. Differences include that YHWH is portrayed as having a physical place in which to dwell, namely the Holy of Holies, in which YHWH was served by male priests and other functionaries. One thus needs to be able to say that while YHWH/God is the creator of all (Genesis 1–2), God still is said to have chosen some (Exod. 19:4–5) and accepted others on the basis of faith (1 Pet. 2:9–10). Similarly, YHWH/God is also a divine mystery, awesome, and omnipresent, beyond human characteristics and understanding, but "he" is more often than not cast in male garb. Modimo, however, never took any human gender, be it metaphorical or literal. Modimo never occupied a house constructed by humans or a tent among Batswana, designated Batswana as a chosen race, or favored a particular human gender. Modimo's characteristics operate differently from those of YHWH/God within this social context. Similarly, the impact on women's lives of these characterizations will be different.

While the Western feminist approach is to highlight the gender-neutral traits of YHWH/God against the predominantly male images in the Bible, we see male images imposed by the so-called source text, abetted by colonizing and patriarchal translation theories. Since those theories begin from the premise that the source text should keep all its traits, the receptor languages and cultures lose their traits. Cultural and linguistic differences, however, need to be underlined and respected to counteract the colonial ideology that legitimates the subjugation of nonbiblical cultures and languages.

The Divining Set, Modimo, and Gender Justice

When it comes to representation of Modimo in the Setswana spiritual space, the contents of the indigenous divining set, *ditaola*, further illustrate that the domination of one gender, male or female, was not characteristic. That divining set, which is used by *dingaka* (diviner-healers) in Batswana communities, reflects several aspects of Setswana life. The set is made out of the four major *taola* called Kgadi (female adult), Moremogolo (male adult), Jaro (young male adult), and Kgatshana (young female adult). These four indicate an inclusive gender representation in the Setswana spiritual ritual. In addition to the four, there is a *taola* called Thakadu (Antbear), represented as both female and male. Thakadu symbolizes Modimo as well as *Badimo,* both of which reflect the Batswana's understanding of the Divine. *Badimo* are intermediaries between Modimo and people. They include women and men and are always referred to in the plural.

The Batswana *dingaka* (diviner-healers) use Thakadu as their symbol because they say it is like Modimo and *Badimo* in many ways. For example, Thakadu (Antbear) cannot be seen easily except at night. Like Thakadu, Modimo and *Badimo* are hardly seen except through their deeds and at death or in dreams and visions. Thakadu digs big holes in the ground, from which people came to inhabit the world. The Thakadu-made holes were used traditionally as places of refuge during turmoil and wars. This gave people protection equivalent to that received from Modimo and *Badimo,* who enabled them to come out of the same holes to inhabit the world.[5] The practice reminds me of the stories told about many Batswana men who escaped the British Colonial Administration during the Second European War (1939–45) by hiding in *dithakadu*—"holes." This concept had a theological significance for the Batswana, which was that they escaped being taken to the war by the colonial administration because they hid themselves in Modimo.

It is also notable that the *ditaola* gives us the gender-balanced hierophany of Modimo or the Divine. There is no gendered *taola* without a male or female counterpart. Apart from the four main characters of *ditaola* and the two that represent *Badimo* and Modimo, other *ditaola* represent other peoples and different things, but in a compound way that does not reflect one gender. For instance, among the Bakwena group of Batswana, other *ditaola* represent groups like Basarwa, Bangwato, Bakgalagadi, and Makgowa without mentioning their gender. The *ditaola* presents a different picture of the Divine from the gendered Modimo of the colonial Setswana Bible.

According to Batswana beliefs, Modimo cannot have exclusively male characteristics. Rather, Modimo includes both male and female and is above all genders. Modimo is a manifold reality that can act through ancestors, spirits, ghosts, gods, nature, and humanity, irrespective of gender. Thus, any act that relates to any manifestation of the Divine relates to Modimo. For Batswana to present Modimo in isolation from other divine powers or manifestations is ambiguous. The manifestations of the Divine remain part of the whole. Staugard (1985) has observed that, in Modimo, Batswana religious beliefs include the existence of an omnipotent transcendental principle.

When the Christian religion was translated into Setswana, the Modimo of the Batswana was divorced from its context of Batswana beliefs, myths, rituals, ethics, experience, and their general way of life. These elements were dismissed as diabolic and as a "masterpiece of hell's invention" (Gairdner 1910:137). Modimo was taken into the Christian religion, which is highly male, leaving the Batswana traditions without a center. Further, the Modimo as preached in the Christian churches is a denouncer of the Batswana cultures. This strategy of translation became a masterpiece of the colonization of Batswana cultures and people. It left the Batswana religion without a divine spark of its own. Modimo, the Batswana divinity, was taken into the biblical cultures as a "receiver" of biblical beliefs and translated to fight against Batswana people and cultures. Setswana religions were also denied their own adherents, who were now colonized and christianized. They came to identify themselves with the translated Modimo of the Christian Bible and churches. The divinity appeared as a male parent, claimed as a God—not of all the Batswana—but of the chosen, "born again" few who believe in Jesus Christ.

Reading from the Translated and Gendered Modimo

This colonization and gendering of Modimo, the hijacking of Setswana traditions, and the resulting marginalization of women can be observed by following the exiled Modimo in Setswana translations drawn from Wookey's Bible of 1908. An account of that process in both Testaments demonstrates how the translated Modimo now functions, how Modimo is heard by Batswana, and how, in fact, Modimo has been exiled from Batswana and their culture to function apart from and even against them.

In the translated Setswana Hebrew Bible, the book of Genesis presents Modimo as the creator of the universe and humanity (Genesis 1–2). In Gen. 1:26–27, we hear Modimo saying: "Me Modimo oa re: A re diheng motho mo setshwanon ea rona . . . kaha sechwanon sa rona. Me Modimo oa tlhola motho mo chwanon ea ona tota, oa mo tlhola mo chwanon ea Modimo; oa ba tlhola nona le tshadi" ("And God said, 'Let us make humankind in our own image . . .' "). In some English Bible translations, "humankind" is rendered with the generic "man." The verse strives to present both genders as created in God's image, but this is only one step away from likening God more with one gender than the other. Indeed, in the following version of creation, Adam, a man, is created by God, while Eve is made from the rib of Adam and for Adam (Gen. 2:15–25). As Motswana readers continue, they hear how a woman came to be blamed for the sin of humanity and to be subjected to harsh discipline and oppression. The creation story is perhaps the strongest link for casting God in human forms. First, it underlines that people were created in God's image or likeness (Gen. 1:26–27). Then, it slants toward associating male gender rather than female gender with God's image (Gen. 2:21–23). For a Motswana reader, in whose culture Modimo is distanced both from human forms and from gender-exclusive representations, both biblical creation stories are problematic.

As we continue in Genesis, we see Modimo calling and using mainly male figures like Noah, Abraham, Isaac, Jacob, Esau, and the twelve sons of Jacob, who later made up the tribes of Israel. The Setswana Hebrew Bible continues to underline the male gender in Exod. 3:6, in which Modimo says, "I am the Modimo of your Father, the Modimo of Abraham, the Modimo of Isaac, and the Modimo of Jacob. And Moses hid his face; for he was afraid to look upon Modimo." Here Modimo is associated with the male line, to the exclusion of women. Second, Modimo is revealing "himself" to another man. In this scene, it is also implied that if Moses had raised his face, he could have seen Modimo! Third, not only has Modimo been translated from a gender-neutral divinity to a male God, but Modimo works primarily through males. The male figures of Moses and his brother will set the children of Israel free from slavery in Egypt and settle in the promised land. God regularly sends the people prophets, most of whom are males, and eventually, in the Setswana Christian Testament, God sends a male messiah who is called "the only Son of Modimo." But above all, when a Motswana reader reads the translated Bible, they hear that Modimo belongs not to them, but to the Israelites.

In the New Testament of the Setswana Bible, one can go from the Gospels to the Acts of the Apostles, from the Epistles to Revelation, following and highlighting the tragically translated, colonized, gendered, and exiled Modimo. For example, in Matt. 10:8 in Wookey's Bible of 1908, Jesus is said to send out his disciples with the command "kgoromeletsan badimo ntle" (NRSV: "cast out demons"). In the Setswana translation, Jesus, whom that same Bible characterizes as the only son of Modimo, authorizes his disciples to go and cast out *Badimo*— Batswana ancestors. In Setswana religious thinking, *Badimo* are part and parcel of the Divine. They dwell and work with Modimo and represent the people before Modimo. In Wookey's translation, these same *Badimo* are to be "cast out." This command is given for several reasons. First, Jesus is now the only mediator between God and people. Second, the translation has equated *Badimo* with evil spirits and demons, recasting their role from divine to evil. The translation thus shows a Motswana that Jesus is more powerful than *Badimo,* who tremble before the mighty Jesus. This result was achieved by separating Modimo from *Badimo* and from other aspects of the Setswana religious world. It was achieved by replacing the group- and gender-inclusive mediators of *Badimo* with the one and only Son, Jesus Christ.

Undoubtedly, this form of translation christianizes, colonizes, and hijacks many African religious divinities, many of which do not share attributes with the biblical God. Such discourse has made it difficult to teach and learn African traditions without theologizing them. For instance, the religious education curriculum in Botswana across all levels has a problem of freeing the African traditions from the Christian traditions. Setswana and many other African traditions are facing a great threat from the Christian biblical patterns. Since colonial times, it has become an unquestionable right for Christians to define African concepts according to Christian understanding, without giving Setswana and other traditions the right to speak for themselves or to maintain their identity.

It is notable, however, that when reading from *Baebele e e Boitshepo* (1992), a revision of Wookey's Bible carried out by the Batswana under the coordination of Rev. Morolong of the United Congregational Church of Southern Africa in Botswana, a few changes have taken place. First, although Modimo retains gendered male characteristics, in Matt. 10:8 and other cases where *Badimo* had been used to translate "demons," other words—*mewa ee maswe*—are now used for the casting out of "evil spirits." The revision has attempted to decolonize Wookey's translation, but it did not depatriarchalize it. Modimo still remains *Rara* or *Rraetsho* ("Father" or "Our Father"), although the *Badimo* are no longer devils, demons, or evil spirits (Dube 1999). This is instructive to Batswana and other African women, for it indicates that indigenous male translators bring their gender into biblical translation. Unless African women are involved in the translation process, the colonial gendering of their deities is likely to be maintained by indigenous male translators.

Implications of the Colonization and Gendering of Modimo

The gendering of Modimo has been used to support the exclusion of Batswana women in church and in other spheres of power. Many Batswana women are active members of the church, but as Sunday school teachers for young children, as caretakers of the church buildings, and sometimes as deacons. The United Congregational Church of Southern Africa

(UCCSA) in Molepolole, for example—where I live—is divided into numbered "village districts" governed by a district council of deacons. Every district is to be chaired by a male deacon, regardless of whether there is a male deacon in the district. If there is none, the male deacon is borrowed from another district. Several times I asked my mother, a deacon in our *kgaolo*, or district, why women from Kgaolo 6 could not be elected chairpersons for their own district. Her answer was obvious: The church does not allow it.

We still see that, although many denominations in the postcolonial church recognize women for priesthood, the church in many other ways remains dominated by men. The impact of this male domination in the church, of course, is also found in society. Some women who used to have powerful roles, like healers, and who became church members, were forced, in many instances, to denounce these roles beforehand. Unlike men who received new power in the church, the women remain powerless. Ife Amadiume (1987) has studied her people, the Nnobi of Igboland, focusing on the position of women prior to colonialism and the impact of colonialism on their lives and social roles. She notes that while women had their own Goddess, Idemili, and their own crops, and while they ran the marketplace, Christianity, when it arrived, condemned indigenous religious beliefs and replaced them with Christian beliefs. The denunciation was enacted systematically through the church, the school, and the colonial job market, and it was taught in the first Christian lessons. In the end, more men could go to school and get hired in the school, church, or colonial offices. Women were marginalized from education, from their own indigenous religions, and from Christianity, which preferred male church leaders and had male spiritual figures, such as God the Father and Jesus the Son. Like the Nnobi, the Batswana were told to stop following their indigenous religious practices, which the colonial Christians interpreted negatively, as demonstrated by the equation of *Badimo* with demons and evils spirits. Batswana thus moved from largely gender-neutral religious space and symbols to male-centered substitutes. The Christian doctrine as presented claimed that God, who came to be translated as Modimo, was a "he" but not a "she" (Amadiume 1987). Just as Amadiume closely studies the changes that followed the introduction of male-centered religion and its institutions, we cannot overlook how the colonial translation of Setswana spiritual space from gender-neutral to exclusively male has contributed to the marginalization of Batswana women in the society and church.

Conclusion

The assumption that the Christian patterns of thought are universal has led many translators and writers to colonize other religions, particularly African religions. Although we celebrate Modimo and God as the Divine, the different understandings that the two terms convey help us to better understand the Christian and the Batswana traditions. Failure to recognize the uniqueness of African religions, or of the Batswana religion, has resulted in Africans and the Batswana losing their identity as well as their humanness (*botho*). For women, the situation has been worse; they have lost their place in the divine arena, in church leadership, and in social spaces. The Christian God has strong gender characteristics, which is not the case with the pre-colonial Modimo. The current study of African traditions and *"Modimo*logy" is problematic in the sense that time and again it identifies the Christian view of God with African divinities.

The Christian theological assumption that Modimo and God are the same gives the impression that

- the Batswana have knowledge of the Divine, which in many ways exposes the missionary claim that Africans had no knowledge of God as a colonial rhetoric of subjugation;

- the unqualified equation of Modimo with YHWH/God justifies the religion of Batswana as the *praeparatio evangelica;* that is, it cannot be a religious tradition in its own right and for the salvation of its own adherents;

- the tradition of the Batswana is nothing other than the

Christian tradition in another language; hence, many theologians present African Christian theology as the African theology, forgetting that Africa is rich in theologies—African, Jewish, Christian, Islamic, Hindu, Sikh, and many others—that need to be respected for their differences;

• religion can be defined in biblical Christian terms and thought of as belief in God, who is personified and highly gendered, thus hijacking the individual characteristics of Setswana and those of other religious faiths.

In short, I am inclined toward Raimundo Panikkar's (1979) thesis that considers the Divine as "the distinctive, not the uniting, factor of religion." That is, a similar concept in different religious traditions does not imply that those traditions understand the concept in the same way. The similarity in concepts does not call for one universal religious tradition. Religious traditions and concepts differ according to understanding, time, place, and people. Each set of terms is understood fully only at home, in its environment (Hick 1989). The Batswana understanding of the Divine was neither patriarchal nor gendered. Modimo was neither a man nor father, neither a woman nor mother. Rather, Modimo is above gender, above humans, above any other thing. Modimo is "Something." Modimo embraces both genders, as seen in the *ditaola* set, which contains a representation of Modimo (Divinity); *mosadi* (woman) and *monna* (man); animals (males and females); and *merafe* (other ethnic groups). Bible translators of today need to decolonize translation theory to embrace the equal authority of both the so-called source text and the receptor languages. In Botswana, we need to liberate Modimo from the gendered Christian coat that "he" wears today, for it legitimizes the marginalization of women in the church and society. For instance, the Lord's Prayer (Matt. 6:9–13) can be retranslated using Thakadu (Antbear) instead of *Rara* (father), and *mosima* (earth hole or home) instead of "heaven," as follows:

> *Thakadu etsho e e mo matsatseng/mosimeng* (Our Antbear who is the earth hole/home)

Leina la gago a le itshepisiwe (Let your name be sanctified)
Maatla a gago a tle (Let your power come)
Go rata ga gago a go dirwe mo lehatshing, mo matsatseng (Let your will be done on earth and in earth holes/homes)
Re nee gompieno sejo sa rona sa letsatsi (Give us today our daily bread)
Mme o re itshwarele melato ya rona (And forgive us our trespasses)
Jaaka le rona re itshwarela ba ba melato go rona (Just as we forgive those who sin against us)
Mme a o ko o seka wa re isa mo thaelong (And lead us not into temptation)
Mme o re golole mo go yo o bosula (But deliver us from Evil)
Go nne maatla a gago a magolo (For great is your power)
Le thata, le kgalalelo, ka bosenabokhutlo (The power and the glory forevermore)
Ditlhokwa di re robalele. Pula! (Let there be Peace and rain amongst us. Pula!)

Notes

1. See Carroll 1996 for the details of this argument.

2. See Sugirtharajah 1996, where he proposes a new model of translation that does not subscribe to a colonizing ideology.

3. Eric Hermanson is a long-serving staff member of the Bible Society of South Africa, and he has overseen a number of their translations in the country and region. As a translator who fully subscribes to the theory of faithfulness to the "source text," he generally disagreed with my paper. Nonetheless, I found his linguistic comment instructive for my thesis.

4. See Johnson 1996a for the strategies of resistance advanced by Western feminists.

5. The Setswana creation myth holds that people came out of a cave when the rocks were still soft. The myth holds that women and men came out with their livestock and other property.

References

Alverson, H. 1978. *Mind in the Heart of Darkness: Value and Self-Identity among the Tswana of Southern Africa*. New Haven: Yale University Press.

Amadiume, Ife. 1987. *Male Daughters, Female Husbands*. London: Zed Books.

Anderson, Capel J., and Stephen D. Moore. *Mark and Method: New Approaches to Biblical Studies*. Minneapolis: Fortress Press, 1992.

Baebele e e Boitshepo. 1992, 1998. Cape Town: Bible Society of South Africa.

Brown, J. Tom. 1926. *Among the Bantu Nomads*. London: Seeley, Service.

Carroll, Robert P. 1996. "Cultural Encroachment and Bible Translation: Observations on Elements of Violence, Race, and Class in Production of Bibles in Translation." *Semeia* 76:39–53.

Chidester, D. 1996. *Savage Systems: Colonialism and Comparative Religion in Southern Africa*. Cape Town: University of Cape Town.

Collins English Dictionary and Thesaurus. 1993. Glasgow: HarperCollins.

Comaroff, Jean, and John Comaroff. 1991. *Of Revelation and Revolution: Christianity, Colonialism, and Consciousness in South Africa*. Vol. 1. Chicago: University of Chicago Press.

Cox, James. 1998. *Ancestor Rational*. Cardiff: Cardiff Academic Express.

Dube, Musa W. 1999. "Consuming a Colonial Cultural Bomb: Translating *Badimo* into Demons in the Setswana Bible (Matthew 8:28–34; 15:22; 10:8)." *Journal for the Study of the New Testament* 73:33–59.

Eller, Cynthia. 1996. "Goddess." Pp. 130–32 in Russell and Clarkson 1996.

Gairdner, W. H. T. 1910. *Edinburgh 1910: An Account and Interpretation of the World Missionary Conference*. London: Oliphant and Ferrier.

Hick, John. 1989. *An Interpretation of Religion*. London: Macmillan.

Johnson, Elizabeth A. 1996a. "God." Pp. 128–30 in Russell and Clarkson 1996.

———. 1996b. "Images of God." Pp. 149–50 in Russell and Clarkson 1996.

Kanyoro, Musimbi R. 1996. "Translation." P. 303 in Russell and Clarkson 1996.

Knitter, Paul F. 1985. *No Other Name: A Critical Survey of Christian Attitudes towards the World Religions*. Maryknoll, N.Y.: Orbis Books.

Maluleke, T. S. 1998. "Denied, Discovered, and Still Denied: African Traditional Religions in the Christian and Religious Studies of Southern Africa." *UNISWA Research Journal* 12:1–14.

Marquard, L., and T. G. Standing. 1939. *The Southern Bantu*. London: Oxford University Press.

Mogapi, Kgomotso. 1992. *Ngwao ya Setswana*. Mabopane, South Africa: L. Z. Sikwane.

Mojola, Aloo Osotsi. 2000. "Bible Translation." Pp. 30–31 in *Dictionary of Third World Theologies*, edited by Virginia Fabella and R. S. Sugirtharajah. Maryknoll, N.Y.: Orbis Books.

Monnig, H. O. 1967. *The Pedi*. Pretoria: Van Schaik.

Monyaisi, Semakaleng D. P. 1970. *Go sa Baori*. Pretoria: J. L. van Schaik.

Panikkar, Raimundo. 1979. *Myth, Faith, and Hermeneutics: Cross-Cultural Studies*. New York: Paulist Press.

Pauw, B. A. 1970. *Religion in a Tswana Chiefdom*. London: Oxford University Press.

Russell, Letty M., and J. Shannon Clarkson, eds. 1996. *Dictionary of Feminist Theologies*. Louisville: Westminster John Knox Press.

Schapera, Isaac. 1971. *Rain-Making Rites of Tswana Tribes*. Cambridge, England: African Studies Centre.

Schapera, Isaac, and J. L. Comaroff. 1991. *The Tswana: Revised Edition.* London: Kegan Paul International.

Setiloane, Gabriel. 1976. *The Image of God among the Sotho-Tswana.* Rotterdam: A. A. Balkema.

———. 1978. "How the Traditional World-View Persists in the Christianity of the Sotho-Tswana." Pp. 402–12 in *Christianity in Independent Africa,* edited by Fashole Luke. London: Rex Collins.

Setswana-English Dictionary. 1923. Tigerkloof, South Africa: LMS Press.

Smith, Wilfred Cantwell. 1981. *Towards a World Theology.* London: Macmillan.

Staugard, Frants. 1985. *Traditional Healers.* Gaborone, Botswana: Ipelegeng.

Sugirtharajah, R. S. 1996. "Textual Cleansing: A Move from the Colonial to the Postcolonial Version." *Semeia* 76:7–20.

Westerlund, David. 1985. *African Religion in African Scholarship.* Stockholm: Almquist and Miksell.

Young, T. C. 1937. *African Ways and Wisdom: A Contribution towards Understanding.* London: Lutterworth Press.

*Reading with and from
Non-academic Readers*

6

Cultural Hermeneutics:
An African Contribution

Musimbi R. A. Kanyoro

Recent situations have prompted me to think about culture. Often culture is subconscious, so ingrained that we do not hear or see ourselves in our cultural skin. The objective of this essay is to encourage more analytical thinking about culture by writing about my own journey.

I was very involved with nongovernmental organizations (NGOs) in connection with the World Conference on Human Rights (Vienna, 1993). A strong argument was put forward, mainly by Asian and African governments, that human rights are culturally determined and, therefore, that we cannot speak about a universal understanding of human rights. China took the lead in this debate, with support from many other states. Critics of this argument quickly pointed to the human rights record of the nations that were making it. We accused these nations of wanting to hide something, and it is evident that nations like China—and my own country, Kenya—are vulnerable to this charge.

The women at the Vienna conference worked very hard to put women's human rights on the agenda, and we succeeded. At the daily women's caucuses, we struggled to maintain a united front on the issue of universal human rights, because we saw the possibility of using culture to explain away violations of women's rights. We were greatly helped by the worldwide awareness of how violence against women defies borders of culture, race, geography, and class. Media coverage of the horrendous use of rape in the former Yugoslavia was also a fresh memory.

Yet beneath this united front was a discomfort raised only in faint voices. The common agenda of getting women to the discussion table of the UN member states was our immediate priority; although some of us saw possibilities in the culture argument, we did not want to deal at that time with the difficult double-edged nature of culture. I remember an informal conversation while walking to lunch with a woman from Pakistan. We found ourselves talking about all the women who have been and are being raped in war around the world. If Bosnia were not in Europe, we wondered, would there have been such extensive press coverage? And if there were, would global solidarity have been mobilized to the same extent?

The question arises for me again as I see the international coverage of Rwanda and other conflicts. Could we have achieved our objectives in Vienna in another way? Or were we being dishonest with one another and to each other as women when we decided not to discuss the culture argument in connection with human rights? Was this another case in which women stand for a cause only to be forgotten after it is won? Were we standing in solidarity with the global women's agenda, knowing full well that we are only marginally part of that agenda?

I recall a presentation by Nashilogo Elago, a Namibian woman, in a workshop in Bossey in 1988. She said that many black women in Namibia had been raped by white occupying soldiers from South Africa. When the women took the matter to the courts, they were told that it was not a serious issue because, culturally, black people enjoy sex, and African women are used to rough treatment in their homes. Later, I met this kind of thinking again when a missionary doctor stopped in Geneva to brief the ecumenical organizations during the terrible early days of the Liberian war. After telling of the horrible killings and looting, he spoke of the widespread rape of women, which no media reports had mentioned. In the discussion that followed, some of us focused on how to help these women. The missionary doctor replied that he saw no possible traumatic effects of rape on them.

Such encounters have led me to seek more focus on culture

102

in all its forms. It seems to me that there has been little mature analysis of or dialogue on culture in ecumenical and international circles. Rather, culture is a euphemism used to explain biases, to justify actions that might otherwise be challenged, and to foster diversity at the expense of unity. There is a need to challenge this thinking and to face a sincere dialogue on culture. Having underscored the universality of the subordination of women, perhaps women can give credibility to this debate; the current ecumenical focus on gospel and cultures may be one forum in which Christian women can speak about their experiences. Let me use an example to illustrate the conditions that might create a safe environment for cultural dialogue. In a January 1994 conference in Nairobi of African women theologians, Denise Ackermann described her theological journey as a white South African who grew up in the system of apartheid. She was challenged to undertake this painful journey by the feminist analysis that supports doing theology from our experience. Yet she felt left out of the theology represented, for example, by the book *The Will to Arise: Women, Tradition, and the Church in Africa*,[1] in which African Christian and Muslim women speak of their religious experiences within African cultures.

These authors search for the female face of God through analysis of their experiences in culture and in religion, especially the rites of passage. They explore the structures and institutions established to support and maintain these rites: rituals, taboos, initiations that accompany birthing, growing up, marriage, mothering, death; ceremonies to celebrate those occasions; and practices and precautions to ensure a future. They discuss such issues as naming rituals, fertility, dowry, property, ownership, widowhood, sexuality, polygamy. The experiences that help weave the theology around these issues do not exist in Denise Ackermann's African world, although she is familiar with some of them because she was born in Africa, has daily contact with indigenous Africans, and is well-read. But did she have a right to be involved in the analysis of the other African women? How far could she go with her critique? Would her critique inevitably come from the safely distant vantage point

from which she has been socialized to regard traditions of indigenous African people? Would we accept her contribution or
would that kind of participation in our experiences estrange us
from each other and create division?

The Cape Town Circle of Concerned African Women in
Theology, a group of blacks, Asians, colored, and whites whose
religious experiences are Muslim, Christian, and African indigenous, discussed these concerns. Their dialogue led them to
conclude that cultural critique is possible only where the vulnerability of all the participants is transparent. Denise was challenged to lay herself bare on the culture of apartheid.

Listening to her paper in Nairobi made me think more seriously of the theology that African women are doing. Upon reflection, I concluded that theology informed by cultural analysis is not peculiar to Africa, although it is more prevalent there.
It is what Asian women are doing when they address issues
like dowry and the burning of brides in India, what black
Brazilians are doing as they ask for recognition of their indigenous spirituality, what womanist theologians do when they
take into account the peculiar cultural distinctions of African
American women.

It seems to me that something significant is happening to
theological analysis. This new aspect of analysis, brought to
theology mainly by women of the southern hemisphere, deserves its rightful place among theological paradigms. Such
analysis could be called *cultural hermeneutics*. Cultural hermeneutics can help us develop a vision for mature cultural di-
alogues. The complexities inherent in cultural debate require a
safe environment of mutual trust and mutual vulnerability in
order for dialogue to take place.

Applying Cultural Hermeneutics to the Biblical Text

Recognition of the universality of women's subordination
and oppression is the basis of all feminist work. But diver-
gences in feminist critique of culture and in the priorities of the
struggle on issues of culture have divided and silenced

women. Cultural hermeneutics can open our eyes to possibilities that might move us to different commitments. Let me illustrate using both the Bible and the experiences of African women. By so doing, I hope to show what I believe to be difficult questions confronting African women reading the Bible, and to demonstrate that African women are asking different questions from those in the theological debate in general and in women's theology in particular.

The biblical story is that of the three women Naomi, Ruth, and Orpah, as found in the Old Testament book of Ruth. These three widows must begin a new life after the deaths of their husbands. Orpah chooses to return to her own people, and the Bible is silent about what happened to her; in fact, she is mentioned only to contrast her with Ruth, who chose to remain faithful to Naomi and Naomi's people. Alice L. Laffey has done a thorough feminist analysis of this passage and also presents a summary of other feminist views.[2] Some emphasize God's empowering of the powerless through Ruth's marriage to Boaz and the subsequent birth of a son. Others point to the friendship of two women of different ages and different nationalities. Still others highlight the courage of the women as they make decisions for their new lives.

Critics denounce the culture that made women feel powerless if they were not attached to a man, the custom of a widow marrying the next of kin, and the lack of choice and opportunity for women. But this is as far as the critique goes—as if this is a story from long ago and these issues are no longer relevant today.

In fact, requiring widows to marry the brother of their dead husband persists in many parts of Africa, and the church and women themselves have sometimes seen this text as endorsing this cultural practice. Our experiences in these circumstances demand that we stay longer with the text and find a way to rescue the characters from cultural bondage. Women who choose to be Orpahs have no models of blessing from the Bible. How do we support Orpahs? What blessings could we imagine for Orpah, especially when compared with the blessings that befell Ruth when she succumbed to certain cultural possibilities—a reward that culminates in her taking a place in the lineage of salvation (Matt. 1:5)?

Our concern with the biblical text is not just to condemn the culture but to seek tools to analyze culture in order to reach out to women in bondage to it. So we continue the exegesis of Ruth by inquiring of women what message this story conveys to them. Does it encourage them to succumb to cultural expectations? What is the message for women who want to be different? How do we imagine the life of Orpah? What blessings and problems accompanied her? Why? Could we be Orpahs? How does an Orpah mobilize collective solidarity? How does she face communal criticism? The questions are endless. We also ask many questions of Ruth and Naomi.

The feminist analysis of patriarchy sometimes approaches women's oppression by pointing to men as the oppressors. This approach is a nonstarter in Africa. While African women acknowledge men's role in oppression, they do not throw stones, reasoning that this would pose a major threat to women's solidarity. It is easy to discredit struggles that center on cultural oppression with the excuse that they break up the community. Moreover, when dealing with cultural matters, there is a need for collective solidarity. Cultural oppression cannot be addressed in singularity. Since the custodians of indigenous cultures often have little contact with other cultures, a valid analysis must include their views.

For us as African feminists, this understanding is crucial if our feminism is not to be seen merely as a bourgeois deviation resulting from the cultural imperialism of Western women. Lack of consensus on what, when, and how to be critical of cultures makes it difficult for African women to mount a collective resistance either to alien cultural values or to oppressive elements of indigenous cultures. It is difficult when solidarity among women cannot be obtained. This lack of collective solidarity is not a matter of a generation gap or different levels of education or varying religious affiliation, but of cultural loyalty. Rituals and initiation practices are one area in which it is very difficult for women to reach a consensus. This is not a sign of lack of courage or inability to confront issues, but of counting the cost and of taking stock of the gains and losses.

Cultural ideologies regarding gender roles and power in society are deeply embedded in our lived experience. Even on issues of violence and on how male power over women is maintained, it is no easier for African women to agree jointly to condemn the men. In addition to the threat to solidarity among women, some African women reason that they want a future in which men are friends. Building that future does not begin by attacking men but by finding methods of bringing change together with them. This is a tall order, but it is the reality of the lived experience of African women.

Another point that needs to be confronted is that institutionalized cultural violence has ensured that women are not only victims but also, more often than not, perpetrators. Who enforces inhuman rituals on widows in Africa and Asia? Who are the excisors of the female? Who are the instigators of divorce or polygamy when wives are unable to give birth to children or, specifically, to male children? These are areas of *women's* violence against women. We have to break the vicious circle of women violating other women in the name of culture. We cannot continue to bemoan the socialization we have had when lives are at stake. That is what some of our African governments do when they blame every tragedy on colonialism and refuse to be accountable for their own part in the calamity of our continent. Women must come of age, confront ourselves, and address women as the cause of oppression. This is not a refusal to address male oppression, but rather a way of empowering women to remove the log in our own eyes so that we can see clearly the log in other people's eyes.

When I read the story of Sarah and Hagar through the eyes of Elsa Tamez, I was delighted to discover that God had a place for Hagar.[3] But Sarah and Hagar are not biblical women to me. They are my family. I have lived in the middle of their struggle all my life. I am part of their fights day in and day out. I am not able to see one as the oppressor and to exonerate the other. I see envy, jealousy, revenge, competition, and many more ugly things. As an adult Bible-reading woman, I am not looking for models of behavior but rather for clues as to what might change behavior. I do not want to see the help that comes to one of them and begin the vicious circle of envy. I want to see them together, refusing the system that promotes their behavior. I do not want to sustain the syndrome of blaming the other and of not taking personal responsibility. This is where the difficulties in reading the Bible lie for those of us who come from cultures that closely mirror the practices of biblical times.

Let us look at another example. Women and work is an issue that feminist theory has addressed in great detail. Many women have found liberation in moving from the household into paid work. Their personal freedom of movement and earnings have been enhanced. But what has this transition done to those who have stayed at home and to the work they do?

Sometimes even a "women's reading" of the Bible does not answer the questions that bother us. In the Martha and Mary stories (Luke 10:38–42; John 11:1–44), we have found liberation in the affirmation by Jesus of Mary's desire for knowledge. That is good. But what about Martha? A majority of women in Africa are Marthas. We live on a continent stricken with calamities. Hospitality and service are the true hope for the millions of starving and dying. We are a continent in which more than 60 percent of women are illiterate, and no change seems in view. This means that, for us, celebrating Mary's privileged position of learning is very painful. We do it, with reservations, as we see that the privileges of material wealth and Western knowledge determine who lives and who dies. We as African women doing theology are among the privileged, but we carry a burden. How shall we do theology that gives hope to our continent? In *Household of Freedom*, Letty Russell has argued that no theology is adequate if it cannot speak to and from the experiences of its participants, its doers and its hearers. "Women's experiences include the biological and cultural experiences of being female as well as the feminist experience, the political experience of those who advocate a change of society to include both women and men as human beings."[4] We are a long way from this situation.

Questions for Feminist Theories

Here are two testimonies by university-educated women in Mali, interviewed by Awa Thiam?[5]

Case 1 (thirty-five years old, working in a government department):

> I had just turned 12 when I was excised. The excisor was an old woman belonging to the blacksmiths' caste. Here in Mali, it is usually women of this caste who practice ablation of the clitoris and infibulation.
>
> On the threshold of the hut, my aunts exchanged the customary greetings and left me in the hands of the excisor. . . . Once I was inside, the women began to sing my praises, to which I turned a deaf ear, as I was overcome with terror. . . . "Lie down," the excisor suddenly said to me. Two women on each side of me pinned me to the ground. . . . First I underwent the ablation of the labia minora, and then of the clitoris. . . . It was a rule that the girls of my age did not weep in this situation. I broke a rule. . . . I was bleeding. The blood flowed in torrents. Then they applied a mixture of butter and medicinal herbs which stopped the bleeding. Never had I felt such excruciating pain. After this, the women let go their grasp, freeing my mutilated body. . . . "You can stand up now" . . . Then they forced me, not only to walk back to join the other girls who had already been excised, but to dance with them. . . . It was months before I was completely well. . . . Everyone mocked me as I hadn't been brave, they said.

Case 2 (twenty-six years old, divorced with one child):

> I was excised as a child. . . . I am talking about my personal experience. Today I am happy I had the excision operation. . . . It has fulfilled its function as far as I am concerned. I've been divorced for four years and I've never for one moment felt the desire to run after a man, or felt the absence of sexual relations . . . to be a vital lack. That indicates to some extent the function of excision. . . . It allows a woman to be in control of her own body. And that is why I don't in any way consider it as a mutilation. . . . I can't think of excision as practised by our elders as being a mutilation. In fact it boils down to what the intention is, and with them, it isn't to mutilate.

Today, through media campaigns backed by medical reports and novels such as Alice Walker's *Possessing the Secret of Joy*, it has been proven that female circumcision is harmful to the health of women. Feminists see it as a destruction of women's sexual pleasure in the interest of male sexuality. Yet millions of women who continue to practice it see it as their cultural heritage and as affirming their dignity within society. For some, as the second case above illustrates, it is the path to freedom over their own bodies. Feminists have advocated the right of women to freedom over their bodies and their sexuality. The accepted methods include choices in marriage and sexual orientation, control over reproductivity, and, of course, the freedom to make decisions. Feminists often assume that there are specific ways to realize these freedoms. But what about women who choose other ways, including their cultural ways, to reach the same goal?

This presents a real challenge to the current collective struggle to outlaw certain traditional practices. The question calls for formulating an alternative to the feminist analysis, one that will speak to the experiences not only of women opposed to traditional practices, but also to those who, in the practices, find personal empowerment.

It might be argued that empowerment has to be a liberating experience that gives full humanity to women. But who judges what is liberating—the woman herself or someone else? Can we accept that female circumcision has liberated the woman in case 2? What cultures determine the choices that are good for individual women? If women have to change a culture, what process should they use toward that change? What support systems will be available to fill the void? Unless a theoretical analysis sees the people involved, its claim for universal validity will not stand.

Establishing Women's Explanations for Culture

Much work is needed on the history of culture and the structures that maintain it. We need to establish how women explain their cultural practices and then to discover the source of such explanations. Sometimes there are surprises. For example, Awa Thiam reports about a well-known myth among Muslim and Christian West Africans that female circumcision is good for women because it was started by women. At the command of God, Sarah circumcised Hagar. The myth goes like this:

> Long before the time of Mahout, there was a prophet named Ibrahima (Abraham), who was married to his cousin Sarata (Sara). He went up to the land of Gerar, where reigned King Abimelech, who delighted in taking to himself all men's wives who were remarkable for their beauty. Now it happened that Sarata was unusually fair. And the king did not hesitate to try to take her from her husband. A supernatural power prevented him from taking advantage of her, which so astonished him that he set her free. And he restored her back to her husband and made her the gift of a handmaid named Hadiara (Hagar).
>
> Sarata and her husband lived together for a long time but Sarata bore Ibrahima no child. And eventually, Ibrahima took Hadiara to wife; some said that it was Sarata who said to her husband that he should take her handmaid to wife since she herself could bear no children. And so Sarata and Hadiara became co-wives to Ibrahima and Hadiara bore him a son and his name was Ismaila (Ishmael) and Sarata also bore a son to Ibrahima and he was called Ishaga (Isaac). In the course of time, the relationship between the two women deteriorated. And so it came to pass that one day Sarata excised Hadiara. Some say that she only pierced her ears while others maintain she did indeed excise her.[6]

Neither the Bible nor the Quran mentions excision. But how did this myth get to the women of Africa? Why does it circulate only among the groups that circumcise women?

Culture has been a dominant feature in African theology. Christian missionaries tended to see African cultures as barbaric. Liberal explorers romanticized these cultures, in the belief that the African would outgrow them with the adoption of the new "civilization."

In the 1960s and 1970s, African theologians (mainly male) began to practice a theology of inculturation in reaction to the Western cultural imperialism that came with Christianity and colonialism. The general conviction behind the theology is that the message of Christ can be dynamic and communicative to all people, in all cultures, at all times. For Africa, inculturation is a form of liberation theology. It decries the Western imperialism in which Christianity was wrapped and exported to Africa.

Simon Maimela describes inculturation as "an approach which is characterized by the attempt to marry Christianity with the African world view, so that Christianity could speak [to Africans] with the African idiom and accent." Hence African inculturation theology relates to the Africanizing of Christianity.[7] African women theologians have argued that the cry to regain our culture is artificial, because we never lost it in the first place. The parts of culture affected were rather artificial; what actually happened was the addition of foreign cultural elements to African cultures. Women have given evidence for these arguments, but there is still reluctance on the part of men genuinely to come to terms with the question of women and culture.

Descriptions of aspects of African culture exist in many publications. Historically, such works are remnants of diaries, memoirs, ethnographic monographs, and anthropological treatises. The authors were merchants, missionaries, colonialists, anthropologists, and, later, African men. Accordingly, their research on women was not only brief but also secondhand and often distorted. Most of these writers, women included, were socialized within pietistic, patriarchal, or Victorian value systems. Under these circumstances, the task of African women is not only to correct past records but also to provide fresh data on the variety of women's experiences and on the nature of their struggles against oppression. The objective is not merely to write women back into history, but also to record gender struggles as defined by history, culture, race, and class structures in Africa. Aspects of this work share in the analysis done by women from other parts of the world, but, in the area of culture, we see that our experiences offer a uniqueness specific to Africa.

Notes

1. Ed. Mercy Amba Oduyoye and Musimbi R. A. Kanyoro (Maryknoll, N.Y.: Orbis Books, 1992).

2. Alice L. Laffey, *An Introduction to the Old Testament: A Feminist Perspective* (Philadelphia: Fortress, 1988), 205–10.

3. See Elsa Tamez, "The Woman Who Complicated the History of

Salvation," in *New Eyes for Reading: Biblical and Theological Reflections by Women from the Third World* (ed. John S. Pobee and Bärbel von Wartenberg-Potter; Geneva: WCC, 1986).

4. Letty Russell, *Household of Freedom* (Philadelphia: Westminster, 1987).

5. Awa Thiam, *Black Sisters Speak Out: Feminism and Oppression in Black Africa* (London: Pluto Press, 1986), 63ff.

6. Ibid., 59.

7. Simon Maimela, in *EATWOT Africa Conference Report 1991;* cf. M. J. Waliggo, ed., *Inculturation: Its Meaning and Urgency* (Nairobi: St. Paul Publications, 1986), 12.

7

Toward a Post-apartheid
Black Feminist Reading of the Bible:
A Case of Luke 2:36–38

Gloria Kehilwe Plaatjie

The Black Woman Who Carries Us All

In her novel *And They Didn't Die*, a black South African woman writer, Loretta Ngcobo, features Jezile as the main character. Jezile is a young black woman living in the rural and infertile areas, which were assigned to black people during apartheid. When Jezile gets married, her husband, like many black southern African men, is forced by the apartheid economic rules to work in urban areas as a miner. Under this system of migrant labor, he is signed to a long contract, underpaid, and allowed to go home just once a year. Jezile is left with her mother-in-law and other women in this situation, who were struggling for survival. Jezile is portrayed, not as accepting apartheid oppression, but as actively involved in resistance movements against "pass laws." Together with other village churchwomen, Jezile organizes ways of resisting the dehumanizing pass laws, designed by the apartheid government to control black people's movements. The village women have resolved that they are not getting "passes."

Jezile's mother-in-law, however, thinks that Jezile must have a child. Since Jezile's husband is living in the mines and is unlikely to come home, her mother-in-law insists that Jezile follow her husband to get pregnant. Her mother-in-law tells her, in effect, that her worth as a married woman is measured primarily by her capacity to bear children. Jezile, the political activist, surprises the reader, for she compromises her political struggle and bows to the demands of her mother-in-law. She gets a pass in order to follow her husband and to conceive a baby. Indeed, she travels and comes back pregnant. The following year, her husband comes home for a short vacation and leaves her pregnant with another child, but he still does not send money to maintain the children, his wife, and mother. Jezile and her mother-in-law resolve that Jezile must find a job for their own survival.

Like many black women, Jezile goes to work as a housekeeper for a white family. She sends money home for the children and their grandmother. Her white master, however, sexually abuses her. When the white mistress is out of the house, he rapes Jezile, and she becomes pregnant. When the white madam realizes this, she is outraged and throws Jezile out of her house, rendering her jobless. Jezile returns to her mother-in-law. The church learns about her situation and immediately excommunicates her, claiming she has sinned. Her mother-in-law is also enraged. She calls relatives to take Jezile back to her parents, for she has behaved in a way unworthy of a married woman. She is sent home, but her children are left with their grandmother, because in the cultural understanding they do not belong to her, but to her husband. Jezile is thus returned to her family in disgrace. She bears a colored child and struggles to raise her. When this child grows up, she joins the liberation struggle against apartheid and gets military training. One night, while she is visiting her mother, a white soldier who has been keeping Jezile's daughter under surveillance undresses and attempts to rape her. This incident reignites Jezile's memory of her own rape, and she kills the soldier. The book ends with this scene.

This story illustrates the economic, cultural, political, social, and legal position of black women in the apartheid era. A black woman was oppressed by the patriarchal expectations that required her to be married and have children. She was oppressed by white men, who saw her as a sexual object; by white women, who saw her as a servant with no rights; by the church, which was also patriarchal; and, to crown it all, she was oppressed by the apartheid system, which relegated her to the lowest rank. She was among the most economically deprived members of the apartheid South African society, with no economic, cultural, political, legal, or social power. And yet, she had to carry everybody else around, sacrificing her own needs and interests. The black woman of this time internalized her own oppression, as evidenced in Jezile's mother-in-law, who measured her daughter-in-law by patriarchal standards of mothering and blamed her for having been raped. Race, class, gender, and cultural oppression weighed the black South African woman down. Ngcobo shows us that the black woman struggled against race oppression, but not against gender oppression entrenched in the culture, apartheid, and the church. That is, Jezile is an activist against pass laws, and in the process kills a white soldier who is about to rape her daughter. She does not, however, question her mother-in-law's insistence that she must prove her womanhood by bearing children, nor does she challenge the church for holding her responsible for her rape and for excommunicating her, nor does she question the Zulu culture that teaches that she should be divorced for having been raped by her white master.

In the post-apartheid era, it is worth investigating how the black churchwoman of South Africa survives. Has she developed strategies of reading the Bible that empower her to resist the patriarchal and apartheid oppression that victimize her? Has she developed strategies of confronting and challenging Tswana/Zulu/Sepedi cultures, which are patriarchal and oppressive? The Constitution of post-apartheid South Africa is that country's biggest achievement, for it recognizes the racial and gender equality of all South Africans, regardless of color. Indeed, for black South African women who sacrificed all other interests and focused on fighting against apartheid, the Constitution of post-apartheid South Africa is in every way a central and authoritative text. It carries sacred status, for it symbolizes what the black people fought and struggled for: justice and human dignity for all. It symbolizes their hope, their political freedom. It symbolizes their insistence that all human beings are made in the image of God and deserve to be treated with dignity. If we bear in mind how many people died to bring about this dignity, we would agree that the new Constitution is indeed a sacred text, a text that stands next to the Bible for black South African women and other victims of apartheid. Further, if one bears in mind that the Bible is a text that provided the grounds for apartheid ideology, then one realizes that the latter's sacred status remains ambiguous in the social memory of black South Africans.

The question, therefore, is: How does the black woman read the Bible in light of the post-apartheid Constitution that gives her equality? Does she use the Constitution, the product of her struggles, to resist all forms of oppression, be they in South African black cultures or the Bible? Does she use the Constitution to resist economic, political, and cultural oppression in the Bible and in indigenous cultures? If she does not use the Constitution to resist all forms of oppression, how can black women academic readers and black churchwomen cultivate a reading strategy that furthers their liberation? This study investigates and seeks to discover and articulate what constitutes a black post-apartheid feminist strategy of reading the Bible.

"Reading from and with" Black Non-academic Women: Theoretical Pathways

Gerald West's (1996) definition of an ordinary reader of the Bible, that is, a non-academic reader of the Bible, includes people who are illiterate, but who listen to, discuss, and retell the Bible. He explains that these readers have little awareness of historical and no awareness of sociological information related to biblical texts. West explains how most ordinary readers of the Bible read the text. First, they do not read the text as a whole, in its own right. Rather, they read unrelated parts of the Bible together (1995:181); they read the text canonically. What matters to these readers is the central message of the Bible (182). Second, most of the groups West and his colleagues visited read the text existentially. The text is also read contextually: that is, with the South African economic, ecclesiastical, and political situation in mind. Lastly, most groups had not developed thorough analyses of the South African context. He attributes the lack of analysis to the pervasive repression and authoritarianism, and to the need for ordinary readers to have resources and processes for developing analytical tools (183–84). He thus holds that some of these readers may be politicized or conscientized, and that they may have a general critical consciousness toward society and texts, but they do not have the historical and sociological tools to engage critically with the biblical text (199).

It would seem that West's agenda in reading with non-academic readers is best captured by the title of his essay in *Semeia* 73, "Reading the Bible Differently: Giving Shape to the Discourses of the Dominated" (1996). Part of this agenda entails equipping the ordinary readers with academic skills, while West himself is also being reconstituted by their reading methods. West's analytical framework seems to revolve around the interaction of the "trained and non-trained reader." West, who counts himself among "white, middle-class male[s] groomed for greatness" (1996:8), sees himself as empowered, and he seeks to work in solidarity with the less empowered by "reading with" the marginalized ordinary readers, or, as he says, by "giving shape to the discourse of the dominated." West's work tends to focus on reading with black ordinary readers, rather than with white ordinary readers. This approach, while recognized for its empathy and intentions of solidarity, risks being seen as anthropological, or as a white male doing what other white males have always done—namely, writing about and becoming an authority on black people (Segovia 2000:68–72). West's approach has been criticized for a number of reasons. Tinyiko S. Maluleke (2000a:94) holds that West's readings run the danger of becoming academic rhetoric, for they do not connect to grassroots Africans. At the basis of his critique, Maluleke questions West's categories of "trained and untrained reader." First, Maluleke does not see the importance for a hermeneutic of liberation to recognize the existence of these two categories, primarily because these unbalanced relations are not natural in South African society. As Maluleke writes, "The real question is *how, which* and *why* people are trained while others are 'ordinaried'" (2000a:94). He insists on an approach that takes the effects of institutionalized apartheid seriously. Second, Maluleke holds that the adopted categories of analysis are ambiguous, and he is suspicious of West's attempt to supplant the divisions of gender, race, economic locations, and power relations that exist between the trained and untrained readers of the Bible (93). Third, he argues that formulation of the untrained-versus-trained distinction is based on uncritical acceptance of the ideologies, choices, and commitments inherent in the "training" of the so-called trained (94).[1]

I agree with Maluleke that, in a South African context, with its decades of officially orchestrated apartheid institutions and structures, the categories of gender, race, and class need to be explicitly foregrounded in liberation-oriented biblical hermeneutics. The inequalities of South African society were deliberately created and maintained. Although we are in the post-apartheid era, the roots and wounds of apartheid are far from being healed or uprooted. Race remains an issue that must not be underplayed, for it largely determines one's class. How race functions with categories of gender and culture needs to inform all readings that seek to promote human dignity in South Africa. I thus choose to focus on the readings of black South African working-class women in Mankweng, a black community around the University of the North. By virtue of their race and gender, the black women of Mankweng still rank among the lowest in the country's economic hierarchy. In my search for post-apartheid feminist ways of reading, I underline the categories of race, class, gender, and culture in the story of the prophet Anna in Luke 2:36–38.

I do not only seek to "read with," but also to "read from" black, non-academic women readers. This strategy is better articulated by Musa W. Dube in her articles "Readings of *Semoya*: Batswana Women's Interpretations of Matt. 15:21–28" (1996) and "Introduction: How We Come to Be 'Reading With'" (West and Dube 1996). Dube states that she uses the term *ordinary readers* to highlight the grind of global structures of dominance, "which most Africans and Two-thirds World people inhabit and which continue to define reality for them" (Dube 1996:10). *Or-*

dinary readers includes most Two-thirds World readers, who are outside the accepted academic methods of reading the Bible—those on the periphery of global economic structures and who belong to what she terms "suppressed knowledges." Differing from Gerald West's definition, which seems to make a sharp division between trained and untrained readers, Dube counts herself among ordinary readers. She does not consider herself a complete outsider to the political, social, economic, and cultural experiences that have molded the thinking and practice of her non-academic readers (1996:115). Nonetheless, Dube acknowledges her own uniqueness, pointing out that she also belongs to academic interpretative communities that inform her biblical interpretation, which are textual in their focus, Western, and that estrange her from the reading practices of women in African Independent Churches (henceforth AICs).

Dube's position as a black African woman who belongs to those whose knowledges are suppressed and subverted by the global grind of economic structures gives her a different agenda for "reading with" non-academic women of her country. Her aim is to subvert the dominant Western and patriarchal discourses by including different interpretive communities (1996:115). She operates within a framework of women representing a long history of imperial and patriarchal subversion, namely, women in African Independent Churches. From this angle, Dube seeks not just to *read with* non-academic readers, but to *read from* them, for she believes they offer strategies of interpretation born from a struggle with both imperialism and sexism (123). Thus she states that on visiting women in AICs with her research assistants, she often said, "We have come to learn from you"—an assertion which, as Dube says, was "an acknowledgement of my position and their position as belonging to suppressed knowledges and an attempt to subvert the dominant discourses through bringing in different interpretative communities" (115). Dube's strategy of *reading from* black non-academic readers is crucial to my search for post-apartheid black feminist strategies of reading. That is, my approach underlines that, for the most part, black South African women's readings, due to gender, race, culture, and the global oppression that marginalize them, are not found in academic halls. Further, as a black South African academic woman, who is more often than not in academic institutions that are white and male,[2] I have no choice but to count myself with the non-academic black women readers. It is important that I should dedicate myself to making our voices heard by studying these women's methods of reading in order to subvert the alienating structures that continue to marginalize us.

Musimbi Kanyoro's much earlier research on reading with non-academic African women (1995) is also a crucial pathway toward defining post-apartheid black feminist strategies of reading. Kanyoro terms her research "cultural hermeneutics" and maintains that reading with non-academic women readers of the Bible helps us, as black feminist biblical scholars, to critically analyze our own black African cultures, which are subconsciously ingrained in us (18). She emphasizes that black African feminists must have a sincere dialogue with the gospel and with their cultures, without romanticizing either. For Kanyoro, reading with non-academic women creates a forum in which Christian women can speak about their life experiences. Kanyoro also holds that cultural hermeneutics can open our eyes to possibilities that might move us to different commitments (21). These commitments include the recognition that not all women challenge patriarchy in the Bible or in their cultures. Rather, for some women, cultural practices and rituals represent their heritage and affirm their dignity within society. Others see such practices as a path to freedom over their own bodies and their sexuality.[3] These are women who, like Jezile and her mother-in-law, have internalized patriarchal standards as normal. In short, Kanyoro holds that differences between feminist academic and non-academic readers are likely to arise. But, for Kanyoro, the act of reading with non-academic readers becomes a participatory feminist approach, which provides time for the academic and non-academic women to be self-critical and to build feminist consciousness. Kanyoro's research and perspective thus provide a reminder that in seeking to empower post-apartheid black feminist ways of reading that involve non-academic women readers, we must also be self-critical of our African cultures, in order not to embrace their patriarchal perspective uncritically or to endorse cultural indoctrination masquerading as liberation.

Kanyoro's stance is confirmed by Dora Mbuwayesango's recent paper, "Childlessness and Woman-to-Woman Relationships in Genesis and in African Patriarchal Society: Sarah and Hagar from a Zimbabwean Woman's Perspective (Gen. 16:1–16; 21:8–21)" (1997). Focusing on Zimbabwean women from the Ndebele and Shona ethnic groups, Mbuwayesango argues that they have internalized patriarchal culture and read the Bible through patriarchal lenses. She argues that in the story of Hagar and Sarah in Genesis and in the Ndebele and Shona cultures, the role of a woman is closely associated with bearing children, especially male children. In cases of barrenness in the Ndebele and Shona cultures, the women's kin provide another woman to supplement the barren women, and the process is supervised by older kin women. This, for Mbuwayesango, is disturbing because it resonates with Hebrew Bible stories, and hence it endorses the patriarchal role of a woman in Zimbabwean society as child-bearer, which, since it is also biblically attested, is seen as sacred or divine. The importance of Kanyoro's and Mbuwayesango's perspective is that black feminist liberation is not guaranteed in African or biblical cultures. Rather, African feminists in their search for liberation must continue to maintain a critical eye toward these traditions.

My quest for post-apartheid black feminist strategies of reading will draw from strategies highlighted by the above writers. First, I seek to underline non-academic black women as agents of interpretation, as Dube demonstrates, to resist the overly white and male-dominated biblical guild of post-apartheid South Africa. Second, as Maluleke, Kanyoro, and Mbuwayesango argue, I seek to underline race, class, gender, and culture in my analysis. Third, by investigating patriarchy in Sepedi/Setswana and biblical cultures, I also investigate how these women internalize their own oppression. Finally, I recognize that both the Bible and African cultures do not guarantee gender and racial justice. Thus, I argue that the South African post-apartheid Constitution can be instrumental in building a feminist consciousness and a black feminist hermeneutics of liberation against all forms of oppression. Before turning to my reading with and from non-academic women of Mankweng, it is important to highlight the position of black women in black theology, in both the church and the academy. The question is, Has the black theology of liberation integrated gender in its fight against racism?

Black Theology and Black Women: Where We Have Been and Where We Should Go

Undoubtedly, the black biblical hermeneutics of South Africa are vibrant and well-known, as represented by Itumeleng Mosala's *Biblical Hermeneutics and Black Theology in South Africa* (1989). His book has influenced the academy worldwide. Other internationally recognized voices of black theology include Desmond Tutu, Allan Boesak, Takatso Mofokeng, and Manas Buthelezi, among many others. The rise of black theology and biblical hermeneutics was unavoidable, given the international consciousness raised against the apartheid regime. But when it comes to black women theologians of South Africa, hardly anyone from the academy or church comes to the surface nationally or internationally. Roxanne Jordaan (1991: 126–27) and Dorothy Ramodibe (1988:18–20) attribute the lack of a black feminist voice in black theology to the deeply rooted patriarchy in the Bible, church, academy, and South African cultures.

Jordaan's firsthand experience of being undermined by her male counterparts occurred during her ministerial studies at the Federal Theological Seminary. She was pregnant and discovered that her black male colleagues would not receive communion from her (1991:126). In the classroom, she also came to realize that, for most of her male colleagues, feminist concerns were regarded as a subject of laughter. Jordaan thus holds that black women's concerns and issues as well as black feminist theology were not central in the height of the struggle against apartheid and in the rise of black theology, which was predominantly male (125). Jordaan also points out that black feminist theologians at the time were not highly trained and qualified pastors. Most of their black feminist theologies were communicated in grassroots communities through sermons, but they were hardly heard in major national addresses or academic forums. Nonetheless, Jordaan holds that black feminist theology should be valued and respected for its direct and practical engagement in liberatory political tendencies (127). She argues that black feminist theology seeks to instill in black, educated brothers a commitment to view the struggle in a holistic way (127).[4] Jordaan underlines that black South African feminism is concerned with laying the foundations of a theology that makes God relevant to women (128). Jordaan's insistence on the availability and validity of grassroots black feminist readers is central to my quest for post-apartheid black feminist strategies of reading. She underlines Dube's argument that African feminists need to "read from and with" the grassroots or non-academic women readers.

Dorothy Ramodibe complements Jordaan's concerns and takes them a step further. Ramodibe holds that black feminist theologians have brought black theology to a crucial understanding: namely, that black theology cannot be a theology of liberation unless black feminist theology is a fundamental part of it (1988:18–20). Ramodibe holds that the church, which is predominantly male in its leadership, should begin by examining all of its symbols, for they are "polluted by male-dominated culture." She includes the Bible, because it was composed, edited, and compiled in patriarchal cultures and because it uses male symbols. Ramodibe fully acknowledges that black women will not readily accept change, for they have internalized patriarchal values. Like Kanyoro and Mbuwayesango, Ramodibe calls for the deconstruction both of internalized oppression among women and of the patriarchally constructed masculinity. She underlines the need for a new church, one that celebrates the liberation of both genders.

Ramodibe and Jordaan represent the emerging voices of black theology and biblical hermeneutics in a largely white, male academic and church leadership. In the academy, Mmadipoane Masenya's work undoubtedly represents one of the most consistent and growing black feminist voices in South Africa. It is, therefore, crucial to take a closer look at Masenya's work in any quest for a post-apartheid black feminist hermeneutics of the Bible. My question is whether Masenya's feminist hermeneutics has integrated race, class, gender, and cultural analysis. Do Masenya's hermeneutics adequately address the post-apartheid context of black South African women? A closer look at Masenya's work will indicate the strength and weaknesses of her hermeneutics and direct the movement toward post-apartheid feminist ways of reading for liberation.

Since 1996, Mmadipoane Masenya has been working on a *bosadi* (womanhood), feminist hermeneutics. Beginning with her doctoral dissertation, "Proverbs 31:10–31 in a South African Context: A *Bosadi* (Womanhood) Perspective," Masenya has consistently used the book of Proverbs to articulate and illustrate her *bosadi* hermeneutics.[5] Masenya's approach is somewhat akin to African inculturation hermeneutics, which compares biblical and African cultures.[6] A feature that distinguishes Masenya's *bosadi* hermeneutics from inculturation is that she foregrounds gender concerns:

> *Bosadi* comes from the word *Mosadi* (woman) and describes what it means to be a woman in a Northern Sotho culture: what ideal womanhood is; what qualities are expected of a woman in this culture. The *bosadi* approach will focus . . . on the following: Reviving the positive elements (liberatory aspects) of the African culture regarding women as well as criticising the oppressive elements of this culture; . . . Taking note of the interplay of oppressive forces such as racism, sexism, classism and the African culture as factors shaping the way African woman reads. (Masenya 1996:59–60)

Masenya then reads Prov. 31:10–31 from a *bosadi* perspective and concludes that the portrait of the woman as

> manager of household, caring for the needy, and industrious, can partially offer liberating possibilities if the text is read from a *bosadi* perspective. It is liberative for some lost aspects of the African culture, like the significance of industry for people of all races, sexes, and classes in South Africa (including African women who have always worked hard) and the *ubuntu/botho* concept[,] for all can be restored. If Africans can revive and reclaim their culture, they will

125

> hopefully regain their self-worth and self-identity as African Christians without the appendage "Westernised." (1996:66)

On the whole, Masenya's work is a careful attempt to reclaim both a Northern Sotho and biblical culture that affirms women without embracing patriarchal standards. Her categories of analysis also include class, race, gender, and African cultures. Yet this balanced attempt, for a number of reasons, fails to escape a trap. First, reclaiming the concept of *bosadi* itself—what it means to be a woman—is more often than not a patriarchal prescription that tends to uphold the interests of the status quo. One wishes to see Masenya attempt to dissociate *bosadi* from the patriarchal expectations of Northern Sotho culture before advocating its liberational use. Accordingly, the cultural and biblical call that women must be hard workers, as expressed in the Northern Sotho saying that "likens a woman to a baboon" (Masenya 1996:65), is a tricky proverb that often justifies women's multiple roles. Similarly, to claim that women are managers of the household and to cite, as a reason, the migration of labor, which leaves most women alone, is not enough. The crucial question is whether the women were and are managing their own estates for themselves or on behalf of their husbands. Masenya's point could be persuasive if she could argue convincingly that labor migration created matriarchal cultures among Northern Sotho households.[7] But I believe she would agree that if women were household managers and leaders, it was for their absent husbands and sons, who remained known as the heads of the households. In the opening of Ngcobo's novel, both Jezile and her mother-in-law represent such women. On the whole, Masenya's reading walks too close to embracing patriarchal values, such that it becomes difficult to discern what would be liberating without subscribing to the patriarchal values of the Bible and Northern Sotho cultures.

Second, it is not clear how Masenya applies the category of race in her reading. One could hold that her reclamation of African culture is a strategy of resisting racism. But it does not clear the confusion about *bosadi* commitment to race. This confusion is underlined by the fact that Israelites regarded themselves as the chosen nation of God, a claim that could hardly apply to black people in South Africa, and a claim that white people used to formulate and justify the ideology of apartheid. One wishes to see Masenya wrestle with the Israelites' chosenness and its historical impact on South Africa, especially on black people. Third, Prov. 31:10–31, as it relates to class, is particularly problematic for black South African women. Masenya acknowledges that the described woman is an idealized elite. She is described as hardworking, a woman who wakes up early and goes to bed late. Black African women of South Africa could identify with this work ethic without claiming the material benefits. The problem in Masenya's *bosadi* reading is that she fails to question the structural forces at work that allow certain workers to reap the fruits of their labor while others remain poor. Such economic realities are particularly significant in the South African context, in which many black people will never be able to provide sufficiently for their households. Masenya's *bosadi* approach, therefore, does not offer an adequate way to address a crucial issue in the post-apartheid context that has relegated many black people to poverty, especially black women.

Lastly, one major weakness in Masenya's *bosadi* hermeneutics is that it is articulated from above. That is, Masenya neither reads with nor from non-academic Northern Sotho women. She does not let their voices speak for themselves, as Jordaan and Dube advocate. She chooses to speak for them, and places them in the role of subalterns who cannot speak. Rather, she theorizes about the *bosadi* approach and applies it from the comfort of academic halls (an approach that is acceptable in nations in which women and men of different races have been accorded equal access to education and opportunities in the public sector). We thus do not know if the average non-academic or grassroots Northern Sotho woman would interpret Proverbs 31 as Masenya does. On these grounds, it could be rightfully argued that Masenya's *bosadi* hermeneutics offer a gendered black biblical hermeneutics from a middle-class perspective. This statement is further supported by her choice of text, her failure to problematize the ideology of Israelites as a chosen people, and her lack of contact with non-academic or grass-roots readers.

No doubt, Masenya's womanhood or *bosadi* perspective is an important contribution to black theology and biblical hermeneutics, for the field has been and is still largely male. Yet the approach remains inadequate in addressing a number of important factors for a post-apartheid black feminist reader. As both Jordaan and Dube have argued, it is essential to integrate the voices of non-academic readers. At the same time, however, it is important to remain critical of our own culture and of biblical cultures that authorize the oppression of women, as both Kanyoro and Mbuwayesango have underlined.

With this, I turn to read Luke 2:36–38 with Bapedi women of Mankweng, seeking to help define a post-apartheid black feminist hermeneutics of the Bible that is academically and non-academically rooted. My aim is to determine whether the Mankweng women read the text while internalizing their Sepedi and biblical patriarchal cultures. I also seek to document feminist strategies from their interpretations. The Mankweng women are also Northern Sotho (Bapedi women). In fact, they come from the same church and community as Mmadipoane Masenya.

Reading Luke 2:36–38 "from and with" Black South African Women from Mankweng

The following questions and responses will help indicate how black women from Mankweng read the Bible, and how they perceive their Northern Sotho and the biblical cultures.

a. What do you think of Anna the Prophet? The women respondents agree that Anna is an old widow and a prophet who only lived with her husband for seven years. They also hold that Anna lived faithfully in the temple, fasting and praying to God day and night without ceasing. But there are varying and conflicting interpretations on her social status:

1. Some of the women see Anna as an independent woman. Anna is independent because she chooses not to be married again.

2. Some women hold that Anna is a trustworthy woman because of her godly life: she never leaves the temple. Anna is also perceived as an empowering figure in their lives in general because she has great faith in God, and she does everything that is pleasant in the eyes of God and in the eyes of fellow human beings.

3. The prophet Anna is seen as an exemplar for other women. These women maintain that her character and role inspire them to serve God ardently. The prophet Anna is seen as empowering and encouraging other women to live their lives in the community, as God wills.

4. She is also seen as a good exemplar to married women because she is faithful and loyal in her marriage. This group of respondents believes that prophet Anna remains single because she does not want to forget her late husband.

5. These women point out that Anna encourages them to be independent as women, to trust in themselves, and to be trusted by other people in the community.

6. Some respondents specifically read Anna's choice in reference to Sotho-Tswana rituals. They speak of the difficult and degrading widowhood rituals to which women are subjected. They hold that Anna could have married a male relative of her deceased husband, but that she probably did not wish to undergo the rituals of widowhood twice. For these women, not all cultural rituals concerning women are "good" or acceptable. Nonetheless, the married women of this group consent that they will undergo the ritual of widowhood when their time comes, for they feel forced by circumstances beyond their control to submit. One of the prime rea-

sons given is that if a woman does not undergo the rituals of widowhood, she will be accused of witchcraft
and be held responsible for her husband's death.

7. Some women interpret Anna's choice to remain single
    in relationship to her children, believing that she may
    have wanted to protect her children from abuse in a
    second marriage. These women hold that if they were
    in Anna's position they would not marry again in order
    to protect their children from the possibility of an abu-
    sive stepfather.

b. What do you understand by the role of a prophet? The
women believe that a prophet is a woman or man consulted
during times of illness, emotional problems, or when there is
suspicion of witchcraft. According to these women, the role of
prophets is:

1. to restore health and instill hope;

2. to be used by God spiritually to spread the Word of God;

3. to be used by God to speak to God's people;

4. to instill fear in one's life, especially when they proph-
    esy about future misfortune and dangers;

5. to restore health, not only through prayer, but also by
    administering and prescribing healing substances like
    Joko tea, blessed water, and stones to prevent possible
    future dangers and misfortunes that might come their
    way.

c. Do you want to be a prophet in the church and general society?
The women agreed that being a prophet is a call by God, but as
to whether they would wish to occupy such a role, there were
conflicting positions:

1. Some women maintain that it is a difficult task, but if
    they are called to become prophets, they would take up
    the position.

2. Others hold that they would have to abstain from a lot
    of worldly things like having fun with friends.

3. Others maintain that they would not readily give in to such a position because, according to these women, many "prophets" in their communities can easily be accused of witchcraft.

4. Further, a prophet has to be exemplary to the young and counsel them in the church. The women thus agree that if they had a choice, they would be unwilling to take up this heavy responsibility. This was a perspective of younger women, who are unwilling to abstain from the worldly pleasures. Consequently, they may not be the best exemplars for their peers and youth in the church.

In summary, the text on the prophet Anna is particularly interesting. It involves a woman of low class—a widow—who does not seem to have male or female children. She is not necessarily attached to a man or family. Further, she is in a position of public leadership. Most women recognized her independent position, but still others interpreted her within patriarchal expectations.

Women Readers in a Patriarchal Framework

Those who choose to read the prophet Anna within patriarchal expectations believe that her choice to remain single is in fact not a denunciation of marriage nor her wish to be independent as such, but rather her full commitment to her deceased husband. Judging the prophet Anna within patriarchal values is also evident among those who applaud her rejection of marriage but who are hesitant to call her an assertive woman who insists on her independence. They attribute her choice to motherhood: she desired to protect her children from possible abuse in a new family.

The women who read within patriarchal confines also display ambivalence in embracing her as a role model in public leadership. In general they expressed great hesitancy about assuming her public leadership role. These women readers gave a number of excuses for their unwillingness to assume the role of public prophecy, such as that it entailed too much responsibility, or that they would be unwilling to give up worldly desires. One particularly striking excuse is the fear of being accused of witchcraft, an accusation used in many Sotho-Tswana communities to discourage and distance women from the public positions of healers, *dingaka,* and property ownership. Women tend to be labeled witches, thereby preserving the public professions of healing, public leadership, and property ownership for men. Further, those who use age to shy away from public leadership also read within southern African (and biblical) cultures, which are more apt to open leadership in spiritual matters only to women who have reached menopause.[8] This practice points to the association of menstruation with uncleanness, but also ensures that every woman marries and raises a family before she can assume a position of spiritual leadership (see 1 Tim. 5:1–15).

The entrenchment of patriarchy in women readers was also evident in those who named gender oppression but who were unwilling to revolt against it. These were the women who said that widowhood rituals were difficult and degrading, but who said they would not revolt, for they would be accused of killing their own husbands. One notes that accusations of witchcraft are used to enforce patriarchal standards on women. This group of respondents is critical but feels helpless when it comes to asserting its own rights. The readings of these women, however, indicate that their submission to patriarchal cultural practices does not necessarily imply agreement. Rather, as some said, they are not willing or strong enough to deal with the consequences of defying patriarchal cultural expectations. Their stance indicates that they lack another authoritative, social frame of reference outside their own culture. The introduction of the post-apartheid Constitution as an authoritative and sacred document, and the use of reading with and from, would conscientize and empower these women to assert themselves.

Black Women Readers Empowering Themselves

Yet, as some academic women like Jordaan and Dube have asserted, non-academic women do offer feminist readings that empower women against patriarchy and other forms of oppression. Their self-empowering interpretive practices were evident on two fronts: in how they perceived the prophet Anna and in what Anna implies for them as black women of Mankweng.

This group read Anna as an independent woman who chooses not to marry again. This choice is seen as a positive attribute, for women readers hold that "she encourages women to trust in themselves and to be trusted by other people in the community." These women readers essentially say women need not be married or to trust solely in male leadership. Women have not easily embraced other women leaders, given that, in family, school, church, and government, women grow up in societies in which public leadership is rare or unknown. If the women of Mankweng assert that a woman can trust herself and be trusted by others, they are reading against patriarchal values that have taught many women not to trust in themselves and other public figures who are women. They are offering a strategy of resistance.

In regard to Anna's position, these women of Mankweng unhesitantly regard her as a prophet and make no attempts to distinguish her role from that of a male prophet. Rather, they say that this position is held by both women and men, and that a prophet is someone called by God. Their answers indicate that they hold that God calls both women and men to public leadership, regardless of gender. Further, they do not see Prophet Anna as an ancient woman far removed from their lives, but rather as an excellent role model who inspires them to serve God ardently. They see the prophet Anna "empowering and encouraging other women to live their lives in the community as God wills." Given that they are lower-class black women, it is clear that they do not regard their class, gender, or race as a deficiency. For the women of Mankweng, God does not discriminate on the basis of class, race, or gender (Gal. 3:28). Their values of reading are essential to the young post-apartheid society, which is beginning to learn how to live with its racial diversity.

In the women's description of the prophet's role, it is clear

133

that a prophet is someone used by God to serve the community, and s/he is looked upon as having a public voice and role. A prophet is a healer, bringer of hope, preacher, and sometimes a person sent by God to speak urgent messages to the public. These readers point out that it is a demanding responsibility. They nonetheless assert that they would take up this position if God called them to become prophets. What remains unclear is whether the Mankweng women see the church and general society embracing the values of equality espoused in the post-apartheid Constitution. If the church and society are not creating the enabling environment that embraces racial, class, and gender justice, how can these women ensure that justice is realized? This is where I believe that reading the Bible with and through the new South African Constitution is imperative.

Conclusion: Toward a Black Post-apartheid Feminist Reading of the Bible

The starting point for a black post-apartheid feminist reading of the Bible should be the disadvantages that black South African women have suffered in all spheres. Black women and others—for decades, if not centuries—have been economically, legally, politically, and socially disadvantaged by a constitutionally orchestrated program of apartheid; their oppression remains largely in place in the new South Africa.[9] The agenda of a post-apartheid feminist should be to seek ways for black women to empower themselves, and to work for the creation of enabling environments. Given that black women were lawfully and wilfully disadvantaged under the apartheid regime, it is imperative that a post-feminist strategy should involve and embrace the use of a post-apartheid Constitution that recognizes their rights. Black South African women, of course, do not constitute a homogenous group. They are rural, suburban, and city dwellers; schooled, semi-illiterate, and unschooled; married, cohabiting, and unmarried; Christian, African traditional religious adherents, and Muslims; young, middle-aged, and old; professional and nonprofessional. Black South African women also come from different ethnic groups. These categories shape their lives and experiences, yet it is no exaggeration that the race and gender identity of being black women relegated them to the lowest rung in apartheid and post-apartheid South Africa. Black South African women like Jezile still face problems of poverty, violence, marginalization, and unfair and unequal gender relations. They are still confronted with lack of access and control over means of production and reproduction. Jezile's story accentuates that class, custom, patriarchy, race, gender, religion, and the law must become critical analytical categories in understanding black women's past and present experiences, as well as in charting black women's empowerment in post-apartheid South Africa. We cannot expect that which was lawfully orchestrated to be corrected outside the law. Our post-apartheid Constitution must be a central part of our liberation. It must become the instrument by which we scrutinize our current institutions, structures, and ideology for the effects of decades of deeply entrenched apartheid, and the instrument that helps create equal opportunities and enabling environments for all people in South Africa, especially black women.

In this background of entrenched apartheid and patriarchal oppression against and marginalization of black women, it is clear that the Bible as a sacred, authoritative, and analytical text for social consciousness and change is not enough. The Bible itself indulges in both patriarchal and apartheid oppression. Black women ought to know that the country's post-apartheid Constitution is another authoritative and sacred text. It contains and recognizes their human rights. Many women fought for the post-apartheid Constitution, as illustrated by Jezile and her rural women, and they should enjoy the benefits of their struggle. How can non-academic and academic black women use the Constitution to empower themselves and to claim their rights in the church and society? How can we integrate the post-apartheid Constitution into our biblical reading practices to empower black women? I suggest that certain challenges, conditions, and strategies must be recognized and followed.

Challenges and Conditions in Reading the Bible through the Post-apartheid Constitution

There are a number of hindrances in using the post-apartheid Constitution with non-academic women. First, legal language can be a barrier to outsiders, although this should not deter non-academic women and black feminist scholars from getting access to the Constitution, and from understanding and using it as an analytical tool. The problem of legal language can be overcome by organizing courses given by persons trained in the law. These courses can be arranged by churchwomen with legal backgrounds as well as by women in larger society. Second, due to decades of apartheid, most South African black women are not literate. This can be overcome by participatory and interactive methods of communication such as radio, television, graphics, and community education programs on the law, or through mass media or theater (or, alternatively, through Sunday school plays in the church or community halls).[10] Using this approach, the law, especially the Constitution, can be understood and used as a strategy to attain black women's full human dignity.

Prior to applying the Constitution, however, the reader must understand it as well as a number of related assumptions or conditions.

1. The legal status of women has improved, but the social effects of gender discrimination have remained.

2. The legal framework for gender equality merely provides a framework from which to promote women's legal human rights.

3. Patriarchal forms of authority are still deeply embedded in social and cultural life, and, consequently, upholding human rights in practice is a major challenge.

4. Black feminist readers of the Bible should also seek a good understanding of the political, economic, social, and ideological reality in which women live.

5. Women's legal rights in practice depend on their socioeconomic situations, rate of literacy, ideological con-

sciousness, and their strength as a group (Maboreke 1990:5).

Strategies of Reading the Bible through and with the Post-apartheid Constitution

Once one knows and understands the post-apartheid Constitution and the accompanying challenges and conditions, one can use it as a lens through which to read the Bible with and from non-academic women. An essential part of a post-apartheid agenda in reading the Bible with and through the Constitution is to empower black women in practical ways against entrenched patriarchy and apartheid. This effort seeks ways of empowering black women against decades of institutionalized poverty and illiteracy, which has relegated them to the lowest class in South Africa. The following strategies can be applied as part of a post-apartheid black feminist way of reading the Bible:

1. Reading the post-apartheid Constitution as an alternative to the Bible, or even in relation to the Bible as a holy text, can become a strategic tool to attain the black woman's rightful position in society.

2. Utilizing the post-apartheid Constitution in country-wide work of reading with and from non-academic women can be part of a program to help these women develop literacy skills. Imparting basic literacy skills to black women, denied education under the apartheid regime, can serve as an incentive for bridging the gap between academic and non-academic women, thus creating a forum for consciousness raising. The approach also challenges the few educated academic black women to give back to their communities.

3. The post-apartheid Constitution and the Bible can be discussed as part of a program of HIV/AIDS prevention and care. This approach will underline the gendered and class-based pathways of the HIV/AIDS infection, thus highlighting that the black woman is the hardest-

hit by the epidemic. It is imperative to adopt ways of reading that empower black women against this form of patriarchal, racial, and class oppression.

4. Specific themes can become the focus of reading the Bible with the post-apartheid Constitution. In this way, the limitations of the Bible and of our black African cultures will hopefully be surfaced and deconstructed. Developing workshops on these themes can be a step toward formulating a post-apartheid black feminist hermeneutics of liberation. Some of the most crucial tasks are:

   a. Comparing biblical and South African post-apartheid constitutional law on women. Such a study can advance the conscientization and empowerment of black women in the public sphere.

   b. Studying African customary law, post-apartheid constitutional law, and biblical law.

   c. Analyzing institutions to find underlying gender and race discrimination and what the Bible, the post-apartheid Constitution, and South African black cultures would say to these structurally entrenched oppressions.

   d. Studying the available institutions that serve the current Constitution—the Bill of Rights, the Gender Commission, the Human Rights Commission, the Truth and Reconciliation Commission, and the Land Commission.[11] The aim is to see how these instruments can help empower black women in the church, academy, and society in general.

   e. Searching and documenting ways in which the Bible can be read in agreement with the post-apartheid Constitution.

To conclude, South African black feminist scholars cannot

separate themselves from non-academic women, given the apartheid history and patriarchal cultures that have made the academy largely white, male, and middle class, and a place that for the most part excludes black women. Black academic women can and must read "from and with" non-academic readers of the Bible in order to subvert institutionally entrenched apartheid and patriarchy as well as to get in touch with their own communities (Jordaan 1991; Dube 1996). Further, black women cannot and should not uncritically romanticize their African cultures (Kanyoro 1995; Mbuwayesango 1997), although they should rightfully preserve their positive parts (Masenya 1996). They must problematize the oppressive parts of the Bible and their cultures (Ramodibe 1988). It is also imperative for post-apartheid black feminist ways of reading to foreground the categories of race, gender, and class (Maluleke 2000a). In addition to and in the light of all these suggestions, I strongly propose that black South African women read the Bible together with and through the South African post-apartheid Constitution. Their reading practices must seek practical ways of empowering black women after decades of systematically orchestrated gender and racial oppression. This proposal is *not* a final answer in our journey to claim and realize our human rights as black women in South Africa, but it is central, since neither biblical nor African cultures guarantee our rights. My proposal should be seen and heard, therefore, as a journey toward articulating liberative black feminist hermeneutics in the post-apartheid era. Such hermeneutics demand that we continue to fine-tune the post-apartheid Constitution, the church, the academy, and African and biblical cultures. Such practices also demand that we continue to recognize the excluded voices of black, non-academic, grassroots women by reading with and from their communities. This approach will deconstruct the overly white and male academic halls of religion, assert the positive aspects of our black African culture, and open a space for the self-empowerment of black women in post-apartheid South Africa.

Notes

1. See also Maluleke 2000b, in which he continues to problematize Gerald West's framework.

2. See Maluleke 1996 for a more detailed discussion of this subject.

3. Kanyoro refers to rituals of female circumcision. In her article, she uses the interviews by Awa Thiam with two university-educated women in Mali who perceive their circumcision differently. The first thirty-five-year-old women sees her circumcision—performed on her, by an elderly woman, after she had turned twelve—as a mutilation of her body. The second woman, twenty-six years old, divorced with one child, understands this ritual not as a mutilation, but as a means to control a woman's desire for a sexual relationship in the absence of a husband. For this second woman, the ritual achieved its goal as far as she is concerned, for she has never desired to be intimate with a man after having been divorced for four years (Kanyoro 1995:24–25).

4. Perhaps one could say some progress has been made in this direction. For example, in "Half a Century of African Theologies," Tinyiko S. Maluleke, one of the leading academic South African black theologians, speaks highly of the impact of African feminist/womanist approaches. He holds that "African Feminist/Womanist theology is charting a new way. This theology is mounting a critique of both African culture and African Christianity in ways that previous African theologies have not been able to do. From these theologies we may learn how to be truly African and yet critical of aspects of African culture" (*Journal of Theology for Southern Africa* 99 [1997]: 22).

5. For an exhaustive listing of Masenya's works, see West and Dube 2000:785–86.

6. See Martey 1993 for a more detailed analysis of inculturation.

7. See Kuzwayo 1985:19, who holds that black women in fact became overloaded with multiple roles: "She became overnight a mother, a father, family administrator, counselor, child minder, old-age caretaker and overseer of both family and neighborhood affairs in a community which had been totally deprived of its male population."

8. Brigalia Bam (1986) holds that, in her Xhosa culture, women need to reach menopause before being allowed to participate in ceremonies that bring ancestors back to earth.

9. See Maluleke 1997, who argues that we should not confuse cosmetic changes with the uprooting of the entrenched marginalization of black people.

10. Given the legacy of apartheid, most black communities do not have the luxury of a theater in their vicinities. Hence I have suggested an alternative to a theater—namely, Sunday school plays—to achieve this end. Community halls are few, and most often they are used for com-

munal activities, such as the distribution of grants to pensioners. See Schuler 1985:30–31.

11. These commissions were implemented by the post-apartheid government in order to ensure a fair distribution of services and resources to those who had been disadvantaged in the past. The disadvantaged groups include women of all races and black people.

References

Bam, Brigalia. 1986. "Priorities for Women in South Africa." Pp. 363–68 in *Speaking of Faith: Cross-Cultural Perspectives on Women*, edited by D. L. Eck and D. Jain. London: Women's Press.

Currie, Iain. 1994. "The Future of Customary Law: Lessons from the Lobola Debate." Pp. 146–68 in *Gender and the New South African Legal Order*, edited by Christina Murray. Cape Town: Juta.

Devenish, Ge. 1998. *A Commentary on the South African Constitution*. Durban, South Africa: Butterworths.

Dube, Musa. 1996. "Readings of *Semoya:* Batswana Women Interpretations of Matt. 15:21–28." *Semeia* 73:111–29.

———. 2000. *Postcolonial Feminist Interpretation of the Bible*. St Louis: Chalice Press.

Jordaan, Roxanne. 1991. "The Emergence of Black Feminist Theology in South Africa." Pp. 122–28 in *Women Hold Up Half the Sky*, edited by Denise Ackermann et al. Natal, South Africa: Cluster.

Kanyoro, Musimbi. 1995. "Cultural Hermeneutics: An African Contribution." Pp. 18–28 in *Women's Visions: Theological Reflections, Celebration, Action*, edited by Ofelia Ortega. Geneva: WCC.

Kuzwayo, Ellen. 1985. *Call Me Woman*. San Francisco: Aunt Lute.

Maboreke, M. 1990. "Introducing Women's Law." Pp. 1–6 in *The Legal Situation of Women in Southern Africa*, edited by Julie Stewart et al. Harare: University of Zimbabwe.

Maluleke, T. S. 1996. "African Intellectuals, African Culture, and the White Academy in South Africa: Some Implications for Christian Theology in Africa." *Journal of Constructive Theology* 2, no. 1: 3–30.

———. 1997. " 'Dealing Lightly with the Wound of My People': The TRC Process in Theological Perspective." *Missionalia* 25, no. 3: 324–43.

———. 2000a. "The Bible among African Christians: A Missiological Perspective." Pp. 87–112 in *To Cast Fire upon the Earth: Bible and Mission Collaborating in Today's Multicultural Global Context*, edited by Teresa Okure. Natal, South Africa: Cluster.

———. 2000b. "Black and African Theology after Apartheid and after the Cold War: An Emerging Paradigm." *Exchange* 29, no. 3: 193–212..

Martey, Emmanuel. 1993. *African Theology: Inculturation and Liberation*. Maryknoll, N.Y.: Orbis Books.

Masenya, Mmadipoane. 1996. "Proverbs 31:10–31 in a South African Context: A Reading for the Liberation of African (Northern Sotho) Women." *Semeia* 78:55–68.

Mbuwayesango, Dora R. 1997. "Childlessness and Woman-to-Woman Relationships in Genesis and in African Patriarchal Society: Sarah and Hagar from a Zimbabwean Woman's Perspective." *Semeia* 78:27–36.

Mosala, Itumeleng J. 1989. *Biblical Hermeneutics and Black Theology in South Africa*. Grand Rapids: Eerdmans.

Ngcobo, Loreta. 1990. *And They Didn't Die: A Novel*. London: Virago.

Ramodibe, Dorothy. 1988. "Women and Men Building the Church Together in Africa." Pp. 14–21 in *With Passion and Compassion: Third World Women Doing Theology*, edited by Virginia Fabella and Mercy Amba Odoyuye. Maryknoll, N.Y.: Orbis Books.

Schuler, Margaret. 1985. *Empowerment and the Law: Strategies of Third World Women*. Grand Rapids: Eerdmans.

Segovia, Fernando, ed. 2000. *Interpreting across the Borders*. Sheffield: Sheffield Academic Press.

West, Gerald. 1995. *Biblical Hermeneutics of Liberation: Modes of Reading the Bible in South African Context*. 2d ed. Pietermaritzburg, South Africa: Cluster.

———. 1996. "Reading the Bible Differently: Giving Shape to the Discourse of the Dominated." *Semeia* 73:21–41.

West, Gerald, and Musa W. Dube. 1996. "An Introduction: How We Come to 'Read With.'" *Semeia* 73:7–17.

———, eds. 2000. *The Bible in Africa*. Leiden: E. J. Brill.

Womanhood and Womanist Methods

8

A *Bosadi* (Womanhood) Reading of Proverbs 31:10–31

Mmadipoane (Ngwana 'Mphahlele) Masenya

Citing proverbs in my everyday speech as an African is exciting and quite easy. It is easier because one does not have to account for such things as why one prefers to cite certain proverbs to others, why certain words have been used in the coinage of certain proverbs, or when such proverbs originated. Such questions are the territory of scientific approaches. Those approaches complicate what may appear, from a layperson's perspective, to be a simple poem giving praise to a good woman in Prov. 31:10–31.

Several factors seem, in my view, to complicate the poem in praise of a good woman. First, it is a poem, and an acrostic at that. Second, it forms part of the book of Proverbs, which contains many proverbs that are not easy to date. Although there is general consensus that the setting of the book as a whole is postexilic (Camp 1985:233–54; Scott 1965:15), we are not compelled to date the poems of chapters 1–9 and 31 in the era after the exile. It is possible that older works were used anew in the book (Camp 1985:187). Lyons (1987:237) concludes that the image of the ʾ*ešet hayil* appears to presuppose a pre-monarchic ideal of wife and family. Third, the poem we are examining closes the book of Proverbs and apparently resembles some material in both the opening poems of chapters 1–9 and in the intervening material (Camp 1985:208; McCreesh 1985; Brenner 1993:128–29). Commenting on the position of this paean at the end of the book of Proverbs, McCreesh (1985:25–26) contends:

> Prov 31:10–31 draws together the major themes, motifs, and ideas of the book in a final, summarizing statement about wisdom under the

image of an industrious, resourceful and selfless wife. It is the final piece in a symbolic framework that unifies the whole book, including the individual sayings. In turn, the symbolic framework presents a coherent statement about the nature of wisdom.

That this paean has been interpreted differently in the past and today is another proof of its complex nature.[1]

Complexities and Readers' Responses

The poetic nature of Prov. 31:10–31 opens possibilities for interpretations that may not necessarily have been intended by the original writers. Unfortunately, in a book such as Proverbs, with various subsections, it becomes difficult to date individual proverbs and to trace the original authors. According to McCreesh (1985:26), the traditional interpretation of the paean under discussion has been that it portrays the model Israelite wife and mother. Such an interpretation assumes that the poem refers literally to the qualities of a human woman, although the latter is idealized. Aitken (1986:158) concludes that "while there are 'ordinary points' in the portrait which should commend themselves to any housewife—above all that she fears the Lord—as a whole it cannot be read as a kind of blueprint of the ideal Israelite housewife—either for men to measure their wives against or for their wives to try to live up to." In a similar vein, Crook (1954:139) concludes, "The Woman of Worth is an ideal; there never was such a person."[2]

Writers like McCreesh (1985) and Camp (1985) conclude that the poem should be understood as a metaphor that uses a woman as a vehicle for wisdom. According to this view, Prov. 31:10–31 portrays wisdom as a woman.[3] Most such authors see the connections between wisdom personified as a woman ("Woman Wisdom") in chapters 1–9 and the Woman of Worth (*ʾešet hayil*) of 31:10–31. If their view holds, it might be interesting to ask why the authors decided to portray wisdom using female imagery.[4] It is not, however, my intention in the present essay to pursue such a line of thought. Rather, the poetic nature of our paean lends itself to a variety of interpretations. Thus, although Prov. 31:10–31 presents a picture of an ideal Israelite woman, this picture was probably drawn from the everyday lives of the people. Otherwise, the picture might not have made sense to hearers or readers. We can therefore assume that, in ancient Israelite society, an average woman was expected to meet certain expectations. These qualities come to light in this passage when it is read from an African woman's liberation perspective.

An African Woman's Liberation Perspective

It is important to begin by describing what I mean by an African woman's liberation perspective in the South African context. I prefer to call the approach an African woman's liberation perspective on the Bible rather than using the well-known terms *feminist* or *womanist. Feminism,* although used in Euro-American, Latin American, and Asian feminist frameworks, may not be a sufficiently explicit term. Originally and basically a Western concept, the term fails to take into consideration the situation of non-Western (including African) women. Feminism focuses on sexism as the principal enemy of women in society.[5] As a result of feminists' emphasis on gender issues, African American women liberation scholars (particularly those who deal with biblical or theological issues) prefer to call their approach "womanism," rather than feminism.[6] What makes womanism appealing to me as an African woman in South Africa is its concern for the multiple forms of oppression experienced by African American women: racism, classism, and sexism. Womanism is also concerned with reviving lost aspects of the African culture, such as the family and the corporeal mentality of Africans. Toinette Eugene (1992:510) argues that "womanist theology is a signification for a theology that permits African American women to define themselves, to embrace and consciously affirm their cultural and religious traditions, and their own embodiment."

Although the perspective I wish to develop for an African woman's liberation reading of the Bible in the South African context has much in common with the womanist framework in the United States, I do not wish to use the term *womanism* to speak of my unique context. A few examples of our differences are worth noting. African Americans experienced slavery, while Africans in South Africa experienced colonialism and apartheid. African Americans were moved out of their mother country and thus lost touch with the rich cultural heritage of Africa, while we are still in Africa, although we were socialized to look down on almost all aspects of our African heritage. Fortunately, however, we still have or can revive the beautiful elements of our culture—one of my intentions in developing this perspective. African Americans are a minority in the midst of the Whites and thus are highly Westernized, while we are in the majority with a few Whites who, due to the apartheid policy, managed to control us in almost all spheres of our lives. Due to these differences, I feel it is necessary to propose an approach that might be more appropriate for African women's liberation Bible interpreters in South Africa. I prefer to call it a *bosadi* (womanhood) perspective. The word *bosadi* comes from the Northern Sotho word *mosadi,* which means "woman." A *bosadi* perspective investigates what ideal womanhood should be for an African–South African woman Bible reader. This approach includes the following elements:

1. A critique of the oppressive elements of African culture manifested in women's lives, while reviving aspects that uplift the status of women.

2. A critique of the oppressive elements of the Bible, while highlighting the liberative elements. I contend that, although the Bible is a product of patriarchal cultures, it does contain liberative elements, if read from a woman's liberation perspective.

3. The interplay of post-apartheid racism, sexism, classism, and the African culture as significant factors in the context of an African–South African woman, factors that in one way or other shape her reading of the Bible.

4. The concept of *botho/ubuntu,* which, according to Goduka (1995:2), rests on the African proverb and is an integral part of all African cultures and languages spoken

in our country. The Northern Sotho version is *Motho ke motho ka batho*, which means "I am because we are," or "we are because I am." Goduka continues:

> The communality, collectivity and the human unity implicit in the proverb operates in the philosophical thought of Africans, and is the guiding principle for relating with other human beings, and forms a basis for thinking, behaving, speaking, teaching and learning, and is devoted to the advancement of human dignity and respect for all.

Taking the *botho/ubuntu* concept seriously implies that the liberation of all African women in our country calls for the involvement of all Africans (both men and women) and the involvement of all South Africans.

5. The significance of the family for Africans, which is also highlighted by the *bosadi* concept, is of such sociological importance that it cannot be overemphasized. Sick families give birth to sick societies, and the latter breeds a sick world. In my view, a woman's liberation perspective that undermines the family and family-oriented matters is not balanced. I should, however, not be misunderstood as advocating that either of the sexes is supposed to be bound to the family. If, for example, an African man or woman opts for domesticity, he/she should not be frowned upon. In this so-called private sphere, he or she is making a valuable contribution to the family. I should also not be misunderstood as saying that a woman should always lose herself for the sake of the African corporeal mentality. It should be the responsibility of all South Africans—both Africans and non-Africans, men and women—to promote the spirit of communality.

Questions to the Author and His Community

If it were possible to trace the author of this paean, I would ask him[7] a number of questions. For example, why did he choose to present the poem about a Woman of Worth and not include a poem in praise of a Man of Worth? This would seem to have been in line with the apparently equal status enjoyed by both parents in the teaching of their children (except that men only teach sons, according to Prov. 1:8; 10:1; 6:20). Whose standards are used to qualify this woman as worthy or good? Are they YHWH's? Are they standards of a patriarchal society? Why does the author use the problematic title *ba'lh* (Prov. 31:11, 23) for the husband of a woman whose capabilities so conspicuously overshadow him? As McCreesh observes (1985:27), "The husband's 'weighty and honorable' profession among the elders at the city gates (v. 23) pales in significance when contrasted with the whirlwind of activity and achievement that is his wife's." Finally, I would ask which class of males produced this text, and for which class was it intended?

If it were possible to speak to the women of the time, I would ask them questions, too. Do they find the picture of the *'ešet hayil* as presented in this paean liberating? Does it make them feel as if they can hold their own in the world of men? Would they agree with Phyllis Bird that "women are not chattel in Proverbs, nor are they simply sexual objects; they are persons of intelligence and will, who, from the male point of view expressed here, either make or break a man" (1974:60)?

Perhaps these are problematic questions for ancient texts, questions which the ancients might never have bothered to ask. This reminds me of Meyers's warning (1991a:26) about what she calls the misuse of the term *patriarchy* by contemporary feminists:

> Worst of all, their judgmental response to biblical patriarchy unfairly uses contemporary feminist standards (which hope for an elimination of sexist tradition by seeking to promulgate equality between sexes) to measure the cultural patterns of an ancient society struggling to establish its viability under circumstances radically different from contemporary Western conditions.

The preceding questions are, however, part of an attempt by modern readers to appropriate the message of the Bible in their lives. Such questions are necessary, particularly in a context in which the Bible is used to subordinate women. Indeed, in some African church circles, Prov. 31:10–31 is cited as containing the qualities that a "good" Christian wife is expected to have. Questions such as these explore whether the Old Testament, from a patriarchal Hebraic culture, can still be relevant if approached from a *bosadi* perspective.

The Household Manager and the Industrious Woman

The Household Manager

A reading of Prov. 31:10–31 discloses some of the key aspects of women's life in postexilic Jewish society. I focus on two aspects, a woman as manager of the household, and an "industrious woman." As a wife, a Jewish woman was expected to manage the household in which she lived (Camp 1985:85). Meyers (1991b:48–49) notes that "the prominence of the interwoven motifs of woman, household, and instruction for both the personified wisdom of chapters 1–9 and the human woman of chapter 31 is noteworthy." Commenting on the domestic setting as one of the characteristics shared by biblical texts in which the term "mother's house" is found, Meyers observes further that "no matter how broad the ramifications of the women's deeds, the women are related to the household activities. Even Woman Wisdom's cosmic role is couched in the metaphor of the house she builds and the table over which she presides."

Likewise, the *ʾešet hayil* of Prov. 31:10–31 is the controller of household affairs. The Hebrew word *bêth,* "her household," appears frequently in this text (vv. 15, 21, 27). The common *bêt ʾb,* "father's house," is here replaced by *bêth,* "her house," and, interestingly, not by *bêt ʾimmh,* "mother's house." This may be evidence of the fact that, in the book of Proverbs, a woman is not viewed primarily as a bearer of children. According to Phyllis Bird, the term "mother" in Proverbs does not refer primarily to her reproductive function, but to the role she plays in the nurture and education of the child. A mother, Bird says, "is not merely the womb that bears a man but a source of wisdom essential to life" (1974:54; see also Camp 1985:83).

It is no wonder that the paean speaks of *bêth,* for so occupied is the woman with the activities of the household that it

151

makes sense to call the house "hers." She skillfully and righteously manages all aspects of a complex household. She makes an important contribution to the household's subsistence. She directs the servants, and, through her industry and foresight, she sees that her family is well cared for with food and clothing (Meyers 1991b:48; Lyons 1987:238; Bird 1974:58). She also controls the household economy. She does not exist only in the private sphere of the home, for she also goes into the public sphere for her business transactions and other obligations.

The situation portrayed is that of a pre-industrial era in which the household economy was controlled in the home, the domestic sphere. As controller of the domestic sphere, a woman had power over the economy of the household. This is the case with the *'ešet hayil* of our text. The Woman of Worth of Prov. 31:10–31 is a family woman who has the concerns of her household at heart.

Parallels from Northern Sotho Settings

This quality of woman as the controller of the household (family) fits well with the notion of *bosadi* (womanhood) in a Northern Sotho context. A Northern Sotho proverb, *Mmago ngwana o swara thipa ka bogaleng* (literally, "the mother of a child holds the sharp part of the knife"), almost summarizes what has been said about the Woman of Worth above. The tenor of this proverb is that, in trouble in the family, especially trouble pertaining to children, society expects a mother to save the situation. Likewise, the family of the *'ešet hayil* is not scared by adverse weather conditions, for she already would have prepared warm clothes; neither is the family worried about how to cope with subsistence needs, for she is there to take care that such needs are met.

The pre-industrial setting in which the *'ešet hayil* operates reminds one of a pre-colonial African (Northern Sotho) South African context in which the economy of the family formed part of the domestic sphere. Commenting on an African pre-colonial setting, Steady (1981:11) states: "Traditionally, in Africa,

both male and female labour was necessary in food production. Communal ownership of the means of production assures
the woman a certain degree of control over her labour and
some decision-making power relative to her labour input."
Both men and women, but women in particular, played a significant role in the production of crops for the family. Women
were thus valued as significant contributors to the family economy. The situation, however, changed with the capitalistic system of colonialism. With this mode of economy, intensive crop
farming fell into the hands of the powerful, while small-scale
subsistence farming was left to African women. As we know,
most of these women remained and remain both fathers and
mothers, due to harsh migratory-labor policies. Such a system
brought with it a new element in African life, namely, the division between the public (most respected, "manly") sphere and
the private (least respected, "womanly") sphere. What was
done in the public sphere tended to be viewed as more valuable than work performed by women in the private sphere,
probably because "men's work" brought capital (Western
money) to the family. This arrangement disrupted the har-
mony between males and females that had existed in the pre-
colonial African economy.

An African woman, like the Woman of Worth of our text, is
a family woman. The needs of her family, be it nuclear or extended, are at the heart of her existence. It is unfortunate if her
concern for her family is viewed as a weakness—as a position
of powerlessness—as some Western feminists have argued.
The position of an African (Northern Sotho) woman as a controller of the household is, in my view, a position of power, particularly in a situation in which, due to migratory-labor policies, she becomes the sole parent. With domestic work
seemingly one of the few options for African women as they
leave their homes to search for jobs, a woman's position as a
domestic worker becomes one of power. It may therefore be argued that anyone who prefers to make their contribution in the
home should not be despised. Their contribution is as valuable
as contributions in the public sphere. I would argue that the
image of the 'ešet hayil as manager of household can be em-

powering for African women willing to employ a *bosadi* hermeneutics in rereading such texts from Proverbs.

The Industrious Woman

Another key aspect of the life of the Woman of Worth, which comes to light as one reads this poem, is her industry. It would appear that women of the time were expected to be industrious, as seen in the manifold tasks that the *ʾešet ḥayil* performs. I should, however, hasten to argue that even those who opt for a literal interpretation of the poem would agree that we are dealing with an exaggerated portrait. I thus agree with Aitken (1986:158) when he argues that "as a whole it [the paean] cannot be read as a kind of blueprint of the ideal Israelite housewife—either for men to measure their wives against or for their wives to try to live up to." The one-sided picture of the woman as totally virtuous shows that this text depicts an image rather than a reality (see McCreesh 1985). Nevertheless, we may assume that the poem wished to present a picture of a woman who is not lazy and who works hard for herself, her household, and the needy.

Parallels from Northern Sotho Settings

In a Northern Sotho setting, hard work is also viewed as a quality of a good woman (*ʾešet ḥayil*), as seen in the Northern Sotho proverb, *Mosadi ke tšhwene o lewa mabogo* (literally, "a woman is a baboon; her hands are eaten"). Its tenor is that a commendable woman is one who does her (household) duties and also takes care of her husband. Industry is one of the aspects of *bosadi* (womanhood) in an African context. No one can deny the significance of the ethos of industry, which is also one of the general themes of the book of Proverbs. In present-day South Africa, a virtue such as industry has to be revived. We are aware of how, with the advance of political liberation, this virtue has been lost among many people. This virtue has to be revived not only among married women (as the above Northern Sotho proverb seems to suggest), but among South

Africans of all races, classes, genders. In a family, both men and women (including children, and particularly boys) should work hard for the welfare of the family. Nationally, both men and women have a responsibility to work hard to boost the weak South African economy. A culture of boycotts has to give way to a culture of industry in order for us to survive as a nation. If the work ethic can be restored to all family members in Africa, families will be better places for women. Currently, African women, particularly brides, are expected to work very hard at home.[8] The industry of the Woman of Worth may thus be liberative from a *bosadi* perspective that recognizes that it is not for women alone to be selfless, hard-working, and serving others, while African men, middle-class African women, and Whites are "sitting at the gates."

Conclusion

Another interesting fact in Prov. 31:10–31, which seems to shed light on the patriarchal mentality of ancient Israel, is that although the *'ešet hayil* emerges as the key figure, the author constantly mentions her husband, who is referred to as her *ba'al* (master). In that social milieu, it appears that no matter how independent one might have appeared as a woman, one would not have been viewed independently from one's husband (hence the common reference to "the wife of so and so," rather than to the name of the woman). From the poem, it becomes clear that the husband is the most significant member of the household, while children and servants are in the background. While one would not see a problem in a woman's being coupled with a man in marriage, one would take exception if one party is always viewed in terms of the other one (as, in most cases, the woman is viewed in terms of the man) and is seen as living always to enhance the other's interests. While it is good for a woman to have the interests of her husband at heart, it will do both of them good if marriage is not a one-sided affair, as in patriarchal cultures like those underlying Prov. 31:10–31 and the proverbs from Northern Sotho. The

155

marriage should be mutual, because, in my view, man and woman were created in God's image to complement each other.

If the preceding interpretation succeeds in helping to revive some of the lost aspects of African culture, like the family mentality, cooperation between men and women, and the significance of hard work, one would be justified in regarding the hermeneutics of *bosadi* as liberating.

Notes

1. For the various ways this poem has been interpreted, see Wolters 1984 and McCreesh 1985.

2. Because of the almost completely secular presentation of the qualities of this Woman of Worth, Crook (1954:137) joins other commentators who see the "fear of the Lord" as a later insertion.

3. See the thorough treatment of the subject in McCreesh 1985.

4. See Camp 1985; 1987.

5. Some feminists, like E. Schüssler Fiorenza (1992), go beyond gender asymmetry and focus also on multiple forms of oppression experienced by various groups of women.

6. For more details about the differences between these two perspectives, see Hudson-Weems 1993 and works by such womanist scholars as Katie Geneva Cannon, Renita Weems, Jacquelyn Grant, Toinette Eugene, Emilie Townes, and Delores Williams.

7. On the male authorship of this paean, see my doctoral thesis (Masenya 1996). Even the mood of the poem seems to suggest male authorship. Athalya Brenner (1993) differs on this point, however, recognizing a female voice in this text.

8. For a discussion of the situation of African women in families, see Masenya 1995.

References

Aitken, K. 1986. *Proverbs*. Edinburgh: Saint Andrew.

Bird, P. 1974. "Images of Women in the Old Testament." Pp. 41–88 in *Religion and Sexism: Images of Woman in the Jewish and Christian Traditions*, edited by R. R. Ruether. New York: Simon & Schuster.

Brenner, A. 1993. "An F Voice?" Pp. 113–30 in *On Gendering Texts: Female and Male Voices in the Hebrew Bible*, edited by A. Brenner and F. van Dijk-Hemmes. Leiden: E. J. Brill.

Camp, C. 1985. *Wisdom and the Feminine in the Book of Proverbs*. Bible and Literature Series 11. Sheffield: JSOT Press, Almond Press.

————. 1987. "Woman Wisdom as Root Metaphor: A Theological Consideration." Pp. 45–76 in *The Listening Heart: Essays in Wisdom and Psalms in Honor of Roland Murphy, O. Carm,* edited by K. Hogland. Sheffield: Sheffield Academic Press.

Crook, M. 1954. "The Marriageable Maiden of Prov 31:10–31." *Journal of Near Eastern Studies* 8:137–40.

Eugene, T. 1992. "Womanist Theology." Pp. 510–12 in *New Handbook of Christian Theology,* edited by T. Musser and J. Price. Nashville: Abingdon.

Goduka, I. 1995. "A Manual to Empower Educators to Affirm Diversity." Unpublished paper.

Hudson-Weems, C. 1993. *Africana Womanism: Reclaiming Ourselves.* Troy, Mich.: Bedford.

Lyons, E. 1987. "A Note on the Book of Proverbs." Pp. 237–45 in *The Listening Heart: Essays in Wisdom and Psalms in Honor of Roland Murphy, O. Carm,* edited by K. Hogland. Sheffield: Sheffield Academic Press.

Masenya, M. 1995. "Freedom in Bondage: Black Feminist Hermeneutics." *Ned Geref Teologiese Tydskrif* 1:115–23.

————. 1996. "Proverbs 31:10–31 in a South African Context: A (Womanhood) Perspective." D. Litt. et Phil. thesis, Pretoria.

McCreesh, T. 1985. "Wisdom as Wife: Proverbs 31:10–31." *Revue biblique* 92:25–46.

Meyers, C. 1991a. *Discovering Eve: Ancient Israelite Women in Context.* Oxford: Oxford University Press.

————. 1991b. "'To Her Mother's House': Considering a Counterpart to the Israelite *Bêt ʾb.*" Pp. 39–51 in *The Bible and the Politics of Exegesis: Essays in Honor of Norman K. Gottwald,* edited by D. Jobling et al. Cleveland: Pilgrim Press.

Schüssler Fiorenza, Elisabeth. 1992. *But She Said: Feminist Practices of Biblical Interpretation.* Boston: Beacon.

Scott, R. B. Y. 1965. *Proverbs, Ecclesiastes.* Anchor Bible 18. Garden City, N.Y.: Doubleday.

Steady, F. C., ed. 1981. *The Black Woman Cross-Culturally.* Cambridge, Mass.: Schenkman Books.

Wolters, A. 1984. "Nature and Grace in the Interpretation of Proverbs 31:10–31." *Calvin Theological Journal* 19:153–66.

9

A South African Indian Womanist Reading
of the Character of Ruth

Sarojini Nadar

The fate of a Hindu widow has traditionally been a tragic one. In India, she is stigmatized as a woman who has failed to safeguard her husband's life. Under ancient law, her husband is God, and when he dies she is expected to manifest inconsolable grief for the rest of her life. The extreme consequence of this belief is the practice of *sati*, in which a wife burns herself on her husband's funeral pyre. The Indians that emigrated to South Africa about four generations ago fortunately have not carried the practice of *sati* with them. The mind-set behind the practice, however, has certainly carried over, since—even in South Africa—when a woman's husband dies, all her hope of survival dies. That belief has changed gradually in recent times, with more Indian women joining the workforce and thereby gaining independence. But there are numerous stories of women who have nervous breakdowns when their husbands die, because they are not able to provide for themselves

---

I use the term *womanist* in the title as opposed to *feminist* because I am a South African Indian woman, and issues of color and class are a significant part of our lives. Further, my ancestors, like ancestors of African women, stand in the history of discrimination. The term *womanist* takes these important issues into account. It is also significant that Masenya, a South African black woman biblical scholar (1997), proposes a *bosadi* (womanhood) hermeneutics. My only reluctance in using Masenya's term is that it is Northern Sotho in outlook, and I have no claim on the cultural nuances that accompany it. The *bosadi* perspective, however, does contain many similarities to the womanist perspective, especially in its attention to issues of race and class.

or their family. Most times the duty of taking care of the family falls to the eldest son, but if the son is not old enough to work, the situation is dire. The story of Ruth the foreign widow resonates with the stories of many South African Indian women, including that of my mother. It is for this reason that I feel drawn to the story of Ruth and propose the following analysis.

Introduction

For the last two hundred years, historical-critical scholarship has dominated the field of biblical studies. It has been afforded a relatively high status, to the exclusion and dismissal of other methods seen as subjective and unsophisticated. As Segovia (1995:5) has pointed out, "Historical criticism was perceived and promoted not only as the proper way to read and interpret the biblical texts but also as the ultimate sign of progress in the discipline, the offer of the (Christian) West to the rest of the (Christian) world and the means by which the backward and the ignorant could become modern and educated." The basic problem with the kind of mind-set that Segovia describes is that it has dominated the field of biblical criticism and, as such, has made the Bible inaccessible to communities of faith such as the one from which I come. Barr also recognizes this problem when he asserts that the modern biblical scholar (who) "is largely insensitive to literary values . . . looks for the intentions of the original author but cannot see what this product has meant to thousands of faithful religious people down the centuries" (1989:6). Cone makes this point more clearly by relating it to liberation discourses: "It matters little to the oppressed who authored scripture; what is important is whether it can serve as a weapon against oppressors" (1990:31).

A case in point would be my own faith community, in which many people struggle just to survive. When they read Psalm 23, for example, they read it as a source of comfort. They see it speaking directly to their own life situation, especially since they themselves feel as though they "walk through the valley of the shadow of death" much of the time. In other words, their interpretation is informed by their life experience.[1] It matters little to them who wrote the Psalms or the time when the Psalms were written or even what the authors intended the Psalms to mean. Biblical criticism is at a stage at which biblical scholars cannot or should not be satisfied just with historical criticism, with its focus on authorial intention, or with "new criticism," with its focus on the text as an independent and stable entity. As Okure (1995:54) points out, biblical scholars are now "taking full cognizance of the influence that the social location of the interpreter plays on his or her search for meaning in the Bible . . . , [so much so that] a reading of the Bible that is not directly related to the social location of the reader is almost considered out of fashion."

Taking the points above into consideration, the aim of this essay is to read the character of Ruth contextually. The essay seeks to show that the character of Ruth can provide a positive example for women in South Africa today. My methodology is largely literary, but distinctly postmodernist. The distinctiveness of a postmodernist literary analysis is that it does not focus on authorial intention alone. In this case, the interpretive significance lies not in the way in which the author has characterized Ruth, but in the way in which the reader interprets Ruth based on the reader's own social location. The importance of the real or physical reader (what Segovia [1995:3] terms "flesh-and-blood readers") in interpretation is affirmed in postmodernist discourse. To a large extent, a postmodernist reading implies reading autobiographically. An autobiographical reading requires that the reader acknowledge her/his context at the outset. Like contextual Bible study, however, autobiographical interpretation "is not content with (simply) an admission of contextuality." Autobiographical interpretation, again like contextual Bible study, "embraces and advocates context. Commitment to rather than cognizance of context is the real issue" (West 1999:51).

My context as a fourth-generation South African Indian Christian woman, born into a lower-middle-class home, and belonging to a Pentecostal church whose members come from lower socioeconomic classes, is indeed significant for my inter-

161

pretation. However, as stated above, it is not enough to declare my location and to carry on "with business as usual" (West 1999:44). My commitment is to the women in my community, many of whom, like Ruth, are single (either widowed or divorced or having husbands not in residence) and impoverished; many have been oppressed at one time because of their ethnicity. We use the Bible collectively as a crutch on which to lean in difficult times. In other words, our community considers the Bible a foundational religious document that dictates how social and other relations are nurtured. As such, I have to state at the outset that the hermeneutical choices I make within this reading are determined by my ideological position. The community with which I have read the biblical text, and with which I continue to read the biblical text, influences the way in which I read. Before I move to the character analysis of Ruth, I want to say further words about my methodology.

Methodology

Two broad, basic processes are involved in characterization. The first lies at the level of the text and the second at the level of the reader. The first process involves the "revelation" of character, and the second is what Fewell and Gunn (1993:75) call "reconstructing" characters. These two processes do not operate independently of each other. They feed into each other constantly. In other words, in an almost unconscious process of collecting all the clues about the character that the text supplies (revelation of character), and coupling that with her/his own ideological assumptions (reconstructing character), a considerate reader attempts to reconstruct the characters. In the analysis that follows I assume the role of such a reader.

Interpretation is a dynamic process, and, therefore, meaning should not be fossilized. Meaning should be evolving constantly. If biblical texts are used in the modern age as a basis for teaching and preaching, particularly because they are thought to contain examples of right living (as in my church), then we cannot be satisfied with accepting characters as mere literary constructs[2] simply because they come to us via an artistic medium. The tools of reader-response criticism afford us the opportunity to analyze character in the same way that we analyze real persons, because meaning is derived not from the physical words of the text itself but through the temporal process of reading (Fish 1980:67). This implies that, in the process of reading, the narrative world of the character becomes fused with the real world of the reader, and the interpretation of character consequently unfolds as the reader reconstructs the character according to her or his own worldview.

A further implication is that, in the quest for meaning, the interpreter does not look through a window into the world of the biblical characters, but looks into a mirror. Interpretation of character is, therefore, a two-way process. The interpreter looks for attributes in the biblical character to identify with or, in the case of negative characterization, to reject. Thus, the character does not remain merely a literary construct or a plot functionary. The character "as an effect of the reading process and as a paradigm of attributive propositions . . . may seem to 'transcend' the text" (Burnett 1993:3).

In the analysis that follows, therefore, reconstruction does not restrict itself to the character of Ruth as a plot functionary, nor does it restrict her character to the world of the narrative only. Rather, it seeks to open her character and to make her accessible even to contemporary readers who seek to identify with her. The hermeneutical circle begins with the reader. As such, the reader, whether consciously or unconsciously, attempts to identify with the characters because "narrative evokes a world and[,] since it is no more than an evocation[,] we are left free to enrich it with whatever real or fictive experience we acquire" (Chatman, quoted in Fewell and Gunn 1993:51). A character analysis of Ruth follows, using the methodology outlined above.

Character Analysis

Leila Bronner draws the following conclusion about Ruth as a character:

Ruth may be regarded as the paragon of all the virtues the sages believe a woman ought to embody. Ruth's role is to be a faithful, modest daughter-in-law and, by remarrying and bearing a male child, to continue the male line of her deceased husband. As attractive as her character is, Ruth is not independent, autonomous and free of male control; on the contrary she is docile and submissive, and this is why the sages laud and honor her. (Bronner 1993:168)

Bronner argues that the sages in rabbinical literature, along with the biblical text in general, emphasize Ruth's modesty and submissiveness not only to authenticate her fitness as the great-grandmother of David, but also to accent the qualities that they think a woman should possess. I agree with Bronner when she asserts that Ruth possesses loyalty and faithfulness. In the following analysis of the character of Ruth, however, I challenge Bronner's and the sages' assertion that Ruth should be characterized as docile and submissive, and that she does not possess qualities of which feminists would approve. In fact, I argue precisely the opposite: Ruth's character is independent, autonomous, strong-willed, and even subversive. This claim will be supported by an examination of the character of Ruth according to what Berquist (1993:34) terms "role dedifferentiation." Role dedifferentiation is defined as the process by which persons respond to a crisis through adding roles, including roles that would be socially inappropriate in normal times.

Ruth 1: "Do Not Press Me to Leave You"

Our first glimpse of Ruth is in 1:4. Here she is spoken of only as the second Moabite woman whom Elimelech's son married: Her role is defined only in terms of her familial relationship to Elimelech's family, as the wife of one of Elimelech's sons. Glimpses of Ruth in the rest of the first chapter are as Naomi's daughter-in-law. She has already undergone a role dedifferentiation from having been defined in terms of her relationship to a man to being defined in terms of her relationship to a woman, her mother-in-law. This is significant because the narrative is now handed over to Ruth and Naomi, and, in essence, shifts from being a man's story to being a woman's story.

Ruth may be aware that she will have to provide for both

Naomi and herself, since Naomi is too old to work and, being past childbearing age, to remarry. In this regard there is role dedifferentiation, especially in respect to the word *davak*, which is translated as "cling" or "cleave." In 1:14, the narrator says that Orpah turned and left, but Ruth "clung" to her mother-in-law. Berquist (1993:26) asserts that the word *davak* in the Hebrew Bible is most often used in relation to God, but, when used in relation to humans, nowhere else does it describe a woman's act. In Gen. 2:24 ("A man shall leave his mother and his father and cling [*davak*] to his wife, and they shall become one flesh"), "clinging" refers to love and to marriage, and possibly also to sexual relations. The important point that Berquist (1993:27) notes is that *davak*, in Genesis, refers to the male role in initiating marriage. Therefore, "When Ruth *clings* to Naomi, Ruth takes the male role in initiating a relationship of formal commitment, similar to marriage." Therefore, Ruth has added a male role of "clinging" to Naomi as a husband and as a provider, as will be clear in chapter 2.

Ruth 2: "I Am Going to the Fields to Glean"

In chapter 2, Ruth is presented as the breadwinner who goes out to glean in order to provide food for herself and Naomi. Sasson (1979:38) reads Ruth's words as a question. "Should I go to the fields and glean among the ears of grain, in the hope of pleasing him (Boaz)?" (2:2). Sasson uses the third-person masculine suffix to indicate that Ruth is referring to Boaz, with the assumption that Ruth and Naomi have spoken about Boaz before, and, therefore, that Ruth plans to please him. The first problem with Sasson's translation is that it implies that Ruth is submissive to Naomi's will, and that if Naomi had said that she could not go, she would not have done so. However, from our examination of Ruth's character as she appeared in chapter 1, it is clear that Ruth is portrayed as a strong-willed, independent thinker; if a situation arose in which she could take care of her mother-in-law, then she would, whether her mother-in-law granted permission or not.

Therefore, Ruth is not asking her mother-in-law whether she can go to the field; she is telling her that she is going. This is evidenced by the narrator's indications when Ruth speaks (*Vatomer Ruth hamoabiya el-Naomi,* which means, "And Ruth the Moabitess said to Naomi") and when Naomi speaks (*Vatomer la leki biti,* meaning, "And she said, 'Go, my daughter' "). The narrator does not indicate that Naomi answered Ruth, but that Naomi spoke to Ruth. The word *vatomer* is used twice to indicate that each "said" something to the other.

Another example of Ruth's resourcefulness is her action in the fields. A number of commentators have suggested that Ruth did not glean until Boaz had arrived, implying that she was waiting for his permission before she could start.[3] However, the narrator informs us in verse 3, in what is a summary of Ruth's actions before Boaz arrives, *vatalaket basade acharei hakotsrim,* which is translated literally as "she gleaned in the fields behind the reapers." This, therefore, implies that she already had asked the permission of the foreman and had begun gleaning behind the reapers when Boaz arrived. The foreman reports in indirect speech the conversation that transpired between Ruth and himself. He reports that she asked if she could gather *among* the sheaves. This was certainly an unusual request, since the law dictated that people could glean behind the reapers but not among them. The foreman could not grant this request himself. Ruth could glean behind the reapers, however, since the law did not require permission for that. Therefore, it seems that Ruth had hitherto only been gleaning *behind* the reapers.

If we interpret the text as suggested above, then Ruth's first statement to Naomi in 2:2 also makes sense: "I am going to glean *among* the ears of grain in the fields after one in whose eyes I find favor." My initial argument that the phrase "to find favor in one's eyes" means permission to glean fits with this latter assertion, because Ruth was aware that in order to do what she wanted, she needed permission. If she planned only to glean behind the reapers, then, as the law stated, she would not need permission. However, as Berquist (1993:28) points out, "[G]leaning provided subsistence for those lowest in social status. In Ruth's case, with two persons eating one's gleanings, even survival would be questionable. Ruth must find another solution to hunger and poverty." Therefore, I suggest that in order to provide enough for both Naomi and herself Ruth had to request something beyond the scope of the law, namely, to glean *among* the reapers as opposed to simply *behind* them.

In this chapter we find another dimension of the character of Ruth emerging. She is not just a kind and selfless character, as established from the examination of her character in chapter 1, but she is strong-willed, determined, daring, resourceful, and innovative. Her daring and innovative act in chapter 2 sets the scene for an even more daring act in chapter 3.

Ruth 3: "Spread Your Wing over Your Maidservant"

In chapter 3, Naomi has developed a strategy that she hopes will help solve their problem. She asks Ruth to wash and perfume herself, to put on her cloak, to go to the threshing floor where Boaz will be, and, after he has eaten, drunk, and lain down, to uncover his feet and wait for his response. Naomi precedes this instruction with the statement that she wants to find a home for Ruth (3:1) and that "Boaz is our relative" (3:2). Naomi's interest is to get Ruth married to ensure her own and, in the process, Ruth's survival. She finds Boaz to be a suitable suitor, but two things are working against this marriage. The first is that Boaz is a kinsman of Elimelech, not a brother of Mahlon. Therefore, if the possibility existed for a Levirate marriage, it had to be between Naomi and Boaz. But Naomi was too old to have children, and, since having children was the point of a Levirate marriage, such a union would be fruitless. Ruth, therefore, would have to act so that the Levirate marriage would help ensure Naomi's survival. The second obstacle follows from the first, in that if the marriage were to take place between Ruth and Boaz, consideration would have to be made of the fact that Ruth was a foreigner. The terms of Levirate marriage applied to Israelites, but there was no mention of foreigners; since there were laws forbidding the union of foreigners with Israelites, these rules did not cater to the redemption of the foreigner.

It is surprising that Ruth agrees to Naomi's plan readily and openly, without the dispute that occurs in the first chapter, in

167

which Naomi tells Ruth twice that she must return, and twice Ruth says no. That Ruth readily agrees to the plan could mean that she recognized that it afforded a permanent solution to their problems. Ruth's concern has not been to remarry. She gave up that dream in order to take care of Naomi, as demonstrated by her refusal to go back to Moab and to find rest in the home of a husband (1:6–18). Her main concern in the plot until now has been to provide food for Naomi and herself. She has not once indicated that she wants a husband. Now that the opportunity arises, and, in the process, to ensure the survival of both Naomi and herself, she takes it on.

Although Ruth is determined, and says to Naomi that she will do all that Naomi tells her, she does not do it. This is evident in 3:9 when Boaz asks Ruth, "Who are you?" and she answers, "I am Ruth your maidservant. Spread your wings over your maidservant, for you are a redeemer." Naomi told her to lie at Boaz's feet and to wait for him to tell her what to do. Ruth does not wait. She takes charge of the situation by telling Boaz what she wants him to do (Trible 1978:184). With a wordplay, Ruth calls Boaz to act on Yahweh's behalf. In the fields, Boaz had said to Ruth, "May Yahweh repay you for what you have done, may you have the full reward of Yahweh, the God of Israel, under whose wings you have sought shelter" (2:12). Ruth now uses the same word that Boaz has used earlier to indicate Yahweh's protection (*kanaph*, which literally means "wings") when she tells him to spread his "wing" over her. In other words, Ruth is challenging Boaz to act on behalf of the Lord God of Israel, to act on his religious commitments. It is highly likely that Boaz would be open to such an invitation, since his character has been developed as that of a deeply religious man. His portrayal as a devout Israelite is indicated in both his greetings to his workers and in his dialogue with Ruth. Ruth cleverly reappropriates Boaz's religious language. As Trible (1978:184) notes, "She challenges Boaz to be the occasion of divine blessing in her life. And the man who asked it for Ruth is himself capable of fulfilling it."

Ruth is thus undertaking a more daring act than seduction

when she calls on Boaz to spread his wing over her; she is a foreign woman calling on an Israelite man to accept a responsibility that, by law, he does not have to answer.[4] Without having to sacrifice her own dignity in the process, Ruth drives the situation to ensure her own survival and simultaneously to gain her rightful place in the Israelite community. Ruth is ensuring that she can progress from outsider to insider.

Ruth 4: "Your Daughter-in-Law Is More Than Seven Sons!"

We do not hear Ruth speak in chapter 4. She is only spoken about in the deal between the other redeemer and Boaz, who refers to Ruth as the Moabitess. This time he uses her name in juxtaposition to Mahlon. He justifies that he can be a redeemer to Ruth because she had married into an Israelite family, and, therefore, in order to preserve the name of the Israelite family, she can also be redeemed. Van Wolde (1997:102) notes that "Boaz makes the name of the dead men of Judah live on through a foreigner." This is true, but van Wolde fails to mention that Ruth, not Boaz, initiates the process, for it is only through Ruth's actions that we have Boaz's reaction. The foreign woman has called an Israelite man to act in the spirit of the Israelite law regarding redemption. So daring is Ruth that she calls a man to act, even when it is beyond his obligation to do so.

Nielsen (1997:76) notes that "Ruth's unexpected interpretation of the kinsman-redeemer's duty . . . is an expression of her resourcefulness in a difficult situation. It does not follow existing law, but it interprets the spirit behind the redeemer concept: care for the survival of the family. We could say that Ruth acts more like an Israelite than her new fellow countrymen do." Nielsen's observation points to the fact that Boaz is merely acting on Ruth's initiative. Even though Boaz might have taken a keen interest in Ruth, he does not act to ensure that they end up together. It is through Ruth's initiative that Boaz can declare what he declares to the elders and witnesses. It is through Ruth's initiative that they end up getting married.

Role Dedifferentiation and Character Development

Humphreys (1985:84–85) asserts that the genre of the biblical short story requires that characters do not develop. This is in comparison to the novel, in which characters "evolve as they shape and are shaped by events and situations. . . . Jonah, Ruth, and even Daniel and his companions are essentially the same at the end of each story as at the outset; they do not grow or develop before us." From the above examination of the character of Ruth, it is apparent that Humphreys's argument can be seriously challenged. We have seen Ruth develop as a character from a childless widow and a foreigner with virtually no status to a person ranked among the great matriarchs of Israel, one of the highest positions that could be accorded a woman.

The way in which the character of Ruth has developed is directly related to the role dedifferentiation that she has undergone from 1:4 to the end, where she is ranked among the great matriarchs of Israel. The role dedifferentiation began when Ruth accepted the male role of providing for Naomi in chapters 1 and 2. Indications of this additional male role are signified by the word *cling* and through Ruth's dialogue in 2:2, in which she tells Naomi that she is going to the fields to glean.

This action sparks a second role dedifferentiation, in that Ruth not only asks to glean *behind* the reapers, but *among* them. Here she asserts herself to become one of the reapers, so that she might glean enough for both Naomi and herself. By taking the role of gleaner, Ruth provides a short-term solution to their need for food. Berquist (1993:29) asserts that "for the proposed long-term solution, Ruth adds another role: seducer." I have argued that Ruth is willing to take on the role of seducer if necessary, but, in making her proposal to Boaz, she elicits a response ensuring that she does not take this role. The language that Ruth uses to propose marriage to Boaz is highly ambivalent. She says in 3:9, "Spread your wing over your maidservant, for you are a redeemer." As Fewell and Gunn (1989a:50) note, the phrase signifies "either an invitation to have sex, or an appeal for marriage and security, or both."[5] In line with my previous argument that Ruth was keeping her options open and did not do everything her mother-in-law told her (that is, to set the scene for seduction and to wait for Boaz to act), one can deduce that "the choice of interpretation is offered to Boaz. That is the risk that Ruth takes and a measure of her courage" (Fewell and Gunn 1989a:50). Either way, Ruth gets what she wants. Boaz can either have sexual relations with her and, in so doing, take her for a wife, or he can act as *yabam* (albeit bending the law of Levirate marriage) and take her for a wife. The ambivalence of Ruth's discourse points to the power of her discourse. Rashkow (1993:41) points out that Ruth knows what she wants and goes after it. Her discourse is that of power; the power of her discourse is that she succeeds.

By accepting his role as redeemer, Boaz in effect makes Ruth the redeemer. This is another example of role dedifferentiation. Ruth is given ultimate credit for provoking Boaz to take the role of the redeemer. Even though Boaz is the redeemer, he makes no attempt to redeem until prompted by Ruth. The women of Bethlehem note in 4:15–16 that it is Ruth who restores life to Naomi. Therefore, Ruth is the redeemer. It is Ruth who is better than seven sons who can redeem. Hence, as Berquist (1993:35) observes, Ruth's dedifferentiation is active, leading to the solution of the story's problems. By taking the role of mother, Ruth brings fullness to Naomi's emptiness and restores life to the living. The name Ruth is derived from the root *rwh* (to water to saturation). As with the other characters in the narrative, Ruth lives up to her name. She indeed fills Naomi's emptiness and restores life.

The character of Ruth is at the heart of the narrative. It is not surprising, therefore, that the book is named after her. She is the bold initiator of change, and it is through her character that denouement is achieved. Ruth is a subversive character in that she subverts gender and ethnic boundaries through her actions. At the beginning, Ruth is portrayed as oppressed in every sphere. She is a woman, a foreigner, a widow, and childless. By the end, we see that Ruth, through dexterity and intelligent action, has managed to cast aside all oppressive roles assigned to her.

Conclusion

Fish (1995:2) argues that "if you want to send a message that will be heard beyond the academy, get out of it." I do not think that womanist interests or other political interests to which Fish points are "out of the scope of the academy," precisely because it is "flesh-and-blood" readers who interpret; these readers cannot divorce themselves from their own realities. For Fish, the academy might be the only reality. Reality, however, is multifaceted and forms inseparable parts of our personalities and consciousness. So, for example, when Bronner argues that Ruth is docile and submissive, she is clearly reading as a white feminist. Her reality does not require that she read beyond that to see Ruth as a survivor, and, in both Fish's and Bronner's cases, that fact is perfectly understandable and acceptable.

For one reading from my context, however, in which there are many "Ruth situations," Ruth emerges as a woman who takes control of her destiny and who changes it from hopelessness to happiness. She is a survivor, not a victim of circumstance, waiting for a man to change her fate. Reading Ruth in this way shows that she can be a positive role model for women in similar circumstances.[6] For Indian Christian churches that read Ruth, such interpretation can help offset the mind-set of *sati* that has been ingrained for generations. Women in situations similar to Ruth's can, like Ruth, rise to the occasion and initiate actions that will change their hopeless situations into positive ones.

Notes

1. The faith element also plays an important role. As Okure (1993:77) points out, African women's "primary consciousness in doing theology is not method, but life and life concerns—their own and those of their own peoples." Masenya (1997:16) makes the point that "this element of faith may not be left out because for the average African–South African Christian Bible reader, the Bible is regarded as the Word of God capable of transforming life and addressing different life situations, not simply a scholarly book to be critiqued." This way of reading the Bible holds true for Indian South Africans, too.

2. See, for example, Chatman (1978:119), who argues that we allow characters to emerge as persons, not merely as functionaries of the plot.

3. See, for example, Sasson (1979:40), who suggests that Ruth is only preparing to glean and does not start gleaning until Boaz gives her permission.

4. The requirements for the *go'el* did not stipulate that he would have to redeem the woman, only the property. However, Naomi assumes that Ruth can act in a way that will make Boaz want her, and that, in the process, Boaz will redeem the land as well. See also Campbell (1975:132–37), who argues that it is Ruth who combines the function of *go'el* with that of *yabam*.

5. The word *kanaph*, which literally translated means "wing," has also been taken to mean "cloak," or "skirt." If one accepts that the translation means "skirt" or "cloak," one has to agree with Beattie (1978:43), who asserts that "such a close physical proximity is indicated that the expression readily connotes an invitation to sexual relations, just as would an invitation, in English, to go to bed, but I cannot see how the idea of marriage may be found in it." Other scholars, however, accept the expression as a figurative reference to marriage, but one that employs sexually explicit language. Kruger (1984:79–83) suggests a connection between Ruth 3:9 and Ezek. 16:8, in which a "marriage covenant" is made between Yahweh and Israel: "And I passed by you and saw you and behold your time was a time for love. I spread my skirt [wing] over you and covered your nakedness. I swore to you and entered into covenant with you, says the Lord Yahweh, and you became mine." Bush (1996:165) argues that we should reject Beattie's assertion that the expression is a sexual invitation, and accept (with Kruger) that it is a figurative marriage proposal based on Boaz's response. He suggests that Boaz heard something other than a sexual invitation, because his response contains a compliment about Ruth's *hesed. Hesed* in this sense cannot be related to sexual relations. A counterargument is that Ruth washed and perfumed herself as her mother-in-law had told her; therefore, the scene already was set for seduction and overlaid with sexual overtones. Whatever *kanaph* means, I think the ambiguity is deliberate. We are meant to see that Ruth is determined to do whatever it takes to ensure her and Naomi's survival.

6. In reading an earlier version of this article at the international meeting of the Society of Biblical Literature (Cape Town, July 2000), I was challenged about how empowering the figure of Ruth really is. The argument was that all of Ruth's actions and initiatives lead her back to the patriarchal web of roles that entrap women. In other words, Ruth ends up as a wife and a mother. She has no identity of her own. Kumari (1993:153) notes the same of Indian women: "Traditional India has seen a woman only as a member of a family or a group—as daughters, wives and mothers—and not as an individual with an identity or rights of her own." The challenge is valid, but only from a modern perspective. In

other words, the patriarchal world regarded the roles of wives and mothers highly—so much so that survival for a woman in all aspects was impossible without embracing those roles. The point is that Ruth was denied those roles, both because she was a foreigner and because she was a poor woman. She did not accept her situation, however, but acted in ways that changed it. Although the struggles for contemporary women may be different from those of Ruth, in that the struggle is not to be wives and mothers, the struggle for survival is common, especially where women are oppressed because of their gender, ethnicity, and class. The positive message that Ruth holds, especially for women like those in my community who look to the Bible for role models, is that women can find ways of dealing with their oppression.

References

Barr, J. 1989. "The Literal, the Allegorical, and Modern Biblical Scholarship." *Journal for the Study of the Old Testament* 44:3–17.

Beattie, D. R. G. 1978. "Ruth 3." *Journal for the Study of the Old Testament* 5:39–48.

Berquist, J. L. 1993. "Role Dedifferentiation in the Book of Ruth." *Journal for the Study of the Old Testament* 57:23–37.

Bronner, L. L. 1993. "A Thematic Approach to Ruth in Rabbinic Literature." Pp. 146–69 in *A Feminist Companion to Ruth,* edited by A. Brenner. Sheffield: Sheffield Academic Press, 1993.

Burnett, F. W. 1993. "Characterization and Reader Construction of Characters in the Gospels." *Semeia* 63:3–28.

Bush, F. 1996. *Ruth, Esther.* Word Biblical Commentary 9. Waco, Tex.: Word.

Campbell, E. F. 1975. *Ruth.* Anchor Bible 7. Garden City, N.Y.: Doubleday.

Chatman, S. 1978. *Story and Discourse: Narrative Structure in Fiction and Film.* Ithaca, N.Y.: Cornell University Press.

Cone, J. 1990. *A Black Theology of Liberation.* 2d ed. Maryknoll, N.Y.: Orbis Books.

Fewell, D. N., and D. M. Gunn. 1989a. "Boaz, Pillar of Society: Measures of Worth in the Book of Ruth." *Journal for the Study of the Old Testament* 45:45–59.

———. 1989b. "Is Coxon a Scold on Responding to the Book of Ruth?" *Journal for the Study of the Old Testament* 45:39–43.

———. 1990. *Compromising Redemption: Relating Characters in the Book of Ruth.* Louisville: Westminster John Knox.

———. 1993. *Narrative in the Hebrew Bible.* New York: Oxford University Press.

Fish, S. 1980. *Is There a Text in This Class? The Authority of Interpretive Communities.* Cambridge: Harvard University Press.

———. 1995. *Professional Correctness: Literary Studies and Political Change.* New York: Oxford University Press.

Humphreys, W. L. 1985. "Novella." Pp. 82–96 in *Saga, Legend, Tale, Novella, Fable: Narrative Forms in Old Testament Literature,* edited by G. Coats. Journal for the Study of the Old Testament: Supplement Series 35. Sheffield: JSOT Press.

Kruger, P. A. 1984. "The Hem of the Garment in Marriage: The Meaning of the Symbolic Gesture in Ruth 3:9 and Ezekiel 16:8." *Journal of Northwest Semitic Languages* 12:79–86.

Kumari, P. 1993. "Women's Studies: Insight into the Challenge of Women Power." Pp. 153–59 in *A Reader in Feminist Theology,* edited by P. Kumari. Gurukul, India: Gurukul Department of Research and Publications.

Masenya (Ngwana 'Mphalele), M. 1997. "Reading the Bible the *Bosadi* (Womanhood) Way." *Bulletin for Contextual Theology in Southern Africa and Africa* 4:15–16.

Nielsen, K. 1997. *Ruth: A Commentary.* Old Testament Library 8. Louisville: Westminster John Knox.

Okure, T. 1993. "Feminist Interpretations in Africa." Pp. 76–85 in *Searching the Scriptures: A Feminist Introduction,* edited by E. Schüssler Fiorenza. New York: Crossroad.

———. 1995. "Reading from this Place: Some Problems and Prospects." Pp. 52–69 in *Social Location and Biblical Interpretation in Global Perspective* (vol. 2 of *Reading from This Place*), edited by F. F. Segovia and M. A. Tolbert. Minneapolis: Fortress, 1995.

Rashkow, I. 1993. "Ruth: The Discourse of Power and the Power of Discourse." Pp. 25–42 in *A Feminist Companion to Ruth,* edited by A. Brenner. Sheffield: Sheffield Academic Press.

Sasson, J. M. 1979. *Ruth: A New Translation with a Philological Commentary and a Formalist-Folklorist Interpretation.* London: Sheffield.

Segovia, F. F. 1995. "Cultural Studies and Contemporary Biblical Criticism: Ideological Criticism as Mode of Discourse." Pp. 1–21 in *Social Location and Biblical Interpretation in Global Perspective* (vol. 2 of *Reading from This Place*), edited by F. F. Segovia and M. A. Tolbert. Minneapolis: Fortress, 1995.

Trible, P. 1978. *God and the Rhetoric of Sexuality.* Philadelphia: Fortress.

Van Wolde, E. 1997. *Ruth and Naomi.* London: SCM Press.

West, G. O. 1999. "Contextual Bible Study: Creating a Sacred and Safe Place for Social Transformation." *Grace and Truth* 2:51–63.

The Divination Method of Interpretation

10

Divining Ruth for International Relations

Musa W. Dube

The book of Ruth is known for the deep friendship of two women, Ruth and Naomi. Ruth looks into the face of her departing mother-in-law and says:

> Entreat me not to leave you or to return from following you; for where you go I will go, and where you lodge I will lodge; your people shall be my people and your God my God; where you die I will die, and there I will be buried. . . . And when Naomi saw that she was determined to go with her, she said no more. (1:16–18)

Church liturgy has transferred these "woman-to-woman" words into a heterosexual marriage pledge. If, however, we are faithful to the book of Ruth, the marriage is between two women. Ruth leaves her home, travels with Naomi, lodges with her, and finally bears a child to her. Indeed, we are told that when Ruth gave birth to a son, "the women in the neighborhood gave him a name, saying, 'A son has been born to Naomi'" (4:17). That the latter verse is at the close of the book indicates their unbroken marriage.

This seemingly woman-centered book has received many interpretations from women readers, who bring different methods and backgrounds to the many aspects of Ruth. For example, when Musimbi Kanyoro read the book with Kenyan women, they saw Ruth

> as the obedient and faithful daughter-in-law, for [Kenyan] culture dictates that marriage is forever—to a family, not to an individual. Thus the death of Naomi's son did not invalidate the marriage of her daughter-in-law. Ruth was then seen as the normal good woman who does what culture expects of her and becomes blessed. Custom and tradition . . . also stipulate honour and respect and help for older people, be they relatives or not. That Ruth chose to stay with Naomi

was normal to [Kenyan] women as is the rising and setting of the sun. . . .[1]

In her commentary on Ruth, A. J. Levine notes that, while Ruth vows to cling to her mother-in-law forever, "Naomi never acknowledges her daughter-in-law's fidelity. Following Ruth's speech, she is silent."[2] Does this mean that Naomi does not commit herself to Ruth? If not, why? The answer to this question should be clearer by the end of this reading. Women readers' diverse interpretations of Ruth are captured in Athalya Brenner's recent volume, *Ruth and Esther: A Feminist Companion to the Bible.*[3] Among these interpretations, we find a Native American reader, Laura Donaldson, focusing on Orpah, who returned to her mother's house and her gods, instead of on Ruth, who "succumbed to . . . hegemonic culture," and who is a "version of the Pocahontas Perplex."[4] Brenner, a Jewish reader, compares the experiences of Ruth with immigrant laborers into present-day Israel and finds that Ruth's pledge to Naomi is akin to "a slave's love for his master in Exod. 21:2–6."[5] Judith McKinlay, a descendant of colonial settlers of New Zealand, focuses on Naomi's character as an assimilator,[6] while, with my background of orality from Botswana, I ignore both Ruth and Naomi and focus on reading the unpublished letters of Orpah.[7]

These readers attest that Ruth, like any other text, is a mine or mosaic of social relations, where readers can take their pick. We find relations of female to male, mother-in-law to daughter-in-law, mother to son, daughter to mother, wife to husband, woman to woman, master to servant; and relationships formed through friendship, widowhood, courtship, neighborliness, migrant labor, and international contact (Moab and Israel). These social relationships are magnetic, drawing many readers precisely because they see and relate these social relations to their own social relationships. The book, in other words, divines its readers, confirming or confronting their experiences and offering alternatives. In this essay, my focus is on international relationships. I examine Ruth and Naomi—as two women representing two different nations, Moab and Judah—from a divination perspective. First, I give a brief introduction to the biblical text as a divination set. Second, I diagnose the health of international relations as portrayed in Ruth and look for international relationships that are life-affirming.

The Bible as a Divining Set for Social Relations

For Batswana and other southern Africans, reading a divination set with a professional diviner-healer was, and still is, tantamount to reading an authoritative book of social life. Diviner-healers read divining sets to diagnose problems and to offer solutions to consulting (nonprofessional) readers. Divining sets, which could be composed of carved bones, beans, beads, coins, and so on, are not fixed or closed canons or stories. Rather, each consulting reader (henceforth CR) writes and reads her/his own story with the diviner-healer in the reading session.

More than a century and half ago, when Robert Moffat, a missionary, first read and interpreted the Bible to Batswana, their response was to regard it as a "talking book" and as a divination set.[8] Today the Bible has become one of the divining sets among the Batswana African Independent Churches' (AICs) faith healers.[9] Many Christian spiritual healers no longer use only original/traditional divining sets for their CRs.[10] They also open the Bible and read its stories to diagnose the relationships of CRs, that is, to identify the causes of their problems and to seek treatment that heals their troubled relationships as well as their physical ailments. Health among Batswana, and in most southern African communities, is closely associated with social relationships. Illness is thus almost synonymous with unhealthy relationships, while health is closely associated with healthy relationships. Healing physical illness thus begins with attending to all the social relationships of the CR's life, before medication is offered for obvious physical ailments. One's physical body is regarded as part of the larger social body.

With this understanding, professional healer-readers read the Bible to diagnose CRs' social relationships and experiences. They read the Bible to offer solutions to troubled relationships and to encourage, as therapy for hurting bodies, the creation and maintenance of life-affirming relations in society. In Setswana belief, reading divining texts involves the right to live a whole life, to have healthy and affirmative relationships in society, as well as the challenge to create and to maintain healthy relationships, both within the family and wider community. This includes creating and maintaining healthy relationships between the community and the land, and with divine powers. Central to the divination framework is that people are interrelated and that they must stay connected and interdependent. Health means healthy relationships. Ill health means disconnections or unhealthy relationships. As people, we are, therefore, responsible for our own health and the health of the people around us; that is, depending on the relationships we create, we can make ourselves and others ill. It is this ethical thinking that makes southern African divination a reading of social relations in the world.

Undoubtedly, the healer-reader and the divining set itself are important to reading and healing social relationships. The healer-reader is an ethical social figure who interacts with many troubled CRs. S/he sits down with each one to read the divining set, to establish the source physical ailments, and to offer solutions that heal not only the consulting individual, but a set of social relations that surrounds every reader. On these grounds, Frantz Staugard holds that a diviner-healer is a central figure in the society.

But how does a divining set expose the relationships that surround each consulting reader? There are number of factors at work, namely, the involvement of divine powers, the set itself, the diviner, and the consulting reader's contribution. First, as the CR opens the divining set, the diviner-healer asks godly powers to expose the CR's healthy and unhealthy relationships. Godly spirits are asked to write the CR's story. At this stage, the CR is also involved. S/he is asked to be the first to handle, to breathe on, or to open the divination set in order to write his/her story on it. Sometimes, s/he is asked to pick a piece from the set that represents him/her. But the diviner-healer sometimes makes the choice, using the CR's age and gender as a guide. For example, a young woman would be assigned a piece symbolizing a youthful female figure.

Second, the divining set itself includes the central human relationships. Each piece represents a particular figure, such as parent, spouse, and sibling, and there are young, elderly, and male and female figures. The carvings also tell the story of the CR. Last, and most important, the pattern formed by the pieces and the direction they face once the divining set is opened indicate the circumstances surrounding the CR's relationships. The pattern writes a story about one's relationships with her/his neighbors, parents, spouse, divine powers, spouse, life and death, indicating which relationships are healthy and which are unhealthy.

The divining set having written the story, the reading begins. The diviner-healer walks the consulting reader through each pattern and the circumstances that the set reveals, asking the CR to confirm or deny if the patterns represent what s/he knows about his/her life. If the CR is not satisfied, there can be up to three throws of the set; the CR and the diviner-healer will read the patterns and the commentary they provide about the CR's life. If the CR still is not satisfied after the third reading, s/he is free to consult another diviner-healer. The CR is therefore an active and, indeed, an integral participant in the reading and writing of her/his social story from and into the divining set. When the CR cannot attend the reading, close relatives can consult on her/his behalf. After this reading, the diviner-healer will prescribe medication for the physical pains that brought the CR, but, more often that not, the diviner-healer usually lays responsibility on the CR. The latter is charged with righting the wrongs surrounding the social relationships of his/her life.

Reading a divining set is thus not as esoteric as laypersons tend to think. Neither the diviner-healer nor the divining sets possess exclusive knowledge, nor does the CR bring hidden knowledge. The diviner-healer acknowledges her/his limitations by inviting the participation of the divine powers and the CR. The CR also acknowledges her/his limitations by visiting the diviner-healer. Needless to say, the divination set will not write or tell any story until both readers throw it open and read it. Divination is thus a production of social knowledge that demands ethical commitment from all participating readers. It involves the realization that one is socially connected and has a responsibility to create and maintain healthy relationships, as well as to avoid those that negate life. Both readers are charged with undertaking social and physical healing.

These points, I believe, capture most of divination's major characteristics as an ethical method of reading in southern Africa. One can also see how the divining set functions as a social book of life. Reading a divining set, therefore, is an ethical art that entails the production of knowledge. It requires substantial understanding of social relations and that one attend to the interdependence of all relationships. I am drawing on this ancient art not as a pioneer, but by following my regional AICs' healer-readers of the Bible.

In what follows, the book of Ruth itself will be my divining set, and I will be a CR. I regard all other published readers of Ruth as diviner-readers. As a CR, my reading is in communication therefore with published readers of Ruth, although my reading of the divining set remains my own. Not all diviner-readers, however, are healer-readers, save those who regard their reading practices as ethical efforts toward better interpersonal and international relations. This practice involves assessment of all existing social relations and the encouragement of healthy relations. As a CR, the issues that bring me to read Ruth as a divining set are: (1) I seek to decolonize the production of knowledge in biblical studies that tends largely to use Western modes of conceptualization and analysis. (2) I am committed to an interdisciplinary approach in biblical studies, and, with this essay, I seek to focus on international relations, southern African divination systems and practices, and Ruth. (3) My focus on international relations relates largely to my social standing as a citizen of Botswana, indeed, of Africa as a whole—I am increasingly aware of the impact the past, present, and future has on our lives.

Divining Ruth for International Relations

As I open the pages of Ruth and peruse its stories, I read it as a divining set that consists of numerous interdependent social relations. While it must be underlined that divination focuses on all social relationships of the text/divining set in order to interpret the CR's state of connection, I read the book of Ruth with a focus on international relationships. This does not mean that I will not focus on social relations such as gender, race, class, and age, but that I will touch on them insofar as they connect with and highlight international relations. Many readers of Ruth have already attended to these relations. As an African of Botswana, I am particularly conscious of international relationships and their impact on past and present economic, ecological, political, and social life. In eagerness to understand these relationships in a time of globalization, I ask the following questions: What international relationships emerge from Ruth? What is the state of connection? Are the relationships healthy or unhealthy? If they are good, is the model usable in the present? If the relationships are unhealthy, what is the cause, and what remedy is offered? Although not all of these questions will be addressed directly, they nevertheless inform the contours of my divining of Ruth for international relations.

Reading Ruth and Naomi as Moab and Judah: What International Relations Emerge?

In the days when the judges ruled there was famine in the land, and a certain man in Bethlehem in Judah went to sojourn in the country of Moab, he and his wife and his two sons. The name of the man was Elimelech and the name of his wife Naomi, and the names of his two sons were Mahlon and Chilion; they were Ephrathites from Bethlehem in Judah. They went into the country of Moab and remained there. But Elimelech the husband of Naomi died, and she was left with her two sons. These took Moabite wives; the names of one was Orpah and the name of the other Ruth. They lived there about ten years; and both Mahlon and Chilion died, so that the woman was bereft of her two sons and her husband. Then she started with her

185

daughters-in-law to return from the country of Moab, for she heard in the country of Moab that the Lord had visited his people and given them food. So she set out from the place where she was, with her two daughters-in-law, and they went on the way to return to the land of Judah. . . . (Ruth 1:1–7)

Two countries, Moab and Judah, immediately surface. Judah is reportedly struck by famine, but Moab is fertile. Elimelech and Naomi and their two sons do what seems to be the reasonable thing: they leave Judah and move to Moab, where there is food, fertility, and life. But their experiences in Moab indicate that such a judgment was a gross miscalculation. Soon after relocating, Elimelech dies. Naomi is left with her two sons, who proceed to marry Moabite women, but their marriages are childless. Soon after, both sons die. The divining set tells us that Naomi "was bereft of her two sons and husband" (1:5b). In addition to Naomi we have two young widows, Ruth and Orpah. Events happen quickly in Moab, and they are largely, if not solely, negative. A diviner-reader realizes that the relationship of the people of Judah to Moab is unhealthy: it is characterized by infertility and death. Irony glares in this divining set, for while it seemed at first that Moab is the land of fertility and Judah the land of famine, reality is the other way around. Why? Is this a statement about Moab? This should become clear as the story continues.

But then hope rises for Naomi, who hears "that the Lord visited her people and had given them food" (1:6). Since Moab had dealt bitterly with Naomi, it seemed only reasonable for her to return to her people and land. Naomi insists that her daughters-in-law remain in Moab, for she cannot promise them husbands. Her words reflect the patriarchal arrangements of the time and that women's survival depended on marriage. Orpah pays heed to Naomi's words and returns, but Ruth insists on going with her mother-in-law.

The journey back to Judah and Ruth's insistence that she accompany Naomi is central to reading the relationship between Moab and Judah. In Naomi's return, another woman takes a journey to a foreign country. Ruth travels to Judah through marriage relations, just as Naomi had traveled to

Moab. Similarly, Ruth represents Moab as Naomi had represented Judah. The experiences of Ruth in Judah and the experiences of Naomi in Moab will highlight international relationships between the two lands.

Ruth the Moabite in Judah

The story of Ruth's journey to Judah is modeled closely on Naomi's journey to Moab. Although the text does not say that Moab was struck by famine, this is evident in the three deaths and the childlessness of the marriages. The famine drives them to Judah, and good news of food in Judah precedes their journey back. Some readers may say that food was not Ruth's motivation for taking the journey to Judah; rather, she traveled because of commitment to her mother-in-law. Her reason is not so different from the reason behind Naomi's journey to Moab. Naomi's journey to Moab does not result from her decision or initiative. Instead, the text says that a certain man sojourned to Moab because of famine in Judah and that Naomi, his wife, came along (1:1). Both Naomi and Ruth, therefore, traveled to and lived in foreign countries due to relationships of marriage rather than choice.

Naomi and Ruth arrive safely in Judah. When "they came to Bethlehem the whole town was stirred . . . and the women said, 'Is this Naomi?' She said to them, 'Do not call me Naomi [Pleasant]; call me Mara [Bitter], for the Almighty has dealt very bitterly with me. I went away full, and the Lord has brought me back empty . . ." (1:19–21). While Naomi's words summarize her experiences in Moab, they also make a statement about Judah. That is, even in famine, one's hands in Judah are full, while one suffers famine in Moab even when it seems there is fertility/food. What are Ruth's experiences in Judah? Will Ruth, a foreigner, eat from the fertility of the land, or is there famine disguised in fertility, which Naomi found in Moab? Will Ruth become involved in another childless marriage? Will Naomi lose what she brought with her, including Ruth? Will their experiences be pleasant or bitter? Similarities and differences in the two characters' relationships with Judah will tell us about international relations between Moab and Judah.

Is Judah Pleasant or Bitter to Ruth the Moabite?

In 1:22, the divining set signals Ruth's positive relationship with the land of Judah by stating that "Naomi and Ruth the Moabite . . . came to Jerusalem at the beginning of barley harvest." The beginning of harvest is a season of possessing fruits of the land. Reading further, Ruth takes the initiative by asking Naomi if she could "go to the field and glean among the ears of grain." Naomi allows it, and Ruth happens "to come to the part of the field belonging to Boaz, who was the relative of Elimelech" (2:1–3). Boaz finds Ruth gleaning in his field, and he encourages her to keep her "eyes upon the field they are reaping," and, if she is thirsty, he encourages her "to go and drink what the young men have drawn" and to continue gleaning in his field until the end of the harvest (2:9). Ruth, thankful for his kindness, asks, "Why have I found favor in your eyes, that you should take notice of me, when I am a foreigner?" (2:10). Boaz points to Ruth's commitment to Naomi and commends her for leaving her parents, land, and people. Boaz then pronounces that Ruth will be rewarded by the Lord God of Israel, under whose wings Ruth has "come to take refuge" (2:12). Ruth is not only invited to harvest and drink, she is invited to eat her full and to take leftovers for Naomi. Ruth is also protected, as Boaz repeatedly instructs that she should not be molested, "reproached," or "rebuked" (2:9–15). So far, Ruth is not Mara in Judah, but she is Pleasant.

Through Ruth's pleasant experiences, the divining set indicates a notable difference between Moab and Judah. In Moab, the story remained mum about the riches/fruits of the country. Although the movement of Naomi's family to Moab is associated with famine in Judah, the text says nothing about the harvests and waters of Moab. As a CR, I do not see Naomi harvesting in the fields of Moab or drinking from the waters. I do not see Naomi eating its food (if she did it must have been poisonous enough to eliminate all the members of her family!).

Rather, I see Naomi losing what she had brought to Moab and returning to Judah "empty." Another significant difference in the divining set is the role of the divine powers in Judah and Moab. If Moab did have food and water, the divining set not only refrains from speaking about them, it does not state the sources of Moab's fertility. In Judah, however, the divine role is explicitly recognized as the prime mover. The return of food in Judah (1:6), the experiences of Naomi in Moab (1:19–21), and the protection of Ruth (2:12–13), for example, are associated with the Lord God of Israel.

In Moab, the divine powers are scarce or even absent. I do hear Naomi instructing her daughters-in-law to return to their mothers' houses and evoking divine blessings on them (1:7–9). Her words, however, highlight a number of things. First, I see the Lord God of Israel's absence from Naomi's family in Moab. Naomi herself states that the hand of the Lord God was "against" her and "dealt bitterly" with her in Moab, such that she returned to Judah, "empty." Second, I realize that although Orpah returned, "to her mother and her gods" (1:15), thus indicating that divine powers existed in Moab, the divining set does not say or indicate that Naomi came under the refuge and blessing of the divine powers of Moab. Third, although Orpah returns to her mother and gods, that is, under their protection, I am not told her story: nothing is said about how she enjoyed the harvests, the waters, and the blessing of the gods of Moab. The silence about Orpah's story, however, is not total, for I can use Naomi's experience in Moab to interpret Orpah's life and land. In Orpah's untold story, Moab remains the land of famine as attested by death, childless marriages, and lack of godly powers. This is a major statement about Moab, which, as we shall see, also points to Moab's relationship with Judah.

Following the story of Ruth and Naomi as a narrative of Moab and Judah, the two women cultivate their space further. Ruth moves from gleaning in Boaz's fields to harvesting barley in his house, on the advice of Naomi. She finds him having eaten and drank, and sleeping next to a "heap of grain" (3:7)! Boaz is in the midst of pleasure and plenty. Ruth sleeps at his feet (private parts), and when Boaz wakes she asks him to "spread his skirt over her," since he is the next of kin. As in the fields, Boaz pronounces more blessings on Ruth: "May you be blessed by the Lord, my daughter; you have made this last kindness greater than the first, in that you have not gone after young men . . ." (3:10). With this move, Ruth has successfully proposed a marriage relationship to Boaz. He treats her with respect and promises to consult with other relatives of Elimelech who may be interested in marrying her. Boaz then sends Ruth home early with more barley so that she does not return to her mother-in-law "empty-handed" (3:17).

Boaz begins to negotiate his marriage to Ruth right away. He convenes a legally witnessed meeting with the closest relative who might be interested in Ruth, but Boaz does not openly discuss marriage. Rather, he negotiates about a piece of land that belonged to Elimelech and asks the man if he wishes to redeem it (4:1–6). The man agrees. Boaz informs him that "the day you buy the field from the hand of Naomi, you are also buying Ruth the Moabite, the widow of the dead, in order to restore the name of the dead to his inheritance" (4:5). It hit me unexpectedly to see Boaz making such a direct connection between the land and the woman, Ruth. The man withdraws. Perhaps he was also surprised. Boaz then openly declares responsibility for the widow of Mahlon. Those gathered accept Boaz's move, declaring a blessing on the marriage and that Ruth, like Leah, Rachel, and Tamar, should build the house of Israel, prosper, and bear children. The divining set quickly confirms that Obed, who becomes "the father of Jesse, the father of David," is born (4:17).

Ruth, who leaves Moab in order to cling to Naomi, marries Boaz. Is this betrayal? The narrative gets more interesting, for just when we think that Naomi has disappeared—when we think that Ruth's pledge to her mother-in-law cannot involve marriage to another man—the text reasserts its earlier perspective:

> So Boaz took Ruth and she became his wife; and he went in to her, and the Lord gave her conception and she bore a son. Then the women said to Naomi, "Blessed be the Lord, who has not left you

this day without the next of kin; and may his name be renowned in Israel! He shall be to you a restorer of life and a nourisher of your old age; for your daughter-in-law who loves you, who is more to you than seven sons, has borne him." Then Naomi took the child and laid him in her bosom, and became his nurse. And the women of the neighborhood gave him a name saying, "A son has been born to Naomi." (4:13–17a)

The latter part of the story helps divine the state of relations between Judah and Moab. As a CR, I ask myself, What makes Ruth, a young woman married to a young man in Moab, childless, and widowed, marry an older man and immediately bring forth a child? Medically, a number of good answers could be advanced, such as Mahlon's infertility. Whatever medical explanations we advance, however, they will not contradict the divining set's portrayal of Mahlon as an impotent young man with a short life span. But an older and fertile man, Elimelech, comes to a sudden end in Moab, while his age mate Boaz remains alive in Judah and proceeds to marry the young widow of Elimelech's son and to father a son who brings forth important descendants—namely, David. The question is whether these facts tell us something about the relationship between Judah and Moab. As I probe the divining set further, I am struck by the words of Boaz when he declares his intention to marry Ruth. He says, "Ruth the Moabite, the widow of Mahlon, I have bought for my wife, to perpetuate the name of the dead in his inheritance, that the name of the dead may not be cut off from his native land" (4:10). What a striking event that Ruth is bought! The purchase is not for her own gain, but for perpetuating Mahlon in his land of Judah. Ruth is bought to serve the life of Mahlon in Judah, to "build Israel"—Mahlon is not dead! Hence we realize that the son is born to Naomi, not to Ruth or to both of them.

The reasons for Ruth's marriage to Boaz lead me to the divining set to scrutinize the relationships surrounding the marriages in Moab. Evidently, marriages occur in both nations, but the difference is in their fruits. In Moab, Ruth and Orpah's marriage is childless, while Naomi loses two sons and her husband. Barrenness and bitterness reign in Moab. In Judah,

191

Ruth's marriage is immediately fruitful. A son is born, who becomes an ancestor of David. Ruth, therefore, does not only have access to the fruits of land, but she herself is fruitful. She can fittingly call herself Pleasant—Naomi. With these explanations for Ruth's marriage to Boaz, I am in a position to glean the reasons for barrenness and death in Moab: Mahlon, Elimelech, and Chilion cannot be inherited in the land of Moab, or by that land. They are cut off, for it is not their native place. In Judah they are reinstated, for it is their native land. Ruth's move to Judah, her clinging to Naomi, now appears in a different light as she becomes property bought and used for the perpetuation of Mahlon. I tend to agree with diviner-readers who note that Naomi does not commit herself to Ruth's pledge, signaling that this is not a relationship of equals. This agreement brings me closer to diviner-readers who hold that Ruth's pledge to Naomi has the tones of a slave-to-master relationship rather than an expression of mutual love between women or two friends. This, unfortunately, connotes the relationship between Judah and Moab.

Conclusion: What Healing Befits Our International Relations?

At first reading of the divining set, there is something attractive in the experiences of Ruth in Judah. She arrives as a powerless foreigner with no economic power—gleaning behind the servants (2:3, 7)—and as a childless young widow exposed to danger (2:9, 22). Yet she is allowed to take her own initiative in the midst of dangers, to explore opportunities, and to succeed (2:1–2; 3:9). Further, Ruth takes advice (3:1–5) from the natives of Judah. It is particularly gratifying to note that Ruth is lovingly protected, given respect, blessed, and allowed to retain her identity as "Ruth the Moabite" (2:6; 4:5, 10). On the whole, Judah is a land of plenty, of blessings and of success, where pleasant relationships can be built. In Judah, barley seems to be everywhere, and Ruth has access to it.

But as a CR, I am left aghast by the experiences of Naomi in Moab. I am confronted by silence, irony, death, and barrenness, which, as said earlier, instructs the reader to avoid Moab, or to embrace it at a price of disaster and death. This sharp contrast between lands of blessings and curses does not speak well of the relations between Judah and Moab. Given this sharp contrast, the story of Naomi in Moab makes the wonderful story of Ruth in Judah unusable as a model of liberating interdependence between nations. One can only embrace the story of Ruth in Judah by subscribing to the characterization of Moab as a godforsaken land, whose resources, however, can be tapped for the well-being of Judah.[11] The resources of Judah (Elimelech and his two boys) cannot be tapped for Moab, hence their death and barrenness. It becomes clear that Ruth (Moab) is a wife to Naomi (Judah)—she is the one who leaves her lands, her people, her gods, and, finally, who bears a son to her. Theirs is a patriarchal marriage, a relationship of unequal subjects. Ruth/Moab is a wife, the subordinate one, who leaves her interests to serve the interests of Naomi/Judah, her husband.[12] Not surprisingly, she bears a child to Naomi/Judah and not to herself and Naomi. Ruth is acknowledged for serving the interests of Naomi/Judah: The gain realized by bearing a child is not her gain, nor that of Moab, her land.

The divining set indicates that the relationship between the two nations is not healthy. It is not a relationship of liberating interdependence, but of subordinates and dominators, in which Moab cannot benefit equally from Judah's resources (from Elimelech, Mahlon, and Chilion). According to the divining set, the root of ill health emanates from Judah's refusal to recognize the divine powers at work in Moab. Moab is regarded as a godforsaken land, a cursed land, in which Israelites cannot bloom. Judah is its opposite. This ill health is responsible in the book of Ruth for the death and barrenness.

Who suffers from the unhealthy relationship between Moab and Judah? Moabites, or both nations? Undoubtedly, Moab suffers more, but the suffering affects both nations, precisely because the two nations are connected. Both nations need to acknowledge and develop a relationship of liberating interdependence. The latter describes a relationship in which both subjects are fairly and equally treated for their own good.

Judah attempts to deny that it can, and needs to, depend on Moab, given that the latter is nothing but a land of death and disaster. The denial is a futile exercise, because the connection between the two lands is self-evident. For example, the journey of Elimelech to Moab in the wake of famine in Judah attests to the fact that the strongest nations—even those that regard themselves as blessed lands of plenty—need the support of other nations. Further, Ruth the Moabite gives birth to a son whose line begets David, an outstanding figure in the history of Israel, thus paralleling the stories of Leah, Rachel, and Tamar, other non-Israelite women who contributed significantly to Israel. The relationship, however, is not one of liberating interdependence, since Judah is unwilling to contribute equally to Moab. Judah rejects Moab's right to benefit equally from their relationship—as indicated by the death of three Israelite men and the portrayal of Moab as a wife, Ruth, who must be subordinated. Building a relationship of liberating interdependence demands that the lands' interconnection be encouraged openly—built to be fair to both—and recognized as the core of their existence and survival; nations are not islands. Nations are never pure or independent, but they are interdependent, interconnected, and multicultural.[13] This recognition means that creating and maintaining healthy relations is indispensable medication in healing our world, and in proclaiming life and success within and outside the nations.

Notes

1. Musimbi R. A. Kanyoro, "Biblical Hermeneutics: Ancient Palestine and the Contemporary World," *Review and Expositor: A Quarterly Baptist Theological Journal* 94, no. 3 (1997): 372.

2. Amy-Jill Levine, "Ruth," in *The Women's Bible Commentary*, ed. Carol A. Newsom and Sharon H. Ringe (Louisville: Westminster John Knox Press, 1992), 80.

3. Athalya Brenner, ed., *Ruth and Esther: A Feminist Companion to the Bible*, 2d ser. (Sheffield: Sheffield Academic Press, 1999).

4. Laura Donaldson, "The Sign of Orpah: Reading Ruth through Native Eyes," in Brenner, *Ruth and Esther*, 140–41.

5. Athalya Brenner, "Ruth as a Foreign Worker and the Politics of Exogamy," in idem, *Ruth and Esther*, 159.

6. Judith E. McKinlay, "A Son Is Born to Naomi: A Harvest for Israel," in Brenner, *Ruth and Esther,* 151–58.

7. Musa W. Dube, "The Unpublished Letters of Orpah to Ruth," in Brenner, *Ruth and Esther,* 145–50.

8. While there are other forms of divination, through the Spirit, or through prophecy, visions, and dreams, this essay confines itself to divination that involves reading a text and in which the diviner remains composed. See Jean Comaroff and John Comaroff, *Of Revelation and Revolution: Christianity, Colonialism, and Consciousness in South Africa* (Chicago: University of Chicago Press, 1991), 299.

9. See Musa W. Dube, "Divining the Text for International Relations (Matt 15:21–28)," in *Transformative Encounters,* ed. Ingrid Rosa Kitzberger (New York and London: Routledge, forthcoming), in which I present a more detailed story of the Bible as a divination set among AICs.

10. James Amanze, *African Christianity in Botswana* (Gweru, Zimbabwe: Mambo Press, 1998), 150.

11. The art of portraying the Other negatively, as shown by both gender and post-colonial studies, is an ideology of domination. The dominator (colonizer or patriarchy) characterizes its victims negatively in order to justify their exploitation. What one reads in Ruth compares very well with the portrait of African people and land in Joseph Conrad's *Heart of Darkness.* While the land is a deadly wilderness, it still means profits for the colonizer.

12. The identification of land with women is generally recognized as an ideology of domination. The ideology becomes more pronounced in post-colonial literature, in which foreign lands or targeted colonies are often represented by a woman, and the colonizer by a man, as in the tale of Pocahontas.

13. See Edward Said, *Culture and Imperialism* (New York: Alfred Knopf, 1992), 336.

In Response

11

A North American Feminist Response

Phyllis A. Bird

First, I want to thank the presenters for a very stimulating set of papers exhibiting a rich diversity of approaches and perceptions. Each alone deserves a more detailed response than I could offer in the time allotted to all. I therefore focus on common or recurrent themes, problems, or interests that I discern in several or all of the papers, with limited comments on individual essays.

The second thing that I want to say is that this session and these papers (along with a number of others) give integrity to the choice of venue for this congress. This is a boundary-crossing congress; but the danger of international congresses is that they may simply move the established conversations of Euro-American scholars to an exotic location, crossing geographical boundaries without significantly altering the nature of the conversation. The papers in this session are all examples in themselves of boundary-crossing within the southern African context. This session represents a small but significant effort to save this congress from being simply a transfer of a North American meeting to a South African convention center. But it is only a first step, and I am ambivalent about my role in it as the only North American speaker in this session. I would like to see dialogue among the four presenters rather than, or as well as, response by an outsider, and I would like to see each of these papers interacting with others treating the same texts or

This essay responds to papers presented by Musa Dube, Gloria Kehilwe Plaatjie, Gomang Seratwa Ntloedibe-Kuswani, and Mmadipoane (Ngwana 'Mphahlele) Masenya at the Religion 2000 Congress, Cape Town, July 24, 2000.

topics, methods, or ideological commitments. But I am immensely delighted to participate in a session on women's interpretation of the Bible in which *all* of the presenters are *African* women.

Before I begin my interaction with the papers, I want to expand briefly on the note of discomfort I have expressed concerning my role in this session. A session devoted to African women's reading of the Bible has asked a North American woman to respond to the readings. On what basis should I respond? By what authority? I am an outsider to the history and culture of this continent that is hosting this meeting. And although I possess a degree of expertise in certain areas of women's critical reading of Scripture, this does not and cannot include expertise in African women's reading. Moreover, my race and nationality and my methodological commitments identify me with a Euro-American colonial history—including an intellectual history—that the four presenters today rightly see as an enemy. I raise these questions and concerns to suggest that the boundaries this session has been designed to cross (gender, culture, and political history) are among the most important for our discipline, and to signal the problem of fostering dialogue across these boundaries. We must try to avoid setting up those on either side of the cultural divide as antagonists or naively assuming that we can be "partners" or "share insights" when our interpretations are rooted in political and cultural realities that have been deeply detrimental to genuine partnership.

I will not try to answer these questions today, but I simply place them on the agenda. And I will offer a premature and overly simple answer to my question about my role as a North American in a discussion of African women's interpretation. I have come to this congress to learn, but not simply to learn. For the nature of scholarly meetings (a distinctively Western institution) is critical interchange, in which each participant expects to broaden her/his knowledge through critical encounter with new ideas and to strengthen her/his arguments by submitting them to critique. So I accept the task of criticism, as a contribution of Western scholarship, a distinct form of interchange that does not reject or displace other ways of knowing and communicating, of hearing and using Scripture. Criticism has only one aim: to make you and me more conscious of what we have overlooked, or misunderstood, or articulated poorly, so that we can form more adequate constructs and argue more persuasively. So I take up the task of respondent, and critic, as tribute to the substantial contributions of each of these papers.

Colonialism and Its Legacy

I begin with an overall appraisal. Despite the diversity of subjects, methods, and judgments, a number of common themes appear in the papers. I want to focus on one that is present both explicitly, and thematically, and implicitly—namely, colonialism and its legacy.

Gomang analyzes the consequences of a colonial translation of the Bible that co-opted an African deity, imposing a "Western" gendered conception of God on a traditional African view of an ungendered, all-encompassing, all-penetrating reality. The gendered Modimo ousts or condemns the ungendered Modimo—with negative consequences for women, she suggests, but also for traditional African views of God.

Gomang's analysis raises questions about the power of translation over against the power of traditional interpretation to impose meaning on the biblical text. She asks, "Did Modimo transform the personified and gendered biblical God or was it the other way around?" Her important question and observations invite a closer look at the biblical text with a more differentiated reading, especially of the Old Testament. Such a reading would show a God that is far more complex—and "contradictory"—than she realizes, and which often bears a closer resemblance to her portrait of Modimo than to the "Christian God" that she has assumed as the "biblical God." Thus, the God of the Old Testament can only be described in metaphors (including rock, spirit, womb, bird, bear, lion, and evergreen cypress) and explicitly rejects the notion that "he" should dwell in a house (1 Kings 8:27; cf. 2 Sam. 7:6).

Musa focuses on international relations in the book of

Ruth, because she sees the economic, political, and social life of her country and of women in her country as deeply affected by international relations, which, in the new forms of globalization, perpetuate patterns of the colonial past.

Musa's focus on international relations to guide her divining has produced some illuminating readings, as well as questions about "fit." What she makes clear, however, is that no reading of the biblical story in an African context can focus simply on interpersonal relations and neglect the international relations that form the backdrop and set the terms of the action, or that at least play a significant role in what may naively be viewed as a "family story."

The colonial heritage of South Africa is also exhibited in these papers and in this session in less recognizable, or non-thematized, ways, namely in the *language* of our discourse and in the *nature* of our discourse.

- In order for these papers to be heard and discussed today by an audience of biblical scholars a colonial language is used.

- The kind of communication in which we are engaged is a cultural product of the world of the colonizers; congresses of scholars who *write* (and then read) scholarly papers for the purpose of critiquing others, and allowing themselves to be critiqued, is an enterprise of Western scholarship.

All of the contributors to this session show that they have mastered the rules of scholarly engagement (the "rules of the game") required for participation in this arena of debate. But each of the papers also shows ways in which these contributors have *revised* the rules of the game, as well as bringing new content and perspectives.

- Musa has given us a new category of biblical interpretation, namely divination. In a creative appropriation of a traditional African form of interrogating a source, she simultaneously introduces a new method and reminds us that similar approaches to sacred texts have been used in the Western world as well, opening the way for new forms of dialogue and sharing between African readers and Western readers.

- Mmadipoane makes a bold move to combine biblical literature with African folktales, bringing diverse canons and diverse literary genres into conversation—with surprising results. Her retelling of the story of Esther using African intertexts highlights similarities that were not apparent on first reading—or hearing—of either. The book of Esther is transformed from a work of nationalist literature into a book of folk wisdom.

- Gloria brings the readings of untrained, and in part illiterate, women to the fore and into the academic forum, with critical commentary. Her paper raises the question of how (Western) critical approaches interact with "traditional" Christian readings—a question that is still relevant in Europe and North America, although it has been excluded almost entirely from the discourse of professional biblical scholars.

There are other aspects of the colonial heritage affecting African biblical interpretation that may not be recognized as such—evidence of the complexity of that heritage. One that I want to lift up is the understanding of the Bible itself and its place in African culture. The Bible was brought to Africa by Christian missionaries, as a holy book, a book of life and death. It is still held in those terms, it appears, by most southern Africans today, including the four presenters. But their papers show a variety of responses to this claim or assumption about the Bible's fundamental character.

- Gomang argues that the gendered Modimo of the missionary translation misrepresented the Batswana God and introduced an element of sexism in which colonial patriarchy found divine sanction in a patriarchal Bible. This Bible appears to be a threat to traditional African belief; it appears to be a book of death rather than life.

  It is not clear to me whether Gomang believes that the

Bible can be liberated from its patriarchal history and its patriarchal origins. This is not a new question for feminists, but it is presented here in a new cultural context with a new set of particulars. The question her paper raised for me is: How shall we approach the cultural particularity of the Bible, which includes its androcentric and patriarchal bias? Can we honor the cultural particularity and still find a message for us as women, African women, or American women? Is the non-gendered Modimo of African religion more supportive of the full equality of women? How are the larger socioreligious and ethical systems related to these two representations of the divine, and how do they compare? Finally, can translation alone carry the full burden of cross-cultural interpretation involved in reading the Bible?

- Gloria finds that the Bible as interpreted by African women members of the Assemblies of God in Mankweng reinforces traditional roles of women that are in conflict with the national Constitution of South Africa. For her, the set of values articulated in the Constitution represents a better view of women's place in society than either the "biblical" view or the traditional African patriarchal view. The Bible presents itself, then, as a problematic book.

- Mmadipoane finds that the book of Esther as typically interpreted in the Christian church, but also as understood by critical scholarship, presents a picture that she finds theologically problematic. She observes, however, that "the Bible is a highly esteemed book" in the South African context. Therefore she proposes to devise "empowering readings" for this context. She hopes that her folkloristic reading may rescue the story of Esther from its negative biases "so that it can be embraced heartily" by those at the margins of society. The underlying assumption appears to be that the Bible ought to be a liberating book. When it is not, for reasons either of its interpretation or its original meaning, we should make it so. Thus, Mmadipoane shares some of Gloria's negative judgments about the Bible's view of women, but she determines to reinterpret it in view of its hold on the women of her church.

• Musa approaches the book of Ruth with a therapeutic model of interpretation derived from the practice of African diviners. The aim of reading is ultimately to heal, but the therapeutic aim of her approach stands in a (more) complex relationship to the text. For the text, as a divining set, contains many possible constructions. It is the therapeutic aim of the diviner-reader and the reader consultant that make the text a healing instrument. Thus the therapeutic end may be achieved by a text/divining set that exhibits unhealthy relationships. The healing diviner may accomplish her aim by revealing the negative relationships displayed in the text.

Musa's actual reading stops short of the therapeutic goal that her model invites (if not demands). She determines on the basis of her reading that the relations between Judah and Moab are not healthy, but she does not apply this analysis to the situation in southern Africa, with which she began. Thus the potential that her divining will produce a message for contemporary Batswana readers is not realized in this reading. Nevertheless, Musa's attention to the role of national or ethnic identity and international relations in the story of Ruth suggests many connections with life today (in southern Africa and elsewhere), such as the lot of African women forced by their husband's migrations to make new lives among, and with, strangers. One of the unaddressed questions that Musa's reading raises for me is what place to give to the obvious ethnocentricity of the narrator (who recognizes only Judah as the place where God attends to the needs of "his people") in assessing the view of international relations presented in the book.

Conclusion

I sense in all of these papers an ambivalent attitude toward the Bible that calls for more explicit articulation of assumptions concerning the authority of the Bible and its relationship to other sources of norms for life today, including the norms of women's experience, indigenous African religion, and the constitution of a multiethnic and multireligious state. I applaud the ethical concern apparent in all of the papers and view it as an important contribution of African scholars to the present state of biblical scholarship, in which the connection with the reading habits and expectations of "ordinary readers," as believers, has been almost entirely lost or suppressed. And above all I rejoice in the new voices we are hearing today and look forward to the time when they will be heard outside this small room, in the wider forum of contemporary biblical scholarship.

12

The Bible and African Christianity:
A Curse or a Blessing?

Nyambura J. Njoroge

"TO THE SISTERS SITTING IN THE PEWS"

Black Christian sisters, you've been silent far too long. It's time to ask the difficult questions about church, the Bible, and even Jesus Christ. You've been still far too long. It's time to press, pull, tug at all you've been taught about faith to see if it's really true. You have been theologically naïve far too long. It's time to read for yourselves, interpret for yourselves, and think for yourselves about God. We've listened to what Anglo theologians have said and to what Black male theologians have said. Now it's our turn. And you know, nobody can say it like us![1]

Reclaiming Our Mothers' Legacy

My task in this essay is to respond to three papers written by three southern African women biblical scholars—Musa Dube, Mmadipoane (Ngwana 'Mphahlele) Masenya, and Gloria Kehilwe Plaatjie—in regard to African women's ways of reading the Bible. Let me introduce myself before I engage in conversation with these sisters. I believe it is necessary to declare my context and to state my struggles as an African Christian woman who wrestles with the Scriptures and my faith to make sense out of the African reality at the dawn of the twenty-first century. It is equally important to trace how these African women biblical scholars have come into being in a continent in which academic women theologians are still an exception, rather than the rule. I also find this approach necessary because my point of reference will be my journey of faith in the Presbyterian Church of East Africa, Kenya. The point of reference for the Presbyterian Church of East Africa (PCEA) is six-teenth-century Reformed theology and tradition.[2]

I am a Kenyan and a scholar of African theology and Christian social ethics. I was born and reared in a Presbyterian manse. And, as a former college-mate puts it, I was "crazy" enough to follow my father into the ordained ministry of word and sacrament at a very young age, leaving behind a teaching career. I am a graduate of St. Paul's United Theological College, Limuru, Kenya (1978–80), Louisville Presbyterian Seminary (1984–85), and Princeton Theological Seminary (1986–92), the last two in the United States. I have ministered in several Presbyterian congregations in Nairobi (1980–86), and, since 1992, I have been in ecumenical ministry in Geneva.

In light of this background, I consider myself a "privileged ordinary reader" of the Bible because, unlike many African Christian women, I have access to well-articulated Bible commentaries and other theological writings, as well as the opportunity to interact and learn from "critical readers" of the Bible.[3] By virtue of my ordination in 1982, I am "authorized" to interpret the Bible for others. I am also one of the few African women who has been co-opted to the male model of ministry, in which a few are "set apart" and given "authority" to lead the church, in particular the Western-oriented missionary-founded church in Africa.[4]

In the history of the Presbyterian Church of East Africa (PCEA), established in 1891 by the Church of Scotland mission and autonomous since 1956, women have always had the "authority" to interpret the Bible—more so if these women became "saved" and joined the Revival Movement, in which even the young have the freedom to expound on the "Word of God" during fellowship gatherings, as the Spirit moves them.[5]

Women in the PCEA, despite the fact that only since 1976 have they had "authority" to study at a theological college and to get ordained as ministers, have preached since the days of the missionaries. Some of the pioneering Gikuyu[6] Presbyterian women asked to be trained as evangelists in the late 1920s. During the missionary days, five women were trained and had the official title of Bible Women or Parish Sisters. Their primary duty was to teach the Bible and Christianity to women and children in their homes and at women's gatherings. However, it was not unusual for women to preach in mixed gatherings and from the pulpit, especially if they were deacons and elders. Women were first commissioned as deacons in the 1940s and the first elders were ordained in 1965. Their numbers may not have been many compared to the women who attended Sunday worship, but, nonetheless, that window of opportunity has existed for many years. Furthermore, in the early 1920s, with the help of women missionaries, pioneering Gikuyu Presbyterian women carved an independent space in which they exercise their God-given gifts, which became the official women's organization, the Woman's Guild.

As a child, I used to accompany my mother to Woman's Guild gatherings. The few literate women would read the Bible with the nonliterate women as they searched for guidance and spiritual nourishment. It is interesting to note that, even though these women would faithfully attend the Sunday morning worship (led predominantly by men), they gathered once more in the evening for prayers, as well as on Thursday afternoon. On all these occasions, the Bible was read, and someone reflected on the passage. The Woman's Guild was also known to hold triennial national conventions for five days, in which preaching took center stage. These gatherings were attended by all—young and not so young, women and men. Since the early 1960s, the Woman's Guild has had a whole week for their activities; on Sunday of that week, the women lead worship and preach. Since this is the oldest church-women's organization in Kenya, women in other churches have followed a similar pattern.

It is also important to mention that African women have been known to compose songs and hymns based on Scripture. In the PCEA, women argue that they are following the example of women in the Bible, such as Miriam, Deborah, Hannah, and Mary mother of Jesus. Some of these songs have found their way into the regular liturgy; however, they are mostly sung and danced at social gatherings and weddings. Bibliodrama is common among women.

Even though the majority of African Christian women may not have always enjoyed the center stage of preaching, or the privilege of theological training, they have carved independent spaces, and they have creatively and subversively found ways of using their God-given right to read, hear, perceive, and interpret the Bible. It is also well-known that the majority of Sunday school teachers are women, a more demanding and challenging task than leading worship, in which a book of liturgy is followed and repeated, Sunday after Sunday. Sunday school teachers read the Bible with the children. By and large, African Sunday school teachers do not have the luxury of teaching materials, nor are they trained as Christian educators.

By reading the Bible with their nonliterate sisters and children, women in the PCEA discovered women in the Bible who had leadership roles. Eventually, women leaders started to question their exclusion from the ordained ministry of elders and ministry of word and sacrament. This questioning and arguing that the male leadership should open all doors, allowing women to exercise leadership and to be "licensed"[7] to preach and to administer sacraments, led the church to give women authority to undertake theological education and to be ordained. These pioneer women paved the way for theologically trained women (mostly in pursuit of ordination) to read the Bible with ordinary readers. Consequently, today we can speak of academically trained women biblical scholars, the "critical readers" who can be considered the third category of African women studying the Bible with "ordinary readers."

This legacy of women reading and interpreting the Bible is not limited to women in the PCEA. Discussing women leaders in the African Instituted Churches and the Roman Catholic Church, the late Nigerian Roman Catholic nun and theologian Rosemary Edet and the Kenyan Roman Catholic theologian Bette Ekeya write:

> Women in such leadership positions desire to know more of the biblical background of their faith and more especially concerning the significance of women in the Bible for the church, and for Christian theology. Women's theology in Africa is being done in Bible studies, where women cease to be the docile and passive recipients of the

wisdom/doctrine of the clergy. They are questioning the established order of things. In fact, the awakened awareness of the traditionally unquestioning women has scared some ecclesiastics into phasing out diocesan programs involving women's development and leadership. It has become uncomfortable for the clergy concerned to head a congregation of women who demand to know the wherefore, the what, and the how of their church's teachings and practices.[8]

By reflecting on this historical background, I wish to acknowledge that when African women biblical scholars read the Bible with "ordinary readers," they are reclaiming a legacy that has existed, but which has to a large extent been neglected by the methodologies of male Euro-centered and Euro-constructed biblical scholarship. This legacy, like the legacy begun by Elizabeth Cady Stanton, affirms women's God-given right to read and interpret the Scriptures from their experiences and perspectives. In my view, these are subversive strategies against male dominance in biblical reflection.

Disempowered Christianity:
A Spiritual Battle for Truth

Having traced this legacy, it is equally important to recognize that these spaces in which women can exercise their God-given gifts were carved out within the patriarchal-colonial mission church. That means that these new women's structures had to conform to European, male-articulated and -dominated decision making as well as patriarchal African cultures in the larger church. More so, women's understandings of Christianity and the church were based on a Eurocentric and patriarchal understanding and interpretation of the Bible.

To a large extent, this kind of patriarchal-colonial Christianity and theology left African adherents disempowered and disoriented; cultural imperialism was central in the process of christianizing and civilizing the African. Consequently, Africans internalized an inferiority complex and self-hatred. Colonial Christianity waged a severe attack on African culture and ways of living in the world and was far from liberating. Western cultural imperialism and colonial domination led to the resistance movements that created African Instituted Churches, as well as the political associations that struggled for political independence. One would have to study critically the history of Kenya since the infamous Berlin Conference of 1884 to appreciate the impact of colonialism on the Kenyan people. Kenya was meant to become a white man's country, in accord with the thinking that shaped apartheid in South Africa.

Regarding women, although condemning practices such as female genital mutilation may be considered liberating, the patriarchal church and sexist-racist theology, to a large extent, did not equip Christian women to be agents of transformation and to analyze creatively and critically the social, political, economic, and cultural forces that keep women oppressed and marginalized.[9] In other words, Christian women may have gained the insight and wisdom to challenge some patriarchal and colonial practices, but policy toward women was far from being holistic and liberating. The same is true with men. It is no wonder that today we come across theologians and preachers like Timothy Murere Njoya, a Kenyan Presbyterian theologian and minister preaching on "Re-empowering the Dis-empowered Christianity,"[10] or Harvey Sindima, a Malawian Presbyterian theologian and minister, who declares Christianity an ideology:

> Missionaries also brought other baggage with them; they identified Christianity with their culture, values and history. The result of such uncritical appropriation of cultural views made Christianity an ideology of western civilization. As an ideology, Christianity was arrogant, and quickly destroyed everything and everyone in its way. *Being a cultural ideology it was used by both the colonialist and the missionary alike to promote cultural superiority. . . . The "Christian" vocabulary is by and large foreign. In short, Africans are unable to see, hear, feel, think, and do differently or live an authentic African life because missionary praxis destroyed their world.* There is great need for change; a need to reconstruct the African world so that people can live and praise God in an authentic African way.[11]

Such a disempowering and disorienting Christianity drives me to ask critical questions, such as the question I pose in the title of this essay: are the Bible and African Christianity a curse or a blessing to the citizens of Africa? I believe that we must be

212

analytical and not accept everything that we hear or read as if it is the last word. Some of us have recognized that the many resources in Africa, including its people, have been cursed in the hands of greedy Africans and their foreign counterparts, who since the days of slave trade have reaped from the land many blessings, of which Teresa Okure, a Nigerian Roman Catholic biblical scholar, writes.[12] As I write, gold, diamond, oil, and other minerals have made Africa a graveyard for its young population in Liberia, Angola, Sierra Leone, and the Democratic Republic of Congo.

This critical reflection on African reality creates war inside me: anger, confusion, passion, struggle, and pain, with occasional spells of hope. Theologians and preachers like the ones mentioned are speaking out and naming what is wrong with the Christianity we inherited from the missionaries, and that we continue to perpetuate. Others like Musimbi R. A. Kanyoro have called, if African women are to be liberated from the multifaceted oppressive practices that confront us daily, for cultural hermeneutics alongside biblical hermeneutics. Kanyoro asserts: "I contend that the culture of the readers has more influence on how the biblical text is understood and used in African communities than historical facts about the text. Consequently not knowing the nuances of the culture of modern readers of the Bible has more far-reaching repercussions for biblical hermeneutics than is normally acknowledged."[13] Mercy Amba Oduyoye, Musa Dube, Itumeleng J. Mosala, and Tinyiko S. Maluleke are others whose incisive and thought-provoking writings bring hope to a weary and disturbed spirit like mine.

On the other hand, religious scholars remind us that Christianity in Africa is growing at a fast rate and that there is high demand for the Bible in the many African languages.[14] But what kind of Christianity are we talking about? Do we speak of a Christianity that appears impotent before bushfires of poverty, violence, ignorance, disease, corruption, and greed that are sweeping the continent? What does this Bible, which in my Gikuyu language is called *Ibuku ria Ngai*, "the Book of God," have to offer in the midst of bloodshed among the youth of

213

Africa, of the prime ages of fifteen to forty? What can a book offer that is used to exploit its illiterate and ignorant listeners, the elderly women and men, who watch helplessly when their children and grandchildren die, leaving no name behind to carry on life? What can a book offer that is interpreted to enrich the greedy preachers, the vultures, the crusaders who take advantage of the poor, deaf, cripples, and the dumb? What can a book offer that is used by the so-called messengers of the good news to stigmatize and ostracize those dying from HIV/AIDS? What can a book offer that has been used to keep Africans, women, and slaves "in their place"?[15] No doubt, we know that this same book has also brought hope and life to people's lives and communities. So is this book a curse or a blessing to the weary and lamenting people of Africa?

Such a critical reading of African reality and the plight of its citizens brings the prophet Jeremiah's lament to memory: "My joy is gone, grief is upon me, my heart is sick. Hark, the cry of my poor people from far and wide in the land: 'Is the Lord not in Zion? Is her King not in her?'. . . For the hurt of my poor people I am hurt, I mourn, and dismay has taken hold of me. Is there no balm in Gilead? Is there no physician there? Why then has the health of my poor people not been restored?" (Jer. 8:18–19a, 21–22).

As an African theologian and Christian social ethicist, as one who wrestles with the Scriptures to discover the truth and the good news, I bring this baggage of questions, lament, anger, confusion, passion, and hope to the Bible, especially when in the company of academic biblical scholars. Having been reared in a patriarchal-colonial church, and having chosen to remain in it, also means choosing to be in a continuous spiritual battle for truth. For a patriarchal-colonial church robs people of their dignity, hope, self-worth, and God-given creativity. Hence we wage an ongoing struggle for material and spiritual freedom against violence, ignorance, poverty, greed, exploitation, domination, and control.

In light of this reality, I embrace the call of Musa W. Dube for us to consider the oral-Spirit framework:

While the patriarchal, imperialist and many other oppressive aspects of the various world scriptures are being addressed; while the suppressed scriptures of the colonized and women from multiple traditions are being restored and re-interpreted, the various feminist theological discourses must also enter and operate from the arena of the oral-Spirit aggressively. I say oral, because women's history and sacred words have remained largely unrecorded, although they have always been articulated; instead of being seen as lamentable, this situation can be claimed as a space of speaking new life-affirming words. I also add Spirit, because it is a theological discourse that recognizes divine partnership. *The oral-Spirit framework can be a creative space, then, where women articulate their own sacred, life-affirming and liberating words of wisdom. In the feminist oral-Spirit space, responsible creativity that involves attentive listening to many oppressed voices and empathy; active prophecy that speaks against oppression and seeks liberation; and intent praying that seeks partnership with the divine, can begin to hear, speak and write new words of life and justice.*[16]

My fellow Africans, enough is enough! We have lived with too many lies. We must get up, arise (*talitha cum*), and discover the truth for ourselves.[17] We call on our technicians, our biblical scholars, to come to our aid—to help us read, hear, perceive, interpret, and liberate the word of life promised in the Bible, in the face of the bushfires spreading throughout Africa. We call on our sisters and brothers to help us unveil layers of distorted messages; these messages have been added to a message already hidden in layers of historical, cultural, social, economic, and religious realities that shaped the writing of the Bible over one thousand years, let alone its translation into many languages.[18] Christianity over the years has been shaped primarily by the way we read, hear, perceive, and interpret the Bible. For African Christianity to be life-giving, creative, healing, and authentic, African biblical scholars, albeit a small number, must rescue the Bible from the misuse and misinterpretation that has disadvantaged faithful followers of Christ, especially women. With this appeal in mind, let us turn to the task at hand.

In my response, I focus mainly on Musa Dube's paper, considering both her methodology and her reading of Ruth and Naomi's story. With Mmadipoane Masenya and Gloria Kehilwe Plaatjie's papers, I focus on methodologies and in particular their claims of an African worldview as a canon (Masenya), and of the post-apartheid constitution as an authoritative, sacred text (Plaatjie). Out of the three biblical narratives read in these papers (those of Ruth/Naomi, Esther, and the prophet Anna), I have chosen to concentrate on Ruth/Naomi, because this narrative is read on more occasions related to women, such as in patriarchal wedding ceremonies in the church. Thus, I feel it deserves critical attention, especially by one who was treated to its interpretation on her wedding day, and who is an ordained minister herself. I conclude by proposing an interdisciplinary approach in our search for a holistic feminist reading of the Bible.

The Art of Divination and Empowering Hermeneutics

When I first read Musa Dube's writing on the art of divination, I was shocked. I had no idea what she was talking about until I started to recollect my parish experience in Nairobi in the 1980s, when I learned with "shame" that some of my female parishioners were consulting *mundu mugo*, a diviner! Maybe relationships with their husbands and the extended family were unbearable, and the church was not providing effective counseling; thus, they took off in secret to consult a traditional healer. This experience reminded me that we cannot generalize the impact of missionary cultural imperialism because, in my context in the Presbyterian Church in Kenya, divinatory practices were condemned as evil, but such does not appear to have been the case in Dube's context in Botswana.

I therefore find Dube's paper insightful and challenging as she invokes the art of divination to read the book of Ruth. By doing so she is not only acknowledging and affirming the "ordinary readers" in the African Instituted Churches who have kept this rich art in operation, she also brings to our attention the need to listen carefully to the women and men in the pew. By concentrating on the "reading" of the divining set by the consulting reader (CR) and the diviner-healer, Dube brings to her audience's attention that "Scripture" is not limited to the written word as in the Bible.

What I consider the central message of Dube's paper is how she relates the divination framework to social relationships. More specifically, Dube ties social relations to health. Given the state of affairs in Africa as highlighted above, acknowledging Africa's wounds while yearning for healing and well-being is a great concern of mine. In my view, African citizens can experience neither liberation nor freedom without paying attention to the unhealthy relationships that exist among many groups. I return to this point at the end of my response. Suffice it to add, however, that John S. Pobee, a Ghanaian Anglican priest and biblical scholar, has underscored the importance of healing in the African church, in particular the African Instituted Churches.[19]

Before examining Dube's focus on international relationships in the book of Ruth, a few comments must be made on her method. As a newcomer to the art of divination, I appreciate Dube's recognition that all diviner-readers are not healer-readers, but that healer-readers are those who regard their reading practices as ethical efforts toward better interpersonal and international relations. Second, Dube remembers to acknowledge the mutuality between the diviner-healer and the consulting reader and their dependency on the divine powers. Acknowledging mutuality between the consulting reader and the diviner-healer in a patriarchal-colonial church, in which many Christians are subject to the concept of "authority" in who has the right to read and interpret Scriptures or even to be theologically trained, is vital and part of the healing process. Third, Dube's articulation in her essay and in other writings of the decolonization process, and of the postcolonial feminist perspective on the production of knowledge, is a much-needed methodology in a patriarchal-colonial church and indeed in a continent that finds itself struggling under neocolonialism and globalization. Elsewhere, Dube explains:

> A post-colonial perspective is a framework that takes into consideration the global experience of imperialism: that is, how the eighteenth-to-twentieth-century imperial powers constructed or construct their subjects and themselves to justify colonialism and imperialism, and how narratives are instrumental in this process. . . .

> [A] post-colonial perspective on the Bible asks what has been the role of the Bible in justifying imperialism and why? It seeks to know how we can read the Bible in the light of its role in imperialism.[20]

Precisely because, as Dube says, many readers and interpreters have concentrated on other social relations, such as gender, race, class, and age, I welcome Dube's focus on international relationships. For those not familiar with Dube's other writings, it is interesting to note that she has focused on international relationships in other articles in creative and imaginative ways—for instance, in dramatically retelling stories of the Samaritan woman (John 4:1–42) and of the bleeding woman (Mark 5:24–43), in the name of African women.[21] I mention this to underscore Dube's commitment to the oral-Spirit framework, mentioned above. Furthermore, she writes:

> Creativity in feminist circles has long been suggested. Yet it is only too true that such a method has lacked the courage of application. To this day, we cannot boast of elaborate feminist re/writing of sacred texts from Africa, Asia, Australia, Europe and the Americas. The various feminist theological discourses have largely remained content with re-reading ancient patriarchal and colonizing scriptures. . . . The oral-Spirit space needs to be employed to seek and to articulate life-affirming words, which speak justice with, for and to all the oppressed people. This, I would argue, is a necessary feminist theological step that will take both patriarchy, imperialism and other forms of oppression seriously in the scriptures of the world as well as *allow women to speak their own sacred words.* Simultaneously, it will also be a feminist theological step that seeks to open a space for cultivating dialogue and articulating liberation across cultures.[22]

Like Dube, I am a consulting reader who is particularly conscious of the international relationships that leave Africa struggling under globalization, as I have tried to explain above. My main concern, though, is to discover if good can come out of Moab, a country that Dube rightly associates with barrenness and bitterness. How do the people of Judah treat this foreigner, Ruth, and their kinswoman, Naomi, who has tasted the emptiness and death of Moab? In the context of patriarchal society, economic insecurity, barrenness, and death, which is so similar to the African reality, how do women carry themselves in pursuit of well-being and fullness of life? Rather, how do the

International Monetary Fund, the World Bank, the G7, and the five permanent members of United Nations Security Council treat a small, economically deprived country, where famine and death have given it a bad name? How does a male palaver in Judah deal with two strong-willed women who want to leave their bitter past behind and to restore their life, dignity, and self-worth in the land of plenty?[23] Are these women a liability or an asset for powerful and rich Judah, at least in the eyes of Moab?

To begin with, Dube's reading of the divining set helps her acknowledge Ruth's acceptance in Judah and the blessings she encounters in chapters 2 and 3. However, Dube immediately returns to Moab, a land of curses, and confronts the horrible experiences of Naomi's family (chapter 1). She then concludes that the sharp contrast with the story of Naomi in Moab makes the story of Ruth in Judah unusable as a model of liberating interdependence between nations, for one can only embrace the story of Ruth in Judah by subscribing to the characterization of Moab as a godforsaken land, whose resources (namely, Ruth), however, can be tapped for Judah's well-being. Based as it is on the patriarchal marriage in chapter 4, the relationship between the two nations is not one of liberating interdependence, but of subordinates and dominators.

The divining set somehow leads me to the activities of these two women as they deal with the harsh realities in Moab and as they fare in the extended patriarchal family. Being new to the art of divination, I need the help of oral-Spirit, and so my audience will hopefully bear with me for referring them to this framework, which comes to us from Dube. In other words, unlike Dube, I am confronted by the stubbornness and the strong will of Ruth and Naomi, or their assertiveness, wisdom, courage, determination, and readiness to take risks in the face of barrenness, emptiness, bitterness, and economic insecurity. Putting it another way, I am amazed by the way these two women refused to be driven by despair, bitterness, and the limitations of patriarchy. Ruth and Naomi refused to internalize the godforsaken image of Moab; they believed something good could come out of their experiences. They clearly spoke about how they felt and saw things, as well as being clear on what they wanted while back in Judah: restoration of their life, economic security, and dignity despite patriarchy, or because of it. Unlike Dube, Ruth and Naomi do not look back to their grim experiences in Moab, nor do they allow patriarchy to deny them the fruits of their hard work—the work of plotting Ruth's marriage to a wealthy next of kin. Rather they obtain for themselves a restorer of life and nourisher of their old age, which was vital for their survival in a patriarchal culture.

Ironically, Dube does not seem to recognize that both Ruth and Naomi operate within the oral-Spirit framework. Hence she concludes that theirs was an unhealthy relationship and not liberating, as seen through the eyes of the relationship between Moab and Judah. In light of this interpretation, given our patriarchal-colonial context, I think there is the danger of misreading Ruth's decisions and actions and blaming them on what Dube calls "a patriarchal marriage." No doubt, Levirate marriage is a patriarchal marriage, but Ruth, like Orpah, Naomi's other daughter-in-law, did not have to follow Naomi and therefore be subjected to Judah's patriarchal mind-set.

Whereas I agree with Dube's reading of Naomi's journey to Moab, I read Ruth's actions differently, although it is hard to imagine why she demonstrated such a strong commitment to Naomi. The only explanation I can think of are the divine powers that Ruth invokes: "Where you die, I will die—there will I be buried. May the Lord do thus and so to me, and more as well, if even death parts me from you" (1:17). Are these not sacred words? It is true that returning to Judah was not Ruth's idea, but, in the end, it was purely her decision to join Naomi (1:14–16). If this was not Ruth's own decision, then I fail to understand what one's decision is.

Second, Dube notes that the relationship between Ruth and Naomi was based on the marriage relationship of Naomi's son, but Ruth had a choice, like Orpah, to sever the relationship. Ruth has no one to blame for her decisions, choices, and actions. Whether Ruth was driven by economic factors or by her deep admiration and love for her mother-in-law, it is still her choice. As a matter of fact, Naomi is the person left without a choice whether to be accompanied by Ruth or not.

In the end, what I would call Ruth's stubbornness or strong will, which I associate with divine powers, left Naomi temporarily speechless. When she recovered her speech, Naomi lamented loudly about her experiences in Moab, giving herself the new name Mara, "bitterness." Then Naomi was ready to face the uncertain future and to deal with her stubborn, strong-willed daughter-in-law, who also spoke her mind clearly and loudly. This encounter between Ruth and Naomi, in my reading of the divining set, begins their liberation story. The two women have made up their minds, and they are ready to negotiate how to overcome the emptiness and insecurity in their lives. Even though God considered Judah to have come out of its famine, this did not automatically mean that Ruth and Naomi would have plenty to eat. They also needed long-term security, especially in old age. Ruth and Naomi needed to strategize.

In a patriarchal setting, maybe this is the most they could ask for. So how could they make a way in a situation of complete emptiness and bitterness? This is where I see the women embracing the oral-Spirit framework to accomplish their mission, to liberate themselves from emptiness and a grim future. That framework constitutes a creative space in which women—and all oppressed people—articulate their own sacred, life-affirming, and liberating words and actions.

In the end, however, the women's fate is determined by the procedures of a patriarchal marriage. Am I appalled by the treatment of Ruth as a piece of property and by the preference for a male child? Of course I am. Like Dube, I am surprised by the way land is connected with Ruth. But coming from a patriarchal-colonial church in which women's concerns are easily dismissed or debated endlessly with little success, I am shocked that no one openly raised Moab's negative treatment of Naomi's family or whether Ruth's presence in Judah would bring a curse to the house of Boaz, given her association with the godforsaken image of Moab that Dube highlights. I am even more shocked how these strong-willed and assertive women survived this far without being silenced and dismissed. I am surprised that no one seems to come between Ruth and Naomi to weaken their efforts and their togetherness.

As the story concludes, the women at the gate of Bethlehem, who were stirred by Naomi's plight in Moab, gather at Ruth's new home to honor and celebrate the fruits of Ruth and Naomi's hard labor and their ability to overcome emptiness and bitterness. Like Boaz, the celebrating women also articulate life-affirming words (4:14–15). No more words from Ruth and Naomi; it is now time to celebrate the fruits of their decisions and actions. No looking back to the unproductive days of Moab. It is a new beginning.

Dube's conclusion led me to return to the divining set to reread the story. I was again reminded that this is a story of three assertive women who speak their mind clearly, make major decisions, and act despite the patriarchal mind-set and potential conflicts due to different nationalities. They refuse to buy into the way their nations treat each other. This is also a story of daughters-in-law and a mother-in-law who refuse to be docile when destructive forces come their way. We are left to imagine, of course, what happened to Orpah. But, in my view, Orpah's decision to remain in Moab does not mean that she, too, was not strong-willed and assertive and did not plot how to live a new, fulfilling life. If Ruth was able to do so, why not Orpah? Many women who have no option of leaving the violence or natural disasters of Africa are known to struggle against many odds and to put families through hard times. We need only remember the Mozambique women who in March 2000 gave birth in trees and on rooftops during the floods.

It appears to me that patriarchal reading of this story has been so thoroughly internalized that we are tempted always to read it as a marriage between a woman and a man. Maybe it is hard for us to imagine a strong and supportive relationship between daughters-in-law and mother-in-law. Whatever we may say about these women, they seem to act out of freedom, love, and commitment to one another despite or because of the hard times they had in Moab. Similar freedom, love, and commitment followed Ruth and Naomi to Judah in spite of or because of the uncertainty of their future together and the bitter memories of death and barrenness. Rereading chapters 2 and 3 makes me admire Ruth's assertiveness and courage and Naomi's calm mind and wisdom.

In my reading, Ruth's conversations with Naomi demonstrate trust and mutuality, which seem to be lacking in many relationships between mother-in-law and daughter-in-law. Mutuality, respect, trust, love, creativity, wisdom, and commitment are the hallmarks of the relationship between Ruth and Naomi. Unhealthy relationships between Moab and Judah, as Dube claims, do not seem to hinder the two women from establishing a healthy relationship, from which the two nations could learn. Naomi and Ruth also remind us that we should not give up knocking at the doors of patriarchal structures that still lock women out and that usually despise their struggle for liberation and well-being.

In a patriarchal-colonial church, many women in circumstances similar to those of Ruth, Orpah, and Naomi can benefit from the healthy relationships we have highlighted. Such relationships help women decolonize their minds from suspicion, mistrust, disrespect, and mutual devaluation that shadow many relationships between daughter-in-law and mother-in-law. They should also help us decolonize our minds from the docile behavior expected of women in the church. This story teaches us not to internalize negative images of our countries, and not to underestimate the young in the company of older people. As Ruth and Naomi demonstrate, courage, assertiveness, attentive listening, wisdom, creativity, liberating sacred words, and life-affirming actions are what African Christian women need to be empowered, liberated, and healed. Only then can we liberate our nations from unhealthy international relations, and ourselves from the way we read and interpret the Bible. Patriarchy notwithstanding, the book of Ruth is a story of faithfulness, struggle for life, and healing. In a patriarchal-colonial church, women can defy all odds and become agents of resistance, transformation, change, and faithfulness to God in creative and imaginative ways, all helping to dismantle the master's house of domination and control.

The Art of Storytelling:
Affirming the Unwritten African Canon

Mmadipoane Masenya's essay reminds us that, long before the Bible was neatly put together and presented as a book, its content was transmitted orally. She also writes that hearing has primacy in the Bible over reading and seeing, the more so today in societies in which a large percentage of the population is nonliterate. Recognizing that, even so, storytelling is not undermined by the art of writing and reading, Hans-Ruedi Weber cautions:

> This inherent emphasis on hearing in the biblical testimonies is not in the first place due to widespread illiteracy. The literate rabbis of Jesus' time also did not write books; rather, they instructed by discussing with one another and with their disciples. Only around the end of the second century after Christ was their oral teaching from mouth to ear fixed in writing in the Mishnah and other collections.[24]

Many of us in Africa grew up listening to oral teaching in sermons that were interjected with stories, proverbs, sayings, and gestures. This is still the case today in the mission-colonial churches as well as in the African Instituted Churches. However, Masenya does something that these preachers (mostly men) do not do in naming the African stories a canon. Telling African stories alongside Esther's biblical story brings two canons together. Unfortunately, Masenya does not engage us in conversation on what she means by a canon, and on the implications of affirming African stories as another canon. All the same, she does a commendable job demonstrating what we stand to gain by using stories from the Bible and from the African worldview in trying to communicate the Bible as a spiritual resource.

I believe that many readers will not have difficulties with storytelling and even with using African stories. In the back of my mind, however, I cannot help but wonder how Masenya's claim for two canons is heard by those who claim that the Bible is the "Word of God." In Africa, this claim for the Bible was made without scrutiny or critical analysis until Itumeleng J. Mosala wrote *Biblical Hermeneutics and Black Theology in South Africa* (1989).

Again I cannot help but reflect on how the Presbyterian Church of East Africa (PCEA) readership would respond. Despite the fact that many African religious, theological, and biblical scholars have articulated and affirmed the need to take African culture and religion seriously in its shaping of the African church and Christianity, the PCEA, in its constitution and in the worship service,[25] makes no mention of African culture or religion, let alone African ways of knowing, communicating, and worshiping God. Thus, in my view, it would make it difficult for me and other scholars like Masenya to get many Kenyan Presbyterians to consider African stories as a canon alongside the Bible stories. This assertion makes me wish that Masenya had addressed herself to a particular group of academic as well as non-academic readers and hearers of the Bible, to witness firsthand how they would receive her claim. This of course would mean explaining briefly what a canon means with regard to the Bible, and how the Bible came into being as a library of many books. What does Masenya mean by declaring African stories a canon?

With books such as Elizabeth Cady Stanton's *The Woman's Bible* (1895); Elisabeth Schüssler Fiorenza's two volumes, *Searching the Scriptures: A Feminist Introduction* (1993) and *Searching the Scriptures: A Feminist Commentary* (1994); and Katie Cannon's *Katie's Canon: Womanism and the Soul of the Black Community* (1996), one cannot help but desire an in-depth, critical conversation on the Bible from the perspective of African feminist biblical scholarship. As long as we accept the Bible as a central spiritual resource for African Christian identity, we have no choice but to engage in critical conversations in matters pertaining to canon, authority, interpretation, and even the Bible as the Word of God, or containing the Word of God, as some would have it. Fortunately, in *Postcolonial Feminist Interpretation of the Bible* (2000), Musa Dube has set the ball rolling in a mighty way!

Furthermore, given the historical-patriarchal-theological-political-imperial naming of the Bible as a canon,[26] one wishes Masenya had wrestled with and articulated the implications of her claim in post-apartheid South Africa. As Gloria Kehilwe Plaatjie has rightly observed in her essay in this book, "Masenya's approach is somewhat akin to African inculturation hermeneutics, which tends to compare biblical cultures and African ones." In one of her conclusions, Masenya alludes to a comparative approach as a way to confirm the close resemblance between the African and Israelite worldviews, which she says may help many Africans embrace the entire Bible as a spiritual resource.

In my view, I do not see why it is necessary to compare the two worldviews for the sake of making the Bible acceptable to Africans, because it is a well-established fact that the Bible (both Old and New Testaments) plays an important role in the life of African Christians. This is something Masenya herself has observed in her paper and in an earlier article, in which she asserts: "Despite this negative situation [apartheid South Africa], there are still many Black South Africans (in particular women) who have interest in the Bible and regard it as a norm for their lives."[27] In East Africa, similar affirmation has been articulated in a collection of essays, *The Bible in African Christianity*, especially in the article by Nahashon Ndungu, "The Bible and an African Independent Church."[28] I think the comparative approach gives legitimacy to the African worldview as a canon, especially in churches founded through missions and colonialism, which tend to give lip service or no place to the African worldview in the shaping of African Christianity.

Certainly there are many lessons to learn from stories in the Bible and from the African worldview. However, I think that Masenya's most important contribution is in grappling and wrestling with bringing the two canons together, as we search for a life-giving Christianity in a continent with many woes.

The challenge for us as African Christians is to search the Scriptures and African religion and culture to identify value systems that will empower African citizens to struggle against life-destroying attitudes and practices. This challenge leads into the essay by Gloria Kehilwe Plaatjie.

National Constitution:
Yet Another Authoritative, Sacred Text

In 1993, the first time I visited South Africa and, in particular, Alexandria Township, I was very angry with God. Visiting with black South Africans in the township took me back to my pastoral ministry in Nairobi in the early 1980s, when I was exposed to the life of my people in the slum dwellings, and in particular the Mathare Valley. In my eyes, there was no difference between life in Alexandria Township and in the Mathare Valley slums. Yet, whereas I could understand Alexandria Township in the context of the apartheid system, it made no sense why, after thirty years of political independence in Kenya, people would live as if they were in apartheid South Africa. The deplorable human condition I witnessed in both places forced me to ask God whether African people are cursed, as white South Africans claimed. I wondered if soon-to-be independent South Africa would behave like other African nations that, despite many years of political independence, continue to condemn their people to extreme poverty and inhuman living conditions such as in my own country, Kenya. In tears and great anger, I asked out loud if God loved African people as I had always been taught in church, and as I preached and taught people in my parish. Unfortunately, the evil actions that soon followed in the genocide in Rwanda and Burundi and in the wars in Liberia, Sierra Leone, the Democratic Republic of Congo, Angola, and elsewhere, and in the scourge of HIV/AIDS, did not help.

In light of this experience and the ongoing agony confronting millions of African citizens, I am curious to know what is happening in post-apartheid South Africa. I therefore welcome this opportunity to interact with Gloria Kehilwe Plaatjie on her essay, "Toward a Post-apartheid Black Feminist Reading of the Bible: A Case of Luke 2:36–38."

Plaatjie has done a commendable job of letting us glimpse the black South African woman in her struggles against the oppressive apartheid system and of highlighting aspects that hinder her own liberation. Plaatjie goes a step further in summarizing some of the efforts African women have made in biblical and cultural hermeneutics, as well as efforts by a white, male, South African biblical scholar. Plaatjie affirms "reading with and from" non-academic black South African women as her approach to biblical and cultural hermeneutics. She also allows us to hear the voices of these women. Plaatjie's interaction with academic and non-academic readers helps her audience appreciate the complex situation in dismantling apartheid as well as the patriarchal mind-set in her society.

By beginning her essay with the story of Jezile, Plaatjie implicitly acknowledges literary writings as a resource for a post-apartheid black feminist hermeneutics. In a way, she appears to join Katie Geneva Cannon, African American womanist theological ethicist, in asserting:

> I have a solemn responsibility to investigate the African American women's literary tradition by asking hard questions and pressing insistently about the responsibility of this canon of books to the truthful, consistent, and coherent representation of black existence in contemporary society. I am urging that there is a certain distinguishable body of writings by African American women characterized by fidelity in communicating the baffling complexities and the irreducible contradictions of the black experience in America. When seen through critical, theo-ethical lenses, Black women writers skillfully and successfully supply the patterns of conduct, feeling, and contestable issues that exist in the real-lived context that lies behind this literature.[29]

One wishes Plaatjie had discussed literary writings, especially by black South African women, as an important resource (a canon or authoritative text) for a post-apartheid feminist hermeneutics.

On the other hand, like Masenya, Plaatjie adds yet another authoritative text—the national constitution—as a necessary resource in developing a post-apartheid feminist hermeneutics. It is important to note the arguments Plaatjie highlights in justifying her suggestion. In sum, South African women like Jezile fought and struggled for the constitution, it was bought with human life, and it was the greatest achievement in the struggle against apartheid. After all, the Bible was used to formulate apartheid ideology, and African culture is patriarchal, making the Bible and culture inadequate for creating a liberating framework for the black woman. Plaatjie identifies the post-apartheid constitution as an authoritative and sacred text—a claim that again calls us as African women theologians to engage in conversation on what constitutes a canon and sacred text.

In this essay, I have identified the Bible, African stories (and their worldview), literary texts, and the South African Constitution as canons or as authoritative, sacred texts. In the case of Plaatjie, as with Masenya, one wishes she had tested her claim about the constitution with the non-academic women with whom she studied the prophet Anna. Widowhood is one area in which we must engage legal experts to investigate if widow's rights are indeed taken into account in the post-apartheid constitution. How, for instance, does this constitution deal with a widow accused of being a witch if she refuses to undergo cultural widowhood rites? It is one thing to believe that people bought their political independence with human life, it is another to engage in an ongoing critical analysis and evaluation of what is happening in their lives.

We have to bear in mind that many African countries bought political independence with human life, but the woman and man on the street were not involved in making the new constitution. A good example is Kenya, which in the 1950s pioneered in the armed struggle for land and freedom against British colonial rule. Unfortunately, the Kenyan constitution was drafted in Lancaster House in London, with a few Kenyans at the negotiating table. In the end, the new constitution was based on British law, which has little to offer Kenyan people (especially women and, in particular, widows) in search of a liberating framework against domination and control. The new government also uncritically affirmed the unwritten tribal legal systems with regard to patriarchy and other oppressive values.

All the same, Plaatjie has left the reader with a clearly thought proposal and with strategies on how black South African Christian women can subvert institutionally entrenched apartheid and patriarchal mind-sets by reading the Bible through the post-apartheid constitution. She has paved the way for an interdisciplinary approach. In my view, bringing the constitution into this discussion is the most provoking and challenging aspect of her essay. One would hope and pray that Plaatjie's sisters and brothers in South Africa will heed her call, and that the rest of us in Africa will also take her seriously in our search for dignity and full humanity in the midst of the betrayed struggle for freedom and liberation.

An Interdisciplinary Approach: Toward a Holistic African Feminist Reading of the Bible

Africa is on fire! One can hardly keep up with the fast-growing bushfires of poverty, corruption, violence, disease (especially the HIV/AIDS pandemic and malaria), greed, and self-hatred. No doubt, if the Bible and African Christianity are going to play a major role in helping African citizens liberate themselves and in bringing healing and dignity, African Christians must first liberate the Bible from centuries of misuse, abuse, and misinterpretation. Similarly, we must liberate and reempower African Christianity, which has been laid on a patriarchal-colonial and racist foundation since the days of slave trade. We must begin our journey of healing in the slave castles in Cape Coast, Ghana, where the church (Portuguese Roman Catholic, Anglican, and Dutch Reformed) stands tall in the midst of screams and human tragedy. Some of us need to follow the screams of our sisters and brothers who were sold into slavery and who survived the painful passage over the Atlantic Ocean. We also need time to mourn for all those who died, and to lament and repent for our part in the trade.

On the other hand, our healing and liberation will be delayed if we fail to decolonize our minds and to dismantle the master's house, built with steel bars and with stones of divide and rule, domination and control, exploitation and greed, devaluation and self-hatred. Many of us are infested with the commonly known "Ph.D." disease of "pull her/him down," whose virus of devaluing, disempowering, and destroying both the other and the self has perpetuated a culture of violence and senseless deaths. How do we read the Bible in this reality of the twenty-first century?

The three essays discussed in this article demonstrate that, if we take ourselves seriously, we have more resources than we need to subvert internalized and institutionalized oppressive practices and mind-sets in African Christianity and to liberate the Bible. Having said that, it is also clear that there is a lot of work to be done to make the Bible and African culture and religion credible resources for constructing liberating and life-giving value systems in Africa. Destructive and oppressive structures must be dismantled before we can even begin to lay a strong foundation for such values. To extinguish the bush-fires, well-conceived strategies, proposals, and resources, along with determined, motivated people, are needed. We can take a cue from Ruth and Naomi, who successfully strategized for their new beginning and life in Judah.

Musa Dube has treated us to the art of divination in exposing unhealthy international relationships (imperialism), one of the major bushfires that has been spreading since the slave trade. Mmadipoane Masenya and Gloria Kehilwe Plaatjie have challenged us to consider the African worldview known in storytelling, in literary writings, and in the national constitution as an authoritative, sacred text, or as a canon, alongside the Bible. These are powerful approaches and are bound to raise eyebrows among many Christians, including those in the academia. Given the multifaceted human suffering in the continent, however, reading the Bible in Africa needs an interdisciplinary approach. As academic women theologians, it is not enough to "read the Bible with and from" the non-academic

231

women. We also need to engage other professionals with our strategies. Each woman has faith, wisdom, and insight worth sharing.

Plaatjie has already brought legal experts into the conversation. We must also include health experts if we are to discuss the HIV/AIDS pandemic and other health issues. We also need to take into account that one of the biggest problems in Africa is abject poverty, which not only contributes to other problems, but also affects our international relationships and political life. More important, economics is a central theme in the Bible, as Gloria and Ross Kinsler have demonstrated with insight in *Biblical Jubilee and the Struggle for Life*.[30] Similarly, we cannot ignore that African politics has to a large extent failed to produce leaders and leadership styles that deliver healing, dignity, wholeness, and fullness of life. Unfortunately, the patriarchal-colonial church has also failed miserably on this account. Yet some believe that the church occupies a strategic site for social change and is almost the only institution that can help deliver democracy, human dignity, and rule of law in Africa.[31]

It is therefore necessary, even before we choose biblical texts on which to work, to begin our journey of healing by considering who is missing from the circle. We should also learn always to ask what expertise is missing before we look for the tools and resources with which to dismantle the patriarchal, colonial, and racist ways of reading and interpreting the Bible. Today, when African women in different professions have bonded in regional associations like the Circle of Concerned African Women Theologians, the Forum for African Women Educationists, the Federation of African Women Lawyers, and African Women Scientists, among others, we should be prepared to take an interdisciplinary approach in our journey toward a holistic African feminist reading of the Bible and of the African worldview. In a way, this proposal is in line with what Musimbi Kanyoro has proposed, that, in addition to cultural hermeneutics, African women need engendered communal theology. She writes, "A method of theology that gives us African women our own voice and space is timely. The result of personal experience is the creation of new literature in which truths about women of Africa will be told. The new literature from women provides light to new ways of reading the Bible."[32] Moreover, an interdisciplinary approach will be in keeping with the creative space made possible by the oral-Spirit considered earlier in this essay, which Musa Dube has articulated powerfully.

Such a creative process will help us "read with and from" women, men, youth, and people with disabilities, who will bring different knowledge and perspectives to the biblical text and other canons that these essays have highlighted. It is not enough, for instance, to unearth (to create critical awareness of) human rights violations against widows and orphans if we cannot move the next step and help the violated claim justice and safeguard their human dignity through the legal system. Thus, it is more effective if a Christian legal expert, working to help a woman overcome internalized fears as she fights for these rights, understands how the Bible and African culture and religion have been used to keep the woman inferior. It would be helpful for this expert to know how biblical and African cultural perspectives on justice can motivate women to struggle for equality and their rights within their country's legal systems. In many churches in Africa, women are also organized in grassroots churchwomen's organizations, through which the Circle of Concerned African Women Theologians can make a great impact by an interdisciplinary approach to reading the Bible.

Finally, I stand to be corrected. A Bible read and interpreted within a patriarchal-colonial-racist-imperialistic mind-set is more likely to be a curse than a blessing. Likewise, a faith nurtured in similar circumstances can only be disempowering, and it also falls in danger of being a curse. Let us therefore search for ways of reading the Bible and other canons that lead to responsible creativity, healing, and wholeness.

Notes

1. Sheron C. Patterson, *New Faith: A Black Christian Woman's Guide to Reformation, Re-creation, Rediscovery, Renaissance, Resurrection, and Revival* (Minneapolis: Fortress Press, 2000), vii.

2. For further details see *Presbyterian Church of East Africa: The Practice and Procedure Manual* (2d ed.; Nairobi: Publishing Solutions, 1998).

3. For further discussion on reading with "ordinary readers" and "critical readers," see *Semeia* 73 (1996).

4. The issue of authority and of women reading and interpreting the Bible is discussed in *Semeia* 78 (1997): 4, 55.

5. For further reading on women in the Presbyterian Church of East Africa, see my book *Kiama Kia Ngo: An African Feminist Ethic of Resistance and Transformation* (Accra, Ghana: Legon Theological Studies Series, 2000). On the Revival Movement in East Africa, see Hannah W. Kinoti, "Christology in the East African Revival Movement," in *Jesus in African Christianity: Experimentation and Diversity in African Christology* (ed. J. N. K. Mugambi and Laurenti Magesa; 2d ed.; Nairobi: Acton, 1998), 60–78.

6. Gikuyu is the largest tribe in Kenya. Gikuyuland, which occupies most of the central part of Kenya, was the center of the Church of Scotland's mission evangelism. In the 1960s, the PCEA began a campaign to evangelize more areas, and the church has spread to almost all the provinces of Kenya and claims to have three million followers, 10 percent of Kenya's population.

7. In the PCEA, students upon graduation from theological seminary are sent to parish ministry under the supervision of a senior minister, who prepares them for ordination. Licensing of ministers of the word and sacrament takes place before ordination, several months after graduation, when the student is scrutinized by the presbytery (more or less like a diocese) to see if one is fit in character and ability to be a minister. After licensing, ordination can take place after twenty-one days and announcement of the ordination edict. During licensing, the student receives the Dogmatic Collar, and followers are charged to address him/her as Reverend.

8. Rosemary Edet and Bette Ekeya, "Church Women of Africa: A Theological Community," in *With Passion and Compassion: Third World Women Doing Theology* (ed. Virginia Fabella and Mercy Amba Oduyoye; Maryknoll, N.Y.: Orbis Books, 1988), 11.

9. For further reading on patriarchy and the African church, see Mercy Amba Oduyoye, *Daughters of Anowa: African Women and Patriarchy* (Maryknoll, N.Y.: Orbis Books, 1995); and Isabel Apawo Phiri, *Women, Presbyterianism, and Patriarchy: Religious Experience of Chewa Women in Central Malawi* (Zomba, Malawi: Kachere Series, 1997).

10. Timothy Murere Njoya, "Re-empowering the Dis-empowered

Christianity (Romans 1:14–17 and Matthew 28:16–20)," a sermon preached on August 13, 2000, in Kikuyu, Kenya.

11. Harvey J. Sindima, *Drums of Redemption: An Introduction to African Christianity* (Westport, Conn.: Greenwood Press, 1994), 117, emphasis mine.

12. Teresa Okure, "The Beatitude in African Context on Matt. 5:3–11," a Bible study presented in absentia at the Joint Africa Theological Conference, Nairobi, August 14–18, 2000. Okure could not be present because of visa problems.

13. Musimbi R. A. Kanyoro, "Reading the Bible from an African Perspective," *The Ecumenical Review: Echoes from the Harare Assembly* 51 (1999): 20.

14. Hanna W. Kinoti and John M. Waliggo, eds., *The Bible in African Christianity: Essays in Biblical Theology* (Nairobi: Acton, 1997). Some of these essays address the growing numbers of Christians in Africa, as well as the appearance of the Bible in African languages beyond the colonial languages of English, French, Portuguese, and Afrikaans.

15. A good example of an in-depth reflection on this issue is Clarice J. Martin, "The *Haustafeln* (Household Codes) in African American Biblical Interpretation: 'Free Slaves' and 'Subordinate Women,'" in *Stony the Road We Trod: An African American Biblical Interpretation* (ed. Cain Hope Felder; Minneapolis: Fortress Press, 1991), 206–31.

16. Musa W. Dube, "Scripture, Feminism, and Post-colonial Contexts," *Concilium* 3 (1998): 52–53 (emphasis mine).

17. When the Circle of Concerned African Women Theologians was launched in Accra, Ghana, in 1989, the women decided to invoke the story of the little girl presumed dead in Mark 5:21–43, in which Jesus utters the words *talitha cum*, "little girl get up!"

18. Hans-Ruedi Weber tells how the Bible, the book—indeed, a library of books—was written over more than one thousand years in *The Book That Reads Me: A Handbook for Bible Study Enablers* (Geneva: WCC, 1995), viii.

19. John S. Pobee, "Healing: An African Christian Theologian's Perspective," *International Review of Mission* 83.329 (1994): 247–55.

20. Musa W. Dube, "Readings of Semoya: Batswana Women's Interpretations of Matthew 15:21–28," *Semeia* 73 (1996): 121–22. See a more in-depth discussion on the postcolonial perspective and the decolonization process in Musa W. Dube, "Toward a Post-colonial Feminist Interpretation of the Bible," *Semeia* 78 (1997): 11–26.

21. "An African Woman Reflects: Five Husbands at the Well of Living Waters," in *A Decade of Solidarity with the Bible* (ed. Musimbi R. A. Kanyoro and Nyambura J. Njoroge; Geneva: WCC, 1998), 6–28; and "Fifty Years of Bleeding: A Storytelling Feminist Reading of Mark 5:24–43," *The Ecumenical Review: Echoes from the Harare Assembly* 51 (1999): 11–17.

22. Musa Dube, "Scripture, Feminism, and Post-colonial Contexts," *Concilium* 3 (1998): 53 (emphasis mine).

23. *Palaver* in this sentence is used with the African understanding of a group of elders or clansmen gathered to discuss political or societal concerns, seeking consensus. Each member is given ample time to make their case; in some tribes, the members carry sticks which they lay down as they talk. After all have spoken, they look for a solution. There can also be a therapeutical palaver, which, depending on the tribe, helps a person or family going through crisis. As far as I know, African palavers are gender- and/or age-based, including contemporaries who, for example, went through a rite of passage at the same time. A woman-based palaver would deal with issues that affect women and not matters of clan politics or issues with wider social implications, such as the question confronting the men of Judah regarding Ruth and Naomi.

24. Weber, *Book That Reads Me*, 1.

25. See *Presbyterian Church of East Africa: The Practice and Procedure Manual*, 1–27, cited in n. 2 above.

26. See Elisabeth Schüssler Fiorenza, "Transgressing Canonical Boundaries," in *Searching the Scriptures*, vol. 2: *A Feminist Commentary* (ed. Elisabeth Schüssler Fiorenza; New York: Crossroad, 1994), 1–14.

27. Mmadipoane Masenya, "Proverbs 31:10–31 in a South African Context: A Reading for the Liberation of African (Northern Sotho) Women," *Semeia* 78 (1997): 55.

28. Nahashon Ndungu, "The Bible and an African Independent Church," in Kinoti and Waliggo, *Bible in African Christianity*, 58–67.

29. Katie Geneva Cannon, *Katie's Canon: Womanism and the Soul of the Black Community* (New York: Continuum, 1996), 70. In her first book, *Black Womanist Ethics* (Atlanta: Scholars Press, 1988), Cannon investigated the literary writings of Zora Neale Hurston.

30. Gloria Kinsler and Ross Kinsler, *Biblical Jubilee and the Struggle for Life: An Invitation to Personal, Ecclesial, and Social Transformation* (Maryknoll, N.Y.: Orbis Books, 1999).

31. Comment made by Samuel Kobia, a Kenyan Methodist minister and the director of the Cluster of Issues and Themes of the World Council of Churches in Geneva, at a staff forum on November 17, 2000. His comment was based on his research on "Ecumenical Social Responsibility and Democratic Change in Africa."

32. Musimbi R. A. Kanyoro, "Engendered Communal Theology: African Women's Contribution to Theology in the Twenty-first Century," in *Talitha Cum! Theologies of African Women* (ed. Nyambura J. Njoroge and Musa W. Dube; Pietermaritzburg, South Africa: Cluster, forthcoming).

13

African "Ruths," Ruthless Africas: Reflections of an African Mordecai

Tinyiko S. Maluleke

African Feminist/Womanist theologies are charting a new way. This theology is mounting a critique of both African culture and African Christianity in ways that previous African theologies have not been able to do. From these theologies we may learn how to be truly African and yet critical of aspects of African culture. (Maluleke 1997a:22)

The Need for Dialogue

To be asked to write a brief response to this collection of essays is both an honor and privilege. It is an honor to be invited to comment on such a creative ensemble. African women's theologies represent the most creative dimension of African theology during our times. There is no doubt that, in the past twenty years, no dimension of Christian theology in Africa has grown in enthusiasm, creativity, and quality like women's theology. At the start of the new millennium, there is a palpable sense of fatigue in male theology. At one level there is a frivolous search for new metaphors and new labels with very little in-depth engagement with substantial issues of methodology. At another level, African male theology appears to have lost its passion, its compassion, and its prophetic urge. African theology is bewildered and confused by the dismantling of apartheid, increased globalization, the forceful emergence of issues of gender, ecology, and human rights, and the irruption of a new world order. Admittedly, some male theologians have been trying to respond theologically to the new situation. But many of these responses lack the freshness, enthusiasm, creativity, and sharpness that one senses in the writings of African women. A striking feature of much current and allegedly innovative African male theology is its inability to dialogue with and engage the ideas and thoughts of African women. It is a cruel piece of irony that the fountain of creativity—African women's theology—is the place into which tired and frivolous African male theology will not look! There is therefore a sense in which there is little real innovation and change in mainstream African male theology. The same old male African theology marches on, only this time it has adopted a new canon of shibboleths such as "reconstruction," "translation," "Africanization," "ordinary readers," "reconciliation," and so on. A closer look at many of these allegedly new theological offerings will reveal this astounding inability to engage the works and thoughts of African women. It is for this reason that Oduyoye (1995:180) has charged that "sometimes African theology, African God-talk, seems no more than a pretentious smoke screen that dissipates on close examination." If I feel honored to write this response, I am also humbled, for I write as part of the guild of African male theologians, and as one who shares in the neglect and disregard of which I speak.

But why is the occasion to write a response also a privilege? African women have every right to close ranks and to speak between and among themselves without the interference of menfolk, even African men. For too long, African men—like white males—have assumed the right to speak on behalf of, and to speak *at*, African women. African women will no longer tolerate this situation. As a result, some African men have responded (*a*) by saying, in various ways, "our women are not like *that*, so it must be 'foreign influences' that are causing them to speak and act in this manner," and (*b*) by fleeing from dialogue with women by suggesting that, since they are not women, they will not comment on anything to do with gender, feminism, or womanism for fear of being accused of meddling. Both responses are grossly inadequate. The first response is a thin and worn-out excuse, while the other is deception and bigotry of the highest order. This is especially true when African women themselves are calling for dialogue.

The Witch Who Made Me: A Biographical Digression

I was barely three years old. The scene is our homestead in the Northern Province village of Valdezia. The *stoeps* of the four mud huts constituting the homestead were covered with people. Other people sat under the ancestral morula tree in the middle of the homestead. In the distance, a makeshift kitchen was covered in smoke as the women cooked in giant pots. I remember the delicious smell of meat. For some reason, everyone was extra-friendly with me. I was literally being thrown from one bosom to the next. Every member of my family known to me was there. What I did not realize then was that this occasion was a funeral—the funeral of my own mother, who was in her early twenties. Her death had shocked the village and stunned the clan. On the way back from a ten-kilometer trip to the maize mill owned by a local farmer, my mother, with baby on her back, collapsed in the footpath and could not proceed. Several hours later, she was declared dead, leaving four children—two boys and two girls, the youngest seven months old. Accusations of witchcraft began to fly. Members of my clan and family consulted diviners and soothsayers for an explanation.

During the same year, one of my aunts, from the more well-to-do section of the extended family, had also died suddenly. It was time to get to the root of this situation. Eventually the culprit was found. It was my paternal grandmother, an amazing and hard-working woman, Sevengwana the child of Nkami and Yingwana (as she so fondly used to introduce herself). She was the witch who caused the deaths of my mother and aunt. Apart from the social stigma that came with the accusation, she was also banned from subsistence farming for two summers, reducing us to village beggars for that time. Meanwhile, she took over as our "mother." Thank God we did not realize that it was her own "fault" that had landed her in this position. Grandma was a hard-working woman who was last to go to bed and the first to wake, and she demanded the same industriousness of one and all. As she pulled the blankets off our tiny bodies during Valdezia's bitter winter mornings, she would shout and ask rhetorically, "Wake up and go to school; has any-

239

one ever gained anything from sleep?" Since she probably regarded my mother as her child, I imagine that she had been as hard and demanding on her as she later became with us. Naturally, mother could have resented this. But the two women were not mortal enemies. Seeing that they had lived together in rural Valdezia at the mercy of an erratic son and equally erratic weather, I was later led to realize how close the two women actually were.

After my father's death in 1991, I had to sort out his belongings at house number 445a, Meadowlands Zone 8, Soweto. One of the most fascinating was a box containing handwritten letters between my father and my mother, and between my father and grandma. From the letters I could piece together the nature of relations among the three. At one stage, my mother had visited my father in Soweto and was refusing to return to Valdezia, and my father wrote to inform his mother. His mother took the side of the young woman! "She is right to insist on staying right there with you, because you neglect her. Why must she return to Valdezia? To die of hunger?" And yet clan and community had reached consensus that grandma was the witch who killed both my mother and aunt. You cannot begin to imagine the havoc unleashed into the family and clan when the diviner fingered my grandma as the witch. To this day, we live with the consequences not only of the accusation, but of the loss that followed: the loss of grandma through the death of her spirit, even though she outlived my mother by twenty-odd years, and the death of my father, who not only lost a wife, but who had to live with the knowledge that his own mother had been accused of witchcraft. Looking back, I see how much anger, shame, trauma, and fear lay behind my father's many masks of male bravado.

Given this background, how could I pretend that I could refrain from comment on "women's issues," and simply let women get on with it? How could I pretend that I do not realize the oppressive elements in my culture? My grandma's main qualification for the witchcraft accusation was that she was a woman—an African woman. She was old, hard-working, and was only a Maluleke by marriage. Surely witchcraft could never emanate from the Maluleke household, especially the male section. It could only be brought in by a "foreigner." Having identified the malicious "foreign element," the Maluleke men went on with business as usual. All the Maluleke wives now knew what would befall them if they were caught practicing witchcraft. A young white woman the same age as my mother would have been unlikely to meet her end the way mother did. She would not have had to carry kilograms of unground maize on her head for twenty kilometers. A white woman of my mother's age did not have to bear the heartache of a part-time, migrant-worker husband. A white woman would most probably had been rushed to a clinic or hospital in time to save her life. Perhaps it was a mild heart attack that my mother suffered. Maybe it was sheer fatigue mixed with heartache and loss of hope. Perhaps she reckoned it better to die than to face a future of "marriage" to a demanding mother-in-law, while the man she loved came home for two weeks a year due to the legally enforced migratory-labor system in apartheid South Africa. A timely drip, an oxygen mask, some injection, some physio-therapeutic technique, some pill might have saved mother's life. But mother was not only a woman, she was a black, rural, barely literate woman whose life was not that highly prized. Of course, she would have died anywhere had her Mozambican ancestors determined that they needed her company at that precise time, but her ruthless circumstances demand that we remain in doubt about the necessity and timing of her death.

I do not wish to draw general principles and immutable lessons on the basis of my biography. I do not wish to lay down proofs regarding witchcraft and beliefs about witchcraft. Nor do I wish to suggest that, since the accusation against my grandma was allegedly authorized by a diviner, divination is necessarily evil. Most likely, the "divining reader" was put under so much pressure by the "consulting readers" that he or she offered the explanation they demanded. Clearly, mother and grandma were not biblical Ruths and Naomis. Their circumstances were far too ruthless. If we see in them glimpses and aspects of Ruth, these glimpses must be situated within the ruthlessness of the oppression that encircled them. African feminist hermeneutics should therefore be awake to and confront head-on the ruthlessness in which African Ruths must and do live.

Issues Raised in the Essays

Methodological Strengths

The strongest element of this collection lies in the richness and variety of methodological and theoretical proposals. The contributors are clearly seeking to move us beyond the familiar situation in which the data are African and local but the analytical theories and methods must come from elsewhere. In that scenario, African contexts present the raw material and sources but the explanatory strategies are seldom fashioned out of local practices, beliefs, and cultures. Admittedly a good analytical framework is useful regardless of whence it emanates. There is something wrong, however, when analytical frameworks must almost always be derived from outside. In my opinion, a major weakness in black and African theologies—African feminist theology included—is methodology. Almost all the essays in this volume make significant contributions in method and theory.

In her contribution, Plaatjie suggests that, given the complicity of the Bible in apartheid oppression of women and blacks, the Bible is no longer sufficient as an authoritative sacred text. Hence she adds the South African Constitution as another sacred text to be read alongside and/or in place of the Bible. My response to this is brief. I find the attempted equation of Bible and constitution a little stretched and careless. The two documents may indeed be viewed by some as sacred, but they serve different purposes. Be that as it may, the crux is not so much which sacred text is better and less tainted than another. The challenge is one of hermeneutics. Whether we substitute the constitution for the Bible, moral principles for the Bible (as Simon Maimela once suggested), or the Koran or other sacred text for the Bible, human beings must still interpret these sacred texts and thereby seek to guide the texts' impact on life.

The fiercest site of struggle is not so much the sacred texts themselves as the hermeneutics applied to the texts and to life in general.

The four essays of Dube, Masenya (two essays), and Nadar present the most articulate and coherent hermeneutical methodologies. The three hermeneuticians, each in her own unique way, help us realize the complexity of biblical patriarchy. I summarize and address selected aspects of these essays.

Masenya: A Mosadi in Search of Bosadi

For some time, Mmadipoane Masenya has been proposing *bosadi* as a methodology for African women's cultural and biblical hermeneutics. She has suggested it because, in her opinion, neither feminism nor womanism speaks to the situation of African women. There is something admirable in the boldness, concreteness, and consistency of her proposal. For one thing, she resists the temptation to consume ready-made agendas, theories, and tools of white and African American women. She also puts a high premium on local expression and culture, and she does so without giving up on gender issues and liberation. It is my opinion that Masenya's proposal, although not always argued well and often misunderstood, blazes a new trail and holds great potential for future African women's hermeneutics. Unlike many critiques of Masenya, my reticence about *bosadi* has little to do with its ethnic tenor. *Bosadi* is no more "ethnic" than Alice Walker's womanism or Oduyoye's bold and otherwise preposterous declaration that all African women are "daughters of Anowa," an Akan woman. It is inadequate and ineffectual to engage Masenya at this level. Indeed, I would add that to engage her at this level is to misunderstand her intentions. Rather, it is at the level of the content and methodological principles that she ought to be engaged.

My contention is a simple one: *bosadi* is a patriarchal construct with patriarchal functions and intentions, and Masenya does not succeed in dusting the bloodstains off. African patriarchy declares that the place of a woman is in the fields under the burning sun, while a man's place is under the tree. What is Masenya's response? There is power in the labor of the maize fields and in the thankless tasks of the kitchen, she says. But what kind of power is this? Everyone who manages to wake up in the morning has "power," but some powers are greater than others.

Nadar to Ruth's Rescue

Sarojini Nadar has not written as extensively as Dube and Masenya, and therefore the contours of her methodology are not yet fully developed. In the essay included in this volume, however, Nadar presents a compelling reading of the story of Ruth and challenges the established canons of historical criticism of the Bible. Leaning heavily on reader-response hermeneutics, she proposes a "biographical reading" of Ruth, informed by the manner in which Ruth is characterized. On this basis, she presents a meticulous exegesis of the Ruth narrative, whose upshot is that "Ruth emerges as a woman who takes control of her destiny and changes it from hopelessness to happiness." Although Nadar's methodological moves are, in and of themselves, neither original nor local, she displays engaging skills of adaptation and argumentation. It would therefore be fair to encourage readers to look for more from her in the future. Through Ruth's story, Nadar argues that countless other "Ruths" within confined and oppressive spaces find ways to undermine, survive, and even to subvert hegemony.

But Ruth must not and cannot be romanticized. Survival and covert resistance—necessary due to fear of reprisals, lack of power and freedom, or potentially fatal danger—must be lauded, but they must not be transformed too quickly into subversive activity. This is the risk that Nadar runs in her attempt to reshape Ruth into a positive role model. Masenya runs the same risk as she attempts to dust patriarchy off the image, identity, and role of the woman of worth in Proverbs 31. Do not rescue Ruth, I would say. Beware of the woman of worth. Be suspicious of "the real African woman." Do not rush to rescue Esther from the lake, for you might come out with Mordecai instead. Listen to Ruth. Observe her carefully. Note her limitations. Mark her naked fears, her selfish drive for survival, her devious schemes, and her spectacular failures. Stop the cult that wishes to see positive and successful role models everywhere. African women's theological hermeneutics will be the better for it. Why must role models be successful anyway? Many African Ruths are not "successful." Patriarchy, culture, and globalization will not let them succeed. My grandmother was beaten to death, just like my young mother, who probably met an unnecessary and premature death in treacherous, rural South Africa. We can read nuances of survival and resistance into their stories, but when we do that, what do we hear and learn? My suspicion is that when we are too eager to read our Ruths in a positive manner, it is because we the middle class benefit from knowing that the ruthlessness of the systems that keep Ruths in bondage is not crushing. We need to think that Ruths are subversive and successful. We need to believe that. For one thing, it is good for our conscience. For another, we need Ruths and potential Ruths to continue believing that their circumstances are not too bad. We the middle class do not want an open revolution and rebellion, do we? But the stubborn insistence that Ruths are successful and that they are succeeding, even though and even when they are not, may be as cruel as subjecting them to physical oppression. While the relationships between black and white women have been the subject of theological scrutiny, the troubled and potentially explosive relationship between Indian women and other women, especially black African women, has yet to be broached. I hope Nadar will tackle this theme soon.

Divining Dube

With her solid background in in postcolonial hermeneutics, Dube offers the most theoretically astute proposal on feminist hermeneutics in this volume. Hers is a riveting mix of postcolonial concerns that find expression in the theme of international relations and in the revalorization of certain cultural practices of reading, illustrated in the ritual of divination. Because Dube focuses her reading of Ruth on international relations, she eschews or at least suspends the option to rescue or condemn Ruth. The relations under investigation are not merely the relations among two women and the men in their

245

lives, but also the international relations between Judah and Moab, in which Ruth and Naomi are caught. Hence the two women are said to "represent two different nations." Furthermore, Dube notes that both Naomi and Ruth became foreigners through marriage. This international relation is the object of Dube's divination. She suggests that the consultation of healer-readers (i.e., diviners) was usually undertaken to address problems of relations. The divining set, once thrown, often mirrors relationship dynamics that must be read and interpreted. In a similar manner, Dube seeks to "divine" the international relations revealed in the book of Ruth, with a view to determining whether they are healthy or not. Her verdict is that the relations between the two nations were not healthy, and that this is mirrored in the experiences and relations between Ruth and Naomi.

Several things commend Dube's divination hermeneutics. The proposed hermeneutics derives from one of the most deep-rooted and widespread cultural practices in (southern) Africa. This grounds her methodology in the spirit, symbolism, and language of everyday life, and in the instincts of community wisdom. Another strength of the proposal is the assertion of *relations* as a central category and principle of interpretation. In this manner, hermeneutics is presented not merely as a mental, esoteric, and academic activity but as an activity aimed at and based on the quality of human relations. The focus on international relations helps avoid a completely individualist reading of the book of Ruth—a trap that Nadar risks falling into. In this way, readers are pushed to see beyond two women, whatever their virtues or vices, to include the national ideologies under whose spell and influence the two women fall. The temptation to call on individual African women to "rise and shine" as individuals, in spite of the national and international relations governing their lives, is great. Often, the few "successful" African Ruths are hoisted as proof that women can make it, even if the national and international relations remain unjust and unchanged. Hence, many a hermeneutician will call on African women to note the Ruths among them, so that they might be like them and do as they do. This approach, says Dube, would be too simplistic and short-sighted. International relations govern women's lives, women's relations, and human relations in profound ways. In her reading of Ruth, she deliberately foregrounds the burden of international relations on Ruth and Naomi and on their relations with their compatriots. Dube's is a profound insight and an appropriate corrective to individualized and decontextualized readings of women's biographies, and she does this without obscuring the women's individual agency.

The "international leg" of Dube's methodology is strong, but further discussion of the method's "cultural leg," the practice of divination, may not be out of place. I have already lauded the cultural rootedness of the divination ritual. But as hinted in my biographical digression above, divination, like many other aspects of culture in general, can be used as a treacherous weapon. Therefore, we must do more than adapting the practice as a technique for biblical hermeneutics. We need a clearly articulated ideological floor on which divination hermeneutics will be built. Fair and coherent as the divination procedures are, even they can be used to blame women for poor quality of life and poor relations in community. For this reason, we need a critique of the national and patriarchal economy within which divination procedures are situated, even as we adapt divination as a metaphor for assessing human relations. Women and other people of the Two-thirds World—but especially women—pay a high price, both at a personal as well as at national and international levels. The battle, therefore, is not just at the level of technology and tools. It is at the level of hegemony, ideology, and culture. The divining bones of culture and its market forces can be malicious and tyrannical. But perhaps Dube has taken a step in the right direction. Dube has begun to seize the tool from those in power and to divine power relations for the health of our world, and to show us the oppressors and how they oppress us. Hopefully, readers will be willing to become part of the healing process.

Not Quite a Conclusion

In order to avoid a cut-and-dried conclusion, let me return to a refrain I have been sounding throughout this essay. We must appreciate those who try and fail in their resistance and subversion. Praise be to the African Ruths who live in ruthless situations and persist by means of survival instinct. Praise to them who try and eventually fail spectacularly. Praise to Esther, whose survival instinct led her to displace Vashti from the throne. I praise her for agreeing to be manipulated by her uncle so that she could survive. Praise to powerless and fearful Ruth, who used Naomi and Boaz even as they used her. Praise the witch who brought me up, for putting up a stubborn fight even as she hated herself to death.

Let me add a word of appreciation for the attempts to acknowledge difference among and between women. This collection achieves this task by a thoroughgoing contextualization of women readers. Hence, Masenya and Plaatjie write as black South Africans conscious of the gap between literacy and orality; Nadar writes as an Indian South African woman with a pentecostal and lower-middle-class background. Similarly, Dube is anxious to foreground Botswana in particular and Africa in general as her primary context. Our interlocutors are therefore under no naive illusions about homogeneous and universal sisterhoods. This is a helpful theoretical procedure. My sense is that although the Circle of Concerned African Women Theologians is in reality a circle of a higher class of women (and this holds true for chapters of the Circle all over the continent), this reality is not consciously foregrounded in the Circle's self-definition. Within South Africa, my impressions and observations have been that the Circle has been becoming paler and whiter by the year, perhaps because in South Africa the class best positioned and therefore most able to execute the writing, speaking, conferencing, and publishing aims of the Circle are women of a paler shade. There is no doubt in my mind that the same situation obtains in chapters elsewhere on the continent, except that the power dynamics may not necessarily be displayed in skin color. To a certain extent, the "Circle ideology"—to the extent that it does not foreground these kinds of differences overtly and boldly—is an ideology of exclusion. That exclusion is accomplished by means of "imperial" inclusion of one and all—an ideology that denies difference.

Let me conclude by again expressing my heartfelt appreciation for the opportunity to respond to some of the issues raised in this collection. I have responded as an African Mordecai, but hopefully as a not-too-typical African Mordecai. I was unable to respond to all of the rich issues raised in this choice collection. I can only trust that my limited response will spur others to continue the dialogue. My contention is that on the African continent there are many Ruths and many Africas. The Ruths of Africa are not roaring successes. But the Ruths of Africa are human, they are humanizing, and they are real. Unlike Achille Mbembe (1988), however, I would be reluctant to declare the Africas in which African Ruths find themselves *L'Afriques indociles*. Who am I to pronounce these Africas indomitable? Can I, a mere African Mordecai, know the price that African Ruths have to pay for these Africas to appear indomitable, even for a brief moment?

References

Ackermann, Denise, Jonathan A. Draper, and Emma Mashinini, eds. 1991. *Women Hold Up Half the Sky: Women in the Church in Southern Africa*. Pietermaritzburg, South Africa: Cluster.

Dube, Musa W. 1996. " 'Woman, What Have I to Do with You?': A Postcolonial Feminist Theological Reflection on the Role of Christianity in Development, Peace, and Reconstruction." In *The Role of Christianity in Development, Peace, and Reconstruction*, edited by Isabel Pbiri, Kenneth Ross, and James Cox. Nairobi: All Africa Conference of Churches.

———. 1999. "Consuming a Colonial Cultural Bomb: Translating *Badimo* into 'Demons' in Setswana Bible." *Journal for the Study of the New Testament* 73:33–59.

———. 2000. *Postcolonial Feminist Interpretation of the Bible*. St. Louis: Chalice Press.

Jordaan, Roxanne. 1996. "Black Feminist Theology in South Africa." In *Feminist Theology from the Third World: A Reader*, edited by Ursula King. Maryknoll, N.Y.: Orbis Books.

Kanyoro, Musimbi. 1994. "Silenced by Culture, Sustained by Faith." In

249

Claiming the Promise: African Churches Speak, edited by Margaret S. Larom. New York: Friendship Press.

Kretzschmar, Louise, and G. C. Cuthbertson. 1995. "Gender and Mission Christianity: Recent Trends in South African Historiography and Theology." *Missionalia* 24, no. 3.

Landman, Christina. 1994. *The Piety of Afrikaans Women: Diaries of Guilt.* Pretoria: Unisa Press.

Maimela, Simon S. 1995. "Seeking to be Christian in a Patriarchal Society." *Journal of Black Theology in South Africa* 9, no. 2.

Maluleke, Tinyiko Sam. 1997a. "Half a Century of Christian Theologies of Africa. Elements of the Emerging Agenda for the Twenty-first Century." *Journal of Theology for Southern Africa* 99:4–23.

———. 1997b. "The 'Smoke-Screens' Called Black and African Theologies: The Challenge of African Women Theology." *Journal of Constructive Theology* 3, no. 2: 39–63.

———. 2000a. "The Quest for Muted Black Voices in History: Some Pertinent Issues in (South) African Mission Historiography." *Missionalia* 28, no. 1: 41–61.

———. 2000b. "The Rediscovery of the Agency of Africans." *Journal of Theology for Southern Africa* 108:19–37.

Mbembe, Achille. 1988. *L'Afriques indociles: Christianisme, pouvoir et etat en société postcoloniale.* Paris: Karthala.

Mosala, Itumeleng. 1988. "The Implications of the Text of Esther for African Women's Struggle for Liberation in South Africa."*Journal of Black Theology in South Africa* 2, no. 2.

Nadar, Sarojini. 2000. "Subverting Gender and Ethnic Assumptions in Biblical Narrative: Exploring the Narrative Voice of Ruth." *Journal of Constructive Theology* 6, no. 2.

Oduyoye, Mercy Amba. 1990. *Who Will Roll the Stone Away? The Ecumenical Decade of the Churches in Solidarity with Women.* Geneva: WCC.

———. 1995. *Daughters of Anowa: African Women and Patriarchy.* Maryknoll, N.Y.: Orbis Books.

Oduyoye, Mercy Amba, and Virginia Fabella, eds. 1988. *With Passion and Compassion: Third World Women Doing Theology.* Maryknoll, N.Y.: Orbis Books.

Oduyoye, Mercy Amba, and Musimbi Kanyoro. 1990. *Talitha qumi! Proceedings of the Convocation of African Women Theologians 1989.* Ibadan, Nigeria: Daystar.

———, eds. 1992. *The Will to Arise: Women, Tradition, and the Church in Africa.* Maryknoll, N.Y.: Orbis Books.

Phiri, Isabel Apawo. 1996. "Marching, Suspended, and Stoned: Christian Women in Malawi in 1995." In *God, People, and Power in Malawi: Democratisation in Theological Perspective,* edited by Kenneth R. Ross. Gweru, Zimbabwe: Mambo Press.

Sugirtharajah, R. S. 1998. *Asian Biblical Hermeneutics and Postcolonialism: Contesting Interpretations*. Maryknoll, N.Y.: Orbis Books.

Williams, Delores. 1993. *Sisters in the Wilderness: The Challenge of Womanist God-Talk*. Maryknoll, N.Y.: Orbis Books.

Wimbush, Vincent L., ed. 2000. *African Americans and the Bible: Sacred Texts and Social Textures*. New York: Continuum.

Contributors

MUSIMBI R. A. KANYORO is the General Secretary of the World Young Women's Christian Association (World YWCA) in Geneva.

MUSA W. DUBE is a lecturer in New Testament in the Department of Theology and Religious Studies, University of Botswana, Gaborone.

ROSE TETEKI ABBEY is an ordained Presbyterian minister in Accra, Ghana.

MMADIPOANE (NGWANA 'MPHAHLELE) MASENYA is a lecturer in Hebrew Bible in the Department of Old Testament, University of South Africa, Pretoria.

DORA R. MBUWAYESANGO is a lecturer in Hebrew Bible at Hood Theological Seminary, Salisbury, North Carolina.

GOMANG SERATWA NTLOEDIBE-KUSWANI is a lecturer in the humanities in the Distance Education Unit, University of Botswana, Gaborone.

GLORIA KEHILWE PLAATJIE is a lecturer in New Testament in the Deparment of Biblical Studies, University of the North Sovenga, South Africa.

SAROJINI NADAR is a Ph.D. candidate in Hebrew Bible in the School of Theology, University of Natal, Pietermaritzburg, South Africa.

PHYLLIS A. BIRD is Professor Emerita of Hebrew Bible at Garrett-Evangelical Theological Seminary, Evanston, Illinois.

NYAMBURA J. NJOROGE is the Executive Secretary of the Ecumenical Theological Education Programme of the World Council of Churches, Geneva.

TINYIKO S. MALULEKE is a Professor of African Theology in the Department of Theology and Religious Studies, University of South Africa, Pretoria.